The Lukan Voice

The Lukan Voice

Confusion and Irony
in the Gospel of Luke

James M. Dawsey is assistant professor of religion at Auburn University, where he has taught since 1981. After earning degrees at Florida Southern College and Candler School of Theology, Professor Dawsey completed doctoral studies in New Testament at Emory University.

James M. Dawsey

PEETERS

MERCER

The paper used in this publication meets the minimum requirements
of American National Standard for Information Sciences—
Permanence of Paper for Printed Library Materials, ANSI Z39.48-1984.
∞™

Library of Congress Cataloging-in-Publication Data

    Dawsey, James M.
      The Lukan voice.

      Includes bibliographies and index.
      1. Bible. N.T. Luke—Language, style. I. Title.
BS2595.2.D39   1986   226'.4066   86-19173
ISBN 0-86554-193-0 (alk. paper)

Contents

Acknowledgments

Of course, a work such as this one is much more of a group effort than the title page indicates. Among those who contributed in important ways are William Beardslee, Fred Craddock, Elsie Reynolds, Rollin Armour, John Kuykendall, Richard Penaskovic, Ward Allen, and Paul Haines. I thank these friends. I also thank the Auburn University Humanities Fund for supporting the book.

To Dixie
the sweetest woman in the world

Voices in Luke

Introduction

The question of the meaning of Luke is more pressing than it first appears. On the one hand, the gospel is written in an ancient language. The story is set in an obscure world and peopled by characters who in some ways act very differently than do the people of our age. On the other hand, all of the New Testament lies overgrown with the doctrines and practices of twenty centuries. Sermons—in addition to illuminating the meaning of the gospels—have also hidden their meaning. The custom of using scattered portions of the gospels for sermon texts, piecemeal, has worked mischief on the story by removing the sayings and actions of Jesus from their narrative framework. Preachers have had a tendency to sacrifice many of the story characteristics of the gospels, and certainly style characteristics, in favor of some ideational content or other that could more readily be appropriated for a modern age.

This loss of the narrative is not necessarily to be decried. There is something of a wonderful mystery in the way that the gospels mean what they mean for each new age. Readers bring much that is individual and subjective to their understanding. The concerns of the church play an important part in exegesis. There are many ways to listen to a text, and it is a fascinating as well as humbling experience to trace the diverse interpretations of a work such as Luke from Marcion to Irenaeus and Augustine, down through the age of the established Church, into the Reformation and its many denominational branches.

Nevertheless, at some point—behind the individual reader and behind Church tradition, homiletics, theology, ethics, and meditation—lies a text that strains to be understood in its own categories. The Lukan categories that I will examine here are those that are peculiar to the narrative world. Whatever else it might be, the Third Gospel is certainly a narrative. In some ways, its form is more dramatic than that of the other gospels.[1] For example, Luke's Jesus often addresses his audience directly in the second person, while in the parallels the third person is used.[2] An instance of this is Luke's redaction of Mk 13:12.

---

[1]Jerome's statement that the evangelist *inter omnes evangelistas graeci sermonis eruditissimus fuit* is often repeated (*Ep. ad Damasum* 20.4,4). Although somewhat dated, Henry J. Cadbury's *The Making of Luke-Acts* (New York: Macmillan, 1927) and *The Style and Literary Method of Luke* (Cambridge: Harvard University Press, 1920) remain two of the most insightful studies into Lukan literary characteristics. Three more recent significant works are John Drury's *Tradition and Design in Luke's Gospel* (Atlanta: John Knox Press, 1977); and Charles Talbert's *Literary Patterns, Theological Themes and the Genre of Luke-Acts* (Missoula MT: Scholars Press, 1974); and Hans Frei's *The Identity of Jesus Christ* (Philadelphia: Fortress Press, 1975). Although strictly speaking, Frei's work is not Lukan literary criticism, since the depiction of Christ is gleaned from the four gospels, there is some justification for including it here in that Frei drew more heavily on the Third Gospel than the others for the original presentation, "The Mystery of the Presence of Jesus Christ," *Crossroads* (January-February-March 1967). Cf. Amos N. Wilder, "Comment," *The Christian Scholar* 49 (1966): 307-309.

[2]Cadbury, *The Style and Literary Method of Luke*, 124-25; cf. Mt 5:3‖Lk 6:20; Mt 5:5, 6‖Lk 6:21; Mt 7:21‖Lk 6:46; Mt 11:18, 19‖Lk 7:33, 34; Mk 12:38‖Lk 20:46; Mk 12:39‖Lk 11:43; Mt 23:4‖Lk 11:46; Mt 25:1-13‖Lk 12:35, 36; Mt 25:11, 12‖Lk 13:25; Mt 7:22, 23‖Lk 13:26, 27; Mt 8:12‖Lk 13:28; Mt 18:12‖Lk 15:4; Mk 13:12, 13b‖Lk 21:16, 19. See also P. L. Bernadicou, "Programmatic Texts of Joy in Luke's Gospel," *Biblical Theology* 44 (December 1969): 3103.

Mk 13:12	Lk 21:16
And brother will deliver up brother to death, and the father his child, and children will rise against parents and have them put to death.	You will be delivered up even by parents and brothers and kinsmen and friends, and some of you they will put to death.

But it is the matter of voice that will first occupy our attention. The characters in Luke, like the characters in all stories, have different views of the events taking place. The significance of the gospel is not simply laid out as in an essay. There is a sense in which the author backed off from what he told and allowed his characters to speak, to agree and disagree, to use their own language, and so to come alive in the story.

Luke's Use of "Son of Man"

It is well to fix this story quality of the gospel in mind by recalling some instances of how the author distinguished his characters one from another. Good examples are to be found in the way he allowed his characters to use different designations for Jesus. Perhaps the best known of these is the author's association of the title "Son of man" with the direct speech of Jesus in the narrative.[3]

"Son of man" appears with possible reference to Jesus twenty-six times in Luke,[4] twenty-five times in the direct discourse of Jesus. The only time that the title does not appear directly on the lips of Jesus is in Lk 24:7, where the "two men in dazzling apparel" consciously quote Jesus' words of Lk 9:22. Thus "Son of man" is Jesus' peculiar way of referring to himself in the narrative.

Not that this close association of Jesus and title is not present in Mark also; it is. Nevertheless, the pattern in Luke cannot be fully explained by theories of source dependence. In Mark the title appears

---

[3]Cf. William Wrede's famous study *The Messianic Secret,* trans. J. C. G. Greig (Cambridge: James Clarke, 1971). Important studies of the titles for Jesus are Ferdinand Hahn, *Christologische Hoheitstitel* (Göttingen: Vandenhoeck und Ruprecht, 1964) and Vincent Taylor, *The Names of Jesus* (New York: St. Martin's Press, 1953).

[4]Cf. 5:24, 6:5, 22; 7:34; 9:22, 26, 44, 56, 58; 11:30; 12:8, 10, 40; 17:22, 24, 26, 30; 18:8, 31; 19:10, 21:27, 36; 22:22, 48, 69; 24:7. The textual evidence is not good for the title's appearance in Lk 9:56.

fourteen times; nine of these are taken over by Luke.[5] Five times the Markan use is omitted from Luke (Mk 9:9, 12; 10:45, 14:21; 14:41). Three of these occurrences are parts of larger blocks of material omitted by Luke (Mk 9:9-13; 14:38b-42); and Lk 22:22 simply removes the repetition of the title from Mk 14:21 and so improves its style.[6]

The change that occurs at Lk 9:22 (compare Mk 8:31), where a Son of man saying is taken out of Mark's indirect discourse and placed in the direct discourse of Jesus, is certainly significant. The title is appropriate to Jesus' voice, but not to the narrator's voice. One notices, too, that the other instance of indirect discourse in Mark mentioning the Son of man (Mk 9:9) is omitted from Luke. The author did not allow his narrator to refer to Jesus directly by the title. It is also important that there are several instances in which "Son of man" seems to have been edited into Luke's sources, in all of which the term is placed in the mouth of Jesus. The appearance of the title in Lk 22:48 is clearly due to the author's reworking of Mk 14:45. This is also the case in Lk 24:7, where the author reworked Mk 16:7. Several of the passages that appear only in Luke also seem to be products of the author. This is especially the case in Lk 17:22, of which the subject is "the days of the Son of man"; and Lk 18:8, in which the connection is not so much with the parable just told but with the Lukan introduction in Lk 18:1.[7] Pos-

---

[5]Cf. Mk 2:10‖Lk 5:24; Mk 2:28‖Lk 6:5; Mk 8:31‖Lk 9:22; Mk 8:38‖Lk 9:26; Mk 9:9; Mk 9:12; Mk 9:31‖Lk 9:44; Mk 10:33‖ Lk 18:31; Mk 10:45; Mk 13:26‖Lk 21:27; Mk 14:21‖Lk 22:22; Mk 14:41; Mk 14:62‖Lk 22:69.

[6]The omission of the title from Mk 10:45 in Lk 22:27 is the only passage that possibly requires explanation as far as characterization is concerned, but even here one notices that this section of Mark (Mk 10:41-45) is vastly modified in Luke (Lk 22:24-27).

[7]There is a possible parallel to the pericope in Lk 17:22-34 in Mt 24:26-28 that does not mention the saying of Lk 17:22 but does mention the saying that follows (Lk 17:24). One notices that the passage in Matthew (as in Q?) emphasizes the coming of the Son of man. Luke 17:24 introduces the idea of something hidden "now" which is to become clear "later" and provides what seems to be a Lukan time scheme in which the present days of the Son of man are distinguished from the future day of the Son of man; see Hobert K. Farrell, "The Eschatological Perspective of Luke-Acts" (Ph.D. dissertation, Boston University, 1972) 94. Other Son of man passages peculiar to Luke are Lk 9:56 (a "dubious reading"); 19:10; 21:36.

sibly the saying was also introduced into the so-called "Q" material at Lk 11:30 and 12:8.[8] Anyway, it seems clear that the pattern already present in Mark was purposefully emphasized in Luke so that the title Son of man might appear only in the speech of Jesus.

By way of illustrating characterization in Luke, then, it seems that the author thought "Son of man" to be a designation for Jesus appropriate in the mouth of Jesus but not appropriate in the speech of the other characters. Even for his own narrational voice, the author preferred not to use this particular title.

Luke's Use of "Teacher"

But "Son of man" was not the only title for Jesus avoided by the author of Luke when writing in his narrational voice. Other instances were "King," "Son of David," "Master" (ἐπιστάτης), and "Prophet."[9] He also shied away from "Teacher" (διδάσκαλος). Although this title appears with reference to Jesus thirteen times in Luke,[10] it does not appear in the indirect discourse of the narrative or in the descriptive language of the narrator. As with "Son of man," "Teacher" seems to have been used by the author with careful regard to the story character doing the speaking.

In contrast to what is in Mark, one does not find in Luke any disciple intimate with Jesus calling him "Teacher" (compare Mk 4:38∥Lk 8:24; Mk 9:38∥Lk 9:49). At Lk 7:40 Simon the Pharisee calls Jesus διδάσκαλε—at Lk 8:49, a man from the ruler's house; at Lk 9:38, a man from the crowd; at Lk 10:25, a lawyer; at Lk 11:45, one of the lawyers;

---

[8]It is possible that Lk 12:8 is taken directly from Q. More likely, however, Lk 12:8 is Luke's combination of Q (= Mt 10:32) with Mk 8:38; so John M. Creed, *The Gospel According to St. Luke* (London: Macmillan, 1957) 171-72. Luke apparently used Q material at Lk 6:22, 7:34, 9:58; 12:10, 40; 17:24, 26, 30.

[9]For a complete discussion of how these titles fit with the voices in the narrative, see chapter 3 of my dissertation, "The Literary Function of Point of View in Controlling Confusion and Irony in the Gospel of Luke" (Ph. D. dissertation, Emory University, 1983).

[10]If Jesus is speaking of himself in Lk 6:40, as Joseph A. Fitzmyer (*The Gospel According to Luke, I-IX* [New York: Doubleday, 1981] 642) believes, then διδάσκαλος is used 14 times. This would be in character with Jesus' clear reference to himself as "the teacher" at Lk 22:11.

at Lk 12:13, one of the crowd; at Lk 18:18, one of the rulers; at Lk 19:39, some of the Pharisees from the crowd; at Lk 20:21, spies; at Lk 20:28, Sadducees; at Lk 20:39, some of the scribes; at Lk 21:7, some undefined members of the crowd; at Lk 22:11, Jesus himself uses the term indirectly in giving the disciples directions about what to say to someone else.[11]

"Teacher" is a title for Jesus placed by the author both on the lips of Jesus and on the lips of those who had an indefinite opinion of him. His closest associates did not refer to him in this way and neither, with the exception of the covert operators of Lk 20:21, 28, 39, did his bitter enemies. Simon in Lk 7:40 is a Pharisee who invites Jesus for a meal but does not like the way that Jesus receives a sinful woman. In Lk 8:49 the narrative character is simply a messenger. With the exception of the spies in Lk 20:21, the Sadducees of Lk 20:28, and the scribes of Lk 20:39, the other characters who call Jesus "Teacher" are simply characters from the multitude that surrounds Jesus, some more and some less favorably inclined toward him but none showing fervent involvement for or against him. Of this group, the most favorably inclined toward Jesus is the father of the boy with the unclean spirit, who begs Jesus to look upon his son. It should be pointed out, however, that the man is included by Jesus in the "faithless and perverse generation" (Lk 9:41) and included by the narrator among those "astonished at the majesty of God" (Lk 9:43). On the whole, the characters of this group seem almost to function as spectators in the narrative, mildly curious, mildly antagonistic, and mildly respectful of Jesus. Besides Jesus himself, the only characters in the narrative who call Jesus "Teacher" and

---

[11]For a discussion of the passage see I. H. Marshall, *The Gospel of Luke: A Commentary on the Greek Text,* (Grand Rapids MI: William B. Eerdmans, 1978) 269-70. Six "teacher" references are either in material peculiar to Luke (Lk 7:40, 12:13; 19:39) or are edited into his sources (Lk 10:25; 11:45; 21:7). The διδάσ-καλος passages in Mark changed in some way by Luke are Mk 4:38; 9:38; 10:20, 35; 13:1. In Mk 4:38 and 9:38, where "teacher" is changed to "master" (ἐπισ-τάτης) in Luke, the title is spoken by someone intimate to Jesus; as is also the case in Mk 13:1, which in Luke is rephrased in such a way that the title is omitted; and in Mk 10:35, which is either dropped or transferred by Luke. In fact, it is only the omission of διδάσκαλος from Mk 10:20 that is more easily explained by other stylistic traits than narrative characterization.

do not fit this pattern are the covert operators of Lk 20:21, 28, 39. But in this case the title does not signify the real relation of the spies, Sadducees, and some of the scribes to Jesus, but rather their pretense to sincerity.

Again, Luke seems to have been very careful to have only appropriate characters call Jesus "Teacher." In the author's mind, "Son of man" and "Teacher" were not interchangeable designations for Jesus. Although both applied to Jesus, each designation found expression with different speakers, and in a sense belonged to those different speakers.

Luke's Use of "Son of God"

We are all familiar with this kind of characterization. The turmoil and conflict of the narrative world feed off the different perceptions of its participants. Certainly we expect Jesus' enemies and friends to perceive him differently in Luke. The plot, so to speak, is the expression and resolution of different views concerning Jesus.

Another example of the author's feel for appropriate language should help us in this regard. There are three titles for Jesus that are bound together in Luke: "Son of God" (υἱὸς τοῦ θεοῦ), "Son of the Highest" (υἱὸς ὑψίστου), and "Beloved Son" (υἱὸς ἀγάπητος). These "Son of God" titles appear in ten places in the gospel.[12] The narrative characters who employ the titles include the angel (Lk 1:32, 35), a voice from heaven (Lk 3:22, 9:35), the devil (Lk 4:3, 9), demons (Lk 4:41), a man with demons (Lk 8:28), Jesus speaking in a parable (Lk 20:13), and all of the assembly of the elders of the people (Lk 22:70). The pattern itself is simple and pronounced. Unearthly beings recognize that Jesus is the Son of God.[13]

---

[12]Three times the titles appear in Markan material (Lk 3:22||Mk 1:11; Lk 8:28||Mk 5:7; Lk 9:35||Mk 9:7), twice in material from Q (Lk 8:28||Mt 4:3; Lk 4:9|| Mt 4:6), three times in material peculiar to Luke (Lk 1:32, 35; 20:13), and twice edited into the Markan source (Lk 4:41; 22:70).

[13]This is emphasized by Luke's change of Mk 5:2||Lk 8:26. It is a man "with demons" in Luke who calls Jesus "Son of the most High God" (cf. Lk 8:28). In Mark the man has an "unclean spirit," which is much less of a personal being and much more of an impersonal influence; cf. T. H. Gaster, "Demon, Demonology," *Interpreter's Dictionary of the Bible*, 5 vols. (Nashville: Abingdon Press, 1962, 1976) 1:817ff.

It may be significant that Jesus himself employs the title only through the mouth of the owner of the vineyard, a character allegorically intended as God (compare Lk 20:19). In the trial scene, Luke has rewritten Mark (Lk 22:67ff.) in such a way that Jesus perhaps does not claim to be the Son of God.[14] Obviously the assembly of the elders thought him not to be the Son of God.

There is tremendous irony at work in this trial scene. The assembly falsely accuses Jesus of claiming to be the Son of God, and condemns him for it. That the accusation is false is emphasized not only by Jesus' silence, but also by Pilate's repeated reference to Jesus' innocence,[15] and by the way that the author changed the centurion's statement in Mk 15:39‖Lk 23:47. Instead of having the centurion recognize that Jesus was the Son of God, the author had the centurion recognize that Jesus was "innocent" (δίκαιος).

But the falseness of Jesus' enemies and his own innocence are not all that is at stake in this section of the gospel. Even though Jesus' enemies are convinced in the story that he is not the Son of God, and even though Jesus does not claim to be the Son of God, the reader knows full well that that is exactly Jesus' real identity. This scene works so well because of the secret knowledge shared by the readers and the unearthly beings. Throughout the first part of the gospel, the unearthly beings—that is, those who are really in the know, both good and bad— have called Jesus "Son of God." Thus the story receives a special twist as Jesus' enemies from the Temple in the last part of the gospel mis-

---

[14]Mk 14:61ff. joins ὁ υἱὸς τοῦ εὐλογητοῦ to the Christ title and shows Jesus' affirmation of both. Luke consciously separates the two titles.

[15]Hans Conzelmann, *The Theology of St. Luke,* trans. Geoffrey Buswell (New York: Harper and Row, 1961) 138ff. Often a Roman apologetic has been seen in Pilate's actions—especially when coupled with the declaration of Jesus' innocence by the centurion; see G. D. Kilpatrick, "A Theme of the Lucan Passion Story and Luke 23:47," *Journal of Theological Studies* 43 (1942): 34ff.; T. W. Manson, *Studies in the Gospels and Epistles* (Manchester, England: Manchester University Press, 1962) 60-61. The final impression of the scene, however, is not that the Romans thought Jesus innocent, but that they killed him in spite of thinking him innocent. Therefore, instead of being relieved of guilt, the Romans in Luke are presented as more villainous than in Mark.

take his true identity, but at the same time inadvertently recognize him for who he is.

Luke's Use of "Lord"

This contrasting perception of Jesus' identity is an essential ingredient of the gospel's plot. The different characters in the story hold different views of the events. They speak a different language and give different interpretations to what they see occurring with Jesus. The reader, in turn, plays off one view against the other, sorting through and interpreting the story at a different level.

The reader makes his or her way through this process, led by the narrator. So the reader finds it important to peg the storyteller into some appropriate categories—to be able, for instance, to tell when the storyteller speaks seriously and when he speaks tongue-in-cheek; to gauge his motives and anticipate his biases. As readers, we do these things naturally, almost without conscious thought. We not only sort through the views of the characters, but also make mental concessions for the special perspective of the narrator.

One last example taken from the titles of Jesus in Luke will perhaps shed some light on how we as readers evaluate the narrator's voice. Then I will move on to the much more difficult task of trying to define the voices in the gospel, noting how they modify each other and bring forth meaning.

Although the Lukan narrator does not call Jesus "Son of man," "Teacher," or "Son of God," he often refers to him as "Lord," (κύριος). "Lord" appears approximately forty-two times with reference to Jesus in the gospel.[16] Fifteen times it is used by the narrator.[17] It is sig-

---

[16]Κύριος is used of "Jesus," "God," and "man" in the narrative. In the immediate context of Lk 1:76 it is not clear whether Zechariah's reference is to Jesus or to God (cf. P. Vielhauer, *Aufsätze zum Neuen Testament* [München: Kaiser, 1965] 40). In the larger narrative context, however, the use of the title fits in with a tendency in the gospel to subordinate John to Jesus; cf. H. H. Oliver, "The Lucan Birth Stories and the Purpose of Luke-Acts" *New Testament Studies* 10 (1964): 217. In my estimation, the list of likely references of Jesus as κύριος includes Lk 1:43, 76; 2:11; 3:4; 5:8, 12; 6:46; 7:6, 13, 19; 9:54, 59, 61; 10:1, 17, 39, 40, 41; 11:1, 39; 12:41, 42; 13:15, 23, 25; 17:5, 6, 37; 18:6,

nificant that of the fifteen times "Lord" appears in the narration of Luke, only once does the title seem to have been taken over from a source (Lk 3:4‖Mk 1:3; cf. Is 40:3).[18] Thus, "Lord" is a way of referring to Jesus that the author thought singularly appropriate for his narrator.

But other speakers also call Jesus "Lord." Elizabeth (Lk 1:43) describes Mary as "the mother of my Lord." It is worth noting that she is said to be filled with the Holy Spirit at the time of her exclamation. Likewise Zechariah, when filled with the Holy Spirit, probably refers to Jesus as Lord (compare Lk 1:76).[19] The speech of the angel (Lk 2:11) and the quotation from Isaiah (Lk 3:4) are other instances where the title is linked in the narrative with divine speech. Probably Jesus' quotation from the book of Psalms (Lk 20:42-44) is also best taken as God's proclamation that Jesus is Lord.[20] Other than in Lk 20:42-44 Jesus uses "Lord" connected to himself in Lk 6:46; 13:25; 19:31. In each case, however, Jesus uses the title while referring to someone else who calls him Lord.[21] Lk 6:46 is apparently directed only to his disciples (compare Lk 6:20), although spoken in the hearing of a multitude (compare Lk 6:17, 7:1). Lk 19:31 also refers to the disciples' manner of speaking of Jesus. Jesus' audience at Lk 13:25 is unspecified in the narrative,[22]

41; 19:8, 25, 31, 34; 20:42, 44; 22:33, 38, 49, 61; 24:3, 34. Less likely references are Lk 2:26; 6:5; 16:8.

[17]Cf. Lk 3:4; 7:13, 19; 10:1, 39, 41; 11:39, 12:42; 13:15; 17:5, 6; 18:6; 19:8; 22:61; 24:3.

[18]Thirty-two times the title is found in material peculiar to Luke (Lk 1:43, 76; 2:11; 5:8; 7:6, 13, 19; 9:54, 61; 10:1, 17, 39, 40, 41; 11:1, 39; 12:41, 42, 13:15, 23; 17:5, 6, 37; 18:6; 19:8, 25; 22:33, 38, 49, 61; 24:3, 34).

[19]That would have been the way the author of the gospel would have understood κύριος.

[20]For a survey of interpretations of the passage see G. Schneider, *Verleugnung, Verspöttung und Verhör Jesu nach Lukas 22, 54-7* (München: Kösel, 1969) 66-81. Cf. Lk 24:44.

[21]This is also the case in Lk 20:42, 44 where Jesus possibly refers to himself as Lord while quoting David.

[22]There is only an allegorical connection in Lk 13:25 uniting Jesus to the κύριος of the house. The more direct identification is made in 13:23, where someone asks, "Lord, will those who are saved be few?" so prompting the allegory.

but the pattern has already been indicated. Thirteen other times in the gospel "Lord" appears in the direct speech of the disciples.

> Lk 5:8, Simon Peter
> 9:54, James and John
> 9:59, another (of the disciples)
> 9:61, another (of the disciples)
> 10:17, the seventy
> 11:1, one of the disciples
> 12:41, Peter
> 17:37, (the disciples)
> 19:34, two of the disciples
> 22:33, Peter
> 22:38, (the apostles)
> 22:49, those about Jesus
> 24:34, those with the eleven

However, the title is not used exclusively by those who accompany Jesus in the narrative. The narrator, as I have pointed out, uses the title. Others who do not accompany Jesus but nevertheless call him Lord are the leper (Lk 5:12), the centurion (through his friends, Lk 7:6); Martha (Lk 10:40); a man asking about the number to be saved (Lk 13:23); the blind man near Jericho (Lk 18:41); Zacchaeus (Lk 19:8); and those who listen to the parable spoken by Jesus in Jericho (Lk 19:25).

The author did not define the speakers of Lk 13:23 and 19:25. Of the remaining speakers who do not accompany Jesus but nevertheless call him "Lord," Martha shows the closest ties with Jesus. She receives him into her house and serves him. Jesus also visits Zacchaeus. The value structures of Zacchaeus's life became different and he receives salvation. Like Zacchaeus the other three—the leper, the centurion, and the blind man—all show a remarkable confidence in the power of Jesus and a humble attitude before him. The man with leprosy falls on his face before Jesus; the centurion does not deem himself worthy to have Jesus come under his roof; and the blind man at Jericho begs Jesus to have mercy on him. In fact, it seems to be these two qualities of dependence on the power of Jesus and humility before Jesus that best characterize those who call Jesus "Lord." Simon Peter falls at Jesus' knees saying "depart from me for I am a sinful man, O Lord" (Lk 5:8). His request in Lk 12:41, it is true, is not of the same humble type, but in that it is a request it does show the tilt of the relationship.

It is significant that "Lord," when spoken by a disciple is almost always associated with a request (Lk 5:8, 9:54, 59, 61; 11:1; 12:41; 17:37; 22:49). Only in Lk 10:17, 22:33, and 22:38 is the case different. Nevertheless Lk 10:17 and 22:38 still emphasize the recognition by the disciples of dependence on Jesus. The seventy return, rejoicing that the demons are subject to them and realizing that the source of their power is Jesus.[23] Lk 22:38 is not as theologically important as Lk 10:17, but it makes the same character statement about those who say "Lord." Jesus tells the disciples that it is time to buy swords, and so they produce swords.[24] The author associated the recognition of a chain of authority and power with those who say "Lord."[25]

The only place where this chain of authority and power is not recognized by a character using "Lord" to Jesus is in Lk 22:33. In this verse, Peter ignores Jesus' words and claims that he will stand by him unto death. But it is this case that proves the association of the title with the right relationship of authority and power between Jesus and his followers, for the narrative soon poignantly contradicts Peter's statement, as he denies Jesus and asserts himself as his own source of authority and power (compare Lk 22:34, 55-62).[26]

To recapitulate, the narrator refers to Jesus as "Lord," and in so doing associates himself with certain story characters who are aware of Jesus' power and their dependence on that power, Jesus' authority and their position before that authority. By calling Jesus "Lord" the narrator defines himself as part of the believing community. He is like

---

[23]The dependence of the disciples is expressed by their ascensive use of καί coupled with ἐν τῷ ὀνοματί σου.

[24]D. E. Trueblood finds some humor in the disciples' misunderstanding of Jesus' ironic statement; see David Elton Trueblood, *The Humor of Christ* (San Francisco: Harper and Row, 1964). However, there is no consensus among scholars on the intended meaning of Lk 22:35ff.

[25]Paul Minear produces a convincing argument for the gospel's concern with a chain of authority in his exegesis of Lk 7:1-10; see Paul Minear, *To Heal and Reveal* (New York: Seabury Press, 1976) 6ff.

[26]The full significance of the title is summed up in Zacchaeus's appropriation of "Lord" in Lk 19:8, which is followed in the narrative by Jesus' statement that "today salvation has come to this house."

the disciples, and this way of referring to Jesus is appropriate to him in a way that "Son of man," "Teacher," and "Son of God" are not.

One of the beauties of analysis is that it allows us to perceive with clarity that of which we are already aware in a muddled way. Anyone who has read or heard the Gospel of Luke is aware of the interplay of its different voices. Still, it is a pleasant task to look more closely, as I shall, at the voices in Luke. The Lukan author was sensitive to the place of characterization in the gospel, and was careful to dress the people of his story with a proper language. The author's style is in itself a matter of fascination and a subject worth pursuing.

However, we would be wrong to think of the different voices in Luke principally as expressions of style. *What* is said in Luke is irrevocably intertwined with *how* it is said. The different voices not only embellish the story; they are the stuff of the story.

With this we should remember also that literary criticism can offer us much more than an awareness of what we already know. Analysis can unlock long-shut secrets and surprise us with an old understanding that is new to us. In the following chapters I will explore how the author characterized the gospel's speakers, and how that was part of his message. Unfortunately, some of the material must be discussed on a technical level. The first two chapters in particular might seem trying to the nonspecialist. This is the penalty that we pay because Luke was written in a foreign language almost two thousand years ago. We must unearth the idiom of the story characters from the debris of a past culture. Everyday expressions common to first-century Christians are obscure to us, not necessarily in what they denote but in what they connote. Linguistic nuances that would have been understood with ease and that would have allowed the early reader to place the characters in an appropriate context need to be tediously unearthed by twentieth-century readers. The very act of reading Luke as a narrative whole is work to us, so accustomed are we to its interrupted presentation in chapter and verse. But in spite of the technical appearance of some of this material, the difficulties are not inordinate, and the rewards are great. The general idea is simple: the characters and the narrator of Luke are in dialogue with each other and with us. Meaning arises out of the conversation.

I will approach this study by separating Jesus' language and his view of events from that of the chief priests, the disciples, the Pharisees, and others—and especially from the language and view of the third-person narrator. The voices in the narrative can be distinguished one from another in terms of the direct speech of the characters, although that is not the only indicator. Hearing the distinctiveness of the Hellenistic Greek of each character proves difficult, even for the linguist, and it is perhaps easier for us, aliens from a different time, to visualize the individual voices than to hear them. Thus it might be a good idea for readers who wish to follow along in the Greek text to underline the direct discourse of the Lukan characters with different colored pens, leaving the narration unmarked.

I begin the study with the language of the characters, and move toward a more general perception of their views of story events. I will not be as interested in isolated phenomena as in overall patterns of narration. The structure of the narrative is important, and I will discuss it presently.

The Narrator's Voice

Chapter 1

While the technique of giving story characters identifiable patterns of speech is readily associated with such modern-day geniuses as Mark Twain and William Faulkner, it is in fact an old storyteller's device used by, among others, Petronius, Aristophanes, and Homer.[1] It is not so surprising, therefore, to find that the Lukan author distinguished among the voices of the characters in his story, and that when he spoke through them he spoke a very different language than when he spoke through his narrator.[2]

In this chapter I shall illustrate some of the specific characteristics of the narrator's speech, posing and answering a few questions. What is the style of the gospel's narration? How does the shift in the style of

---

[1]See Erich Auerbach, *Mimesis,* trans. W. R. Trask (Princeton: Princeton University Press, 1953) 24-31; Robert G. Ussher, *Aristophanes* (Oxford: Clarendon Press, 1929) 13-28; cf. J. H. Moulton, R. Howard, and N. Turner, *A Grammar of New Testament Greek,* 4 vols. (Edinburgh: T. and T. Clark, 1908-) 2:7; W. B. Stanford, *The Odyssey of Homer* (New York: St. Martin's Press, 1971) 1:xxiv-xxv.

[2]Henry J. Cadbury, *The Making of Luke-Acts* (London: SPCK, 1968) 221ff.

the narration following the prologue (Lk 1:1-4) affect the reader's understanding of the narrator's voice? What do the so-called "Septuagintalisms" in the narration indicate? What is the literary standard of Luke's narration? And what does the narrator's voice tell us about the general setting of the narration?

Characterization in Luke

As I have already pointed out in the introduction, the author associated certain titles for Jesus with certain characters or groups of characters in the gospel. But the author's care, in this regard, should not be seen as pertaining only to a few titles for Jesus. His use of a proper language to dress and give life to the different speakers is much more comprehensive,[3] and suggests a natural and almost unconscious tendency on the part of the author to hear the characters of his story as they spoke dramatically, so paralleling what William Faulkner described in reply to a question concerning his own use of voice patterns.

> You've got to see . . . the scenes you describe. You've got to hear the voice speaking the speech that you put down. You have to hear the vernacular he (that is, the character) speaks in rather than to think of the speech and translate it into the vernacular.[4]

That the author of Luke in fact wrote as if he were listening to an actual conversation between the characters of his narrative can perhaps be seen in his use of λέγω ὑμῖν, λέγω σοι, "I say to you" —a construction used eighteen times by Mark's Jesus.[5] But Luke's Jesus uses the construction forty-six times.[6] The author of the Third Gospel very clearly took over and emphasized a pattern of speech already associated with Jesus by the tradition. However, one notes that the con-

---

[3]See Appendix A.

[4]Frederick L. Gwynn and Joseph L. Blotner, eds., *Faulkner in the University: Class Conferences at the University of Virginia, 1957-1958* (New York: Random House, 1965) 181.

[5]Mk 2:11; 3:28; 5:41; 8:12; 9:1, 13, 41; 10:15, 29; 11:23, 24, 33; 12:43; 13:30, 37; 14:9, 18, 25.

[6]Lk 4:24, 25; 5:24; 6:27; 7:9, 14, 26, 28, 47; 9:27; 10:12, 24; 11:8, 9, 51; 12:4, 5, 8, 22, 27, 37, 44, 51, 59; 13:3, 5, 24, 35; 14:24; 15:7, 10; 16:9; 17:34; 18:8, 14, 17, 29; 19:26, 40; 20:8; 21:32; 22:16, 18, 34, 37; 23:43.

struction, although intensively used in Luke, does not appear as a hardened formula. Its forms are diverse.

ἀμὴν λέγω ὑμῖν	Lk 4:24; 12:37; 18:17, 29; 21:32
δὲ λέγω ὑμῖν	Lk 4:25
σοὶ λέγω	Lk 5:24; 7:14
ἀλλὰ ὑμῖν λέγω	Lk 6:27
λέγω ὑμῖν	Lk 7:9, 28; 10:12; 11:18; 13:24; 15:7; 17:34; 18:8, 14; 19:26, 40
ναί, λέγω ὑμῖν	Lk 7:26; 11:51; 12:5
λέγω σοί	Lk 7:47; 12:59; 22:34
λέγω δὲ ὑμῖν	Lk 9:27; 12:4, 8, 27; 13:35
λέγω γὰρ ὑμῖν	Lk 10:24; 14:24; 22:16, 18, 37
κἀγὼ ὑμῖν λέγω	Lk 11:9
διὰ τοῦτο λέγω ὑμῖν	Lk 12:22
ἀληθῶς λέγω ὑμῖν	Lk 12:44
οὐχί, λέγω ὑμῖν	Lk 12:51; 13:3, 5
οὕτως, λέγω ὑμῖν	Lk 15:10
ἐγὼ ὑμῖν λέγω	Lk 16:9
οὐδὲ ἐγὼ λέγω ὑμῖν	Lk 20:8
ἀμήν σοὶ λέγω	Lk 23:43.[7]

The artistry of the Third Gospel at this point results from its author's ability to give a special stamp to the speech of Jesus without turning it into a caricature of real speech—as perhaps occurs in John's gospel with its self-conscious formula ἀμὴν ἀμὴν λέγω ὑμῖν (σοι), "truly, truly I say to you."[8]

Again, it is unfortunate that many nuances in the points of view in Luke reflected by the characterization of the different voices in the gospel are lost to the modern reader, who no longer finds it easy to associate first-century societal groups with their particular idioms. Some insight into the

---

[7]There are seventeen different forms in Luke for the same basic λέγω ὑμῖν. This variety of construction compares with only six forms in Mark: σοὶ λέγω (Mk 2:11; 5:41); ἀμὴν λέγω ὑμῖν (Mk 3:28; 8:12; 9:1, 41; 10:15, 29; 11:23; 12:43; 13:30; 14:9, 18, 25); ἀλλὰ λέγω ὑμῖν (Mk 9:13); διὰ τοῦτο λέγω ὑμῖν (Mk 11:24); ἐγὼ λέγω ὑμῖν (Mk 11:33); and ὃ δὲ ὑμῖν λέγω (Mk 13:37).

[8]John's Jesus uses some form of λέγω ὑμῖν twenty-six times. Twenty-three of these are ἀμὴν ἀμὴν λέγω ὑμῖν (σοι). Factors of rhythm and assonance might also be at work in Luke.

problem is gained when one realizes that only fifteen years after the death of William Faulkner, an Oxford, Mississippi, native and boyhood friend found it necessary to produce a glossary of Mississippi localisms "while they were still known."[9] Faulkner's fiction has in our day already begun to outlive the world in which it was set.

But although it is difficult the effort to place correctly first-century speech in its social location is not entirely hopeless. Extensive study of the question of Semitisms has provided enough information to allow hints concerning the voices in Luke.[10] A first step is the rediscovery of the distinct features of each voice.

The Language and Style of the Gospel's Narration

Any discussion of the distinct qualities of the voice of the narrator best begins with the prologue to the gospel, not only because it appears first in the sequence of the narrative, but also because it is of singular style in the gospel.[11] The opening sentence of Luke (Lk 1:1-4) is of unusual artistic construction. It stands in the best tradition of classical Greek. Composed as a single unit of six clauses, the sentence shows balance and symmetry. None of the parts is overlong or overshort; the protasis and the apodosis are of even weight; the πολλοί is balanced by κἀμοί, ἀνατάξασθαι διήγησιν by γράψαι, καθώς by the answering ἵνα ἐπιγνῷς.

Besides the balanced structure, the sentence employs a select vocabulary. Thus, the hapax legomenon ἐπειδήπερ, "inasmuch," is used where the less grand ἐπειδή might have been used; the more sono-

---

[9]Calvin S. Brown, A Glossary of Faulkner's South (New Haven CT: Yale University Press, 1976).

[10]For a history of the investigation of Semitisms in Luke, see Matthew Black, An Aramaic Approach to the Gospels and Acts (Oxford: Clarendon Press, 1967) 1-14; Fred L. Horton, "Reflections on the Semitisms of Luke-Acts," Perspectives on Luke-Acts, ed. Charles H. Talbert (Edinburgh: T. and T. Clark, 1978; reprint, Macon GA: Mercer University Press, 1984) 7ff.; and Max Wilcox, Semitisms of Acts (Oxford: Clarendon Press, 1965) 1-19.

[11]So also A. T. Robertson, "Luke's Method of Research," Biblical Review 5 (1920): 171-95. Henry J. Cadbury, "Commentary on the Preface of Luke," The Beginnings of Christianity, ed. F. J. Foakes-Jackson and Kirsopp Lake, 5 vols. (reprint, Grand Rapids MI: Baker Book House, 1979) 2:490.

rous πεπληροφορημένων, "which have been accomplished," appears in place of a possible πληρωθέντον; and the correct Attic form παρέδοσαν, "delivered," is preferred to the more colloquial ἔδωκαν.[12] In all, the sentence is without parallel in the gospel.

But abruptly, with the introduction of ἐγένετο ἐν ταῖς ἡμέραις ("there lived in the days") in the second sentence (Lk 1:5), the author abandoned his elaborate style and never again returned to it. The narration becomes colloquial in flavor, with Semitic idioms and the stringing together of coordinate clauses taking the place of the careful vocabulary and periodic construction of the opening sentence.

But what occasioned this remarkable shift in narrative style from the first to the second sentence? Some have associated the change with a gospel editor who was trained in rhetoric, but who was more interested in compiling sources than in the style of his narrative.[13] It is worthwhile to note, however, that the consequence of this change in style is not to draw attention to sources, but to make the reader aware of the characterization of the third person narrator. As Eduard Norden has so correctly pointed out, the reader, from the very beginning, is made aware that the story could have been told in excellent Attic style, but was not.[14] The change in the standard of speech from the first to the second sentence is accompanied by a change in narrative voice from the first person to the third person. Where the narrator speaks in the first person, his speech is of an Attic literary style. Where he speaks in the third person, his speech is noticeably colloquial. Since the high standard of the first sentence defines the reader's expectations of the narrator's voice, the change in style coupled with the change in voice draws attention to the purposeful na-

---

[12]Friedrich Blass, *Philology of the Gospels* (London: Macmillan, 1898; reprint, Chicago: Argonaut, 1969) 7-11.

[13]Cf. W. L. Knox, *Some Hellenistic Elements in Primitive Christianity* (London: Oxford University Press, 1944) Lecture I.

[14]Eduard Norden, *Die Antike Kunstprosa* (Stuttgart: B. G. Teubner, 1958) 2:483. So also Cadbury, "Commentary on the Preface of Luke," 490-91; Charles C. Torrey. *Our Translated Gospels* (New York: Harper and Brothers, 1936) lvi-lvii; H. F. D. Sparks, "The Semitisms of St. Luke's Gospel," *Journal of Theological Studies* 44 (1943): 129; W. B. Tatum, "The Epoch of Israel: Luke i-ii and the Theological Plan of Luke-Acts," *New Testament Studies* 13 (1967): 195.

ture of what follows.[15] What it does is emphasize the intentional characterization of the voice of the third-person narrator.

When the Gospel of Luke is read with an ear for the interaction of its voices, Lk 1:1-4 qualifies the whole narrative and pulls the narrator

---

[15]Something similar to this occurs in modern literature in William Faulkner's short story "That Evening Sun" (*Faulkner's County: Tales of Yaknapatawpha County* [London: Chatto and Windus, 1955] 339-55). The setting of the story is quickly drawn in the first three paragraphs. Quentin Compson begins his narration as a grown man remembering fifteen years into the past. The writing is of a style and vocabulary appropriate for the grown Quentin. The sentences are generally long, one consisting of 121 words, but show good balance. There is conscious artistry in the emphatic placement of "now" at the end of the first sentence, which is then repeated in the second sentence, and contrasted with "ago" at the beginning of the second paragraph. The syntax of this section is complex and the speech is generally heavy with description. Throughout there is a sprinkling of metaphors and similes, but of a stilted variety. Beginning with the fourth paragraph, however, the speech of the narrator changes. The sentences become short and choppy, often grammatically incorrect, and the vocabulary becomes colloquial; "negro" of the second paragraph giving way to "nigger" in paragraph thirteen. Description lessens, but at the same time becomes more imaginative. No phrase of the opening paragraphs nears the vivid imagery of Jesus "in the kitchen, sitting behind the stove, with his razor scar on his black face like a piece of dirty string" (341). In all, the speech pattern of the narrator changes from that of the adult Quentin Compson to that of the child of fifteen years earlier who saw and experienced the events that he recounts but did not at the time fully understand their meaning. Besides setting the scene for the story, the opening three paragraphs point the reader to the importance of the childlike voice of the narrator that follows, establishing the narrator's point of view. It is integral to the structure of the story that the narrator be perceived as one who sees but cannot fully interpret. This is guaranteed by the opening shift in style, for it draws attention to and emphasizes the characterization that follows; cf. Evans B. Harrington, "Technical Aspects of William Faulkner's 'That Evening Sun,' " *Faulkner Studies* (Milwood NY: Kraus Reprint, 1973) 1:54-59. For the importance of voice to narration, see also M. L. Cecil, "A Rhetoric for Benjy," *Southern Literary Journal* 3 (1970): 32-46; M. Blanchard, "The Rhetoric of Communion: Voice in *The Sound and the Fury*," *American Literature* 41 (January 1970): 555-65; K. Morrison, "Faulkner's Joe Christmas: Character Through Voice," *Texas Studies in Literature and Language* 2 (Winter 1961): 419-43; J. F. Trimmer, "The Unvanquished: The Teller and the Tale," *Ball State University Forum* 10 (Winter 1969): 35-42.

into the story. There is a sense in which he stands center stage, much as does Ivan when he narrates "The Grand Inquisitor."[16] One never loses consciousness that it is Ivan, distinct from Dostoevsky, telling the story to Alyosha, and in the same way the narrator in Luke appears as a distinct character telling the story to Theophilus.

Beginning with his second sentence, the narrator's language is constructed almost exclusively with the particles καί and δέ, "and," "but."[17] Out of approximately 1,260 particles in his speech, 1,064 are either one or the other.[18] The shift from the subordination of clauses in the narrator's prologue to the coordination of clauses in the body of his speech is significant. The exact way in which it is significant, however, is debated. Some have taken the parataxis common to the body of the narrative to be Semitic.[19] As is well known, while the extensive coordination of independent clauses with καί (less often δέ) was not accepted in classical Greek, the equivalent construction was virtually necessary in Hebrew. But the matter is complicated, because parataxis also occurs with regularity in koine nonliterary texts, so that this construction alone is not enough to indicate Semitic overtones in the narration. Only the overuse of the construction might establish such overtones—and at this point the problem becomes yet more difficult as one realizes that although it is abundant in Luke's narration, the paratactic construction appears significantly less than in Mark.[20] Unfortunately, then, the inclination toward sentences

---

[16]Fyodor M. Dostoevsky, *The Brothers Karamazov,* trans. Constance Garnett (Chicago: William Benton, 1952) 127-37.

[17]The exact breakdown of the narrator's use of function words is given in Appendix A.

[18]The figures are approximate and will vary slightly according to the choice of text. Καί and δέ were laboriously counted in *The Greek New Testament,* ed. Kurt Aland, et al. (Stuttgart: Deutsche Bibelstiftung, 1981) Robert Morgenthaler's count of καί and δέ is slightly higher than mine. He found 1,455 καί(compared to 1,435) and 548 δέ (compared to 538); cf. *Statistik des neutestamentlichen Wortschatzes,* (Zürich: Gotthelf-Verlag, 1958) 167.

[19]Notably Henry S. Gehman, "The Hebraic Character of LXX Greek," *Vetus Testamentum* 1 (1951): 81-90.

[20]Total figures for Mark's and Luke's use of καί and δέ by each narrational

formed with καί and δέ is not enough to distinguish clearly a Greek from a Semitic setting for the narrator's voice.

Nevertheless this tendency does help to remind us of the oral nature of the gospel's narration. It has long been observed that while the complex sentence of the prologue has its common matrix in written composition, the short, simply connected, running sentences of the rest of the narration have their matrix in an oral setting.[21] This is a complicated matter that should be pursued at some length, but it is highly suggestive that the narrator's repeated use of καί and δέ displays two of the principal characteristics of spoken language: (1) the average length of the sentences formed with the two particles is much shorter than the literary sentence of the prologue; and (2) the variety of the function words in the body of the narration is proportionately much less than the variety in Lk 1:1-4.

To this oral pattern of the narrator's function words can be added other rhetorical evidence suggesting the recited character of his speech in Lk 1:5-24:53. J. W. Gibson and others have found that oral language displays significantly fewer syllables per word than written language,[22] and as F. Blass and many others have pointed out, the vocabulary of the body of the narration in Luke includes a proportionately larger number of short words than does the prologue.[23] Perhaps a ready example is to be found in the uses of ἐπειδήπερ in the prologue and ἐπειδή in Lk 7:1.

---

group can be compared in the following table.

	καί		δέ		TOTAL WORDS IN GOSPEL	
SPOKEN BY	MK	LK	MK	LK	MK	LK
The Narrator	740	(698)	113	(366)	5,826	(7,690)
Jesus	237	(587)	39	(157)	3,944	(9,038)
Other Characters	70	(150)	3	(15)	1,252	(2,437)
TOTALS	1,047	(1,435)	155	(538)	11,022	(19,165)

[21]F. Blass and A. Debrunner, *A Greek Grammar of the New Testament and Other Early Christian Literature,* trans. Robert W. Funk (Chicago: University of Chicago Press, 1961) 239.

[22]J. W. Gibson, et al., "A Quantitative Examination of Differences and Similarities in Written and Spoken Messages," *Speech Monographs* 33 (1966): 444-51.

In general, oral language can also be identified by the use of relatively few precise numerical terms.[24] How Luke was inclined to leave
out details of number from his sources has been thoroughly detailed
by Henry J. Cadbury in *The Style and Literary Method of Luke.*[25] In fact,
this oral disposition of the gospel is highlighted by the narrator's af-
fection for qualifying numbers with ὡσεί, "about." In all, Cadbury
concluded that Luke "inclines to generalization,"[26] which again is quite
characteristic of oral language.[27] In this regard, Lk 3:1-2, with its dating
and elaborate chronological synchronism, has often been mistakenly
identified as a sign of the author's historical-literary intention."[28] But
Cadbury's conclusion of generalization holds true here also, for actually the passage is not so much concerned with specifying the date
of the beginning of John's ministry[29] as it is with rapidly brushing in a
proper background for the story of Jesus. While comparisons have been
made at this point between Luke and Thucydides,[30] one cannot but notice the yet greater affinities between Lk 3:1-2 and the beginning of Es-

---

[23]F. Blass, *Grammar of New Testament Greek*, trans. Henry St. John
Thackery, 2nd ed. (London: Macmillan, 1905) 280; Torrey, *Our Translated
Gospels*, lviff.; W. L. Knox, *Some Hellenistic Elements*, 1ff.

[24]J. A. DeVito, "Psychogrammatical Factors in Oral and Written Discourse
by Skilled Communicators," *Speech Monographs* 33 (1966): 73-76.

[25]Henry J. Cadbury, *The Style and Literary Method of Luke* (Cambridge MA:
Harvard University Press, 1920) 127ff.

[26]Ibid., 115-18.

[27]DeVito, "Psychogrammatical Factors," 73-76.

[28]John Drury, for instance, saw in Lk 3:1-2 a good example of "Luke's in-
terest in historical dating" (*Tradition and Design in Luke's Gospel* [Atlanta:
John Knox Press, 1977] 124); cf. J. M. Creed, *The Gospel According to St. Luke*
(London: Macmillan, 1957) 46ff.

[29]One should not minimize the important role that John's ministry plays
in the gospel. Nevertheless, if the author's purpose were primarily historical,
one could expect an elaborate dating of the beginning of Jesus' ministry instead of the Baptist's ministry.

[30]Creed, *The Gospel According to St. Luke*, 48.

ther, for example, which belongs in a dramatic rather than historical atmosphere—the recitation at Purim.[31]

Luke's inclination toward ἅπας or πᾶς, "all," and ἕκαστος, "each, every," also hints at the oral character of the gospel's narration. J. A. DeVito has found that oral style is characterized by significantly more "pseudo-quantifying terms" and "allness terms" than written style.[32] Again, it was Cadbury who most clearly demonstrated how such terms are favored by the gospel's author.[33] Perhaps the strongest evidence joining these terms to the narrator's voice is the partial list given by Cadbury, in which πᾶς appears in small summary statements in Luke but is not present in the parallels (Lk 3:15; 7:18; 8:40; 9:43; 13:17; 18:43; 19:37; 24:9).

On the whole, then, the narrator's use of short sentences, the lack of variety in his use of function words, the small number of vocables in his average word, his avoidance of precise numerical terms, his tendency to generalize, and his inclination to use "pseudoquantifying terms" and "allness terms" remind us that his account is directed to the ear as much as to the eye. In modern terms, one could think of the narrator's voice in Lk 1:5-24:53 as characterized as an oral type. This, of course, is not an unexpected discovery, for it seems that for reasons of custom and economics most ancient literature was intended to be read aloud. Nevertheless, it is helpful to think of the narration more in terms of the spoken word and less in terms of the written word than we normally do.[34]

---

[31]Cf. the first paragraph of the prologue and Esther 1:1-3. For the book's association with its festival recitation, see Hayyin Schauss, *The Jewish Festivals* (Cincinnati: Union of American Hebrew Congregations, 1938) 237ff. Although most modern scholars do not think that Esther originated in the festival setting, by the time of Luke the book was closely associated with its recitation at Purim; cf. Israel Bettan, *The Five Scrolls* (Cincinnati: Union of American Hebrew Congregations, 1950) 201ff.

[32]De Vito, "Psychogrammatical Factors," 73-76.

[33]Cadbury, *Style and Literary Method,* 115ff.

[34]Important studies of the oral qualities of the gospels are Norden, *Die antike Kunstprosa;* Amos N. Wilder, *The Language of the Gospel: Early Christian Rhetoric* (New York: Harper and Row, 1964); Walter J. Ong, *The Presence of the Word* (New Haven CT: Yale University Press, 1967); *Interfaces of the Word* (Ithaca NY: Cornell University Press, 1977); *Orality and Literacy* (New

Narrational Formulas

Luke's narration is characterized not only by orality; it is also characterized by several formulaic constructions found frequently in the narration of the gospel but hardly at all in the direct speech of the characters of the story.

1. (Καὶ) ἐγένετο, *"(and) it happened" with a following verb.* This idiom, frequently used in the Septuagint, appears forty times in the voice of the narrator. The construction is highly formalized, occurring thirty-four times followed by ἐν with dative,[35] three times followed by ὡς,[36] and twice followed by μετά with accusative.[37] It is significant that the (καὶ) ἐγένετο appears only once outside of the narration of Luke (compare Lk 19:15).

2. Ἀποκριθεὶς εἶπεν, *"answering, he said."* This idiom appears frequently in the Septuagint.[38] It appears thirty-six times in the voice of the narrator, and only four times otherwise.[39]

York: Methuen, 1982); Werner H. Kelber, *The Oral and Written Gospel* (Philadelphia: Fortress Press, 1983); John Dominic Crossan, *In Fragments* (San Francisco: Harper and Row, 1983). More generally, see Geoffery S. Kirk, *Homer and the Oral Tradition* (Cambridge: Cambridge University Press, 1976) and Donald Lemen Clark, *Rhetoric in Greco-Roman Education* (Westport CT: Greenwood Press, 1977).

[35]Lk 1:5, 8, 59; 2:1, 6; 3:21; 5:1, 12, 17; 6:1, 6, 12; 7:11; 8:1, 22, 40; 9:18, 29, 33, 36, 37, 51; 10:38; 11:1, 27; 14:1; 17:11, 14; 18:35; 20:1, 24:4, 15, 30, 51.

[36]Lk 1:23, 41; 2:15.

[37]Lk 2:46; 9:28. It is followed by a genitive at Lk 11:14.

[38]Cf. F. L. Horton, "Reflections on the Semitisms of Luke-Acts," *Perspectives on Luke-Acts,* 6. J. M. Creed (*The Gospel According to St. Luke,* lxxx) without sound basis thought that ἀποκριθεὶς εἶπεν was probably due to the influence of Aramaic.

[39]Lk 1:19, 35, 60; 3:11, 16; 4:8, 12; 5:5, 22, 31; 6:3; 7:22, 40, 43; 8:21; 9:19, 20, 41, 49; 10:27, 41; 11:45; 13:2, 14, 15; 14:3; 17:17, 20, 37; 19:40; 20:3, 39; 22:51; 23:9; 24:18. To these one might add the construction of ἀποκριθεὶς with ἔφη (Lk 23:3, 40). Outside of the speech of the "narrator to Theophilus" the construction appears at Lk 11:7 (ἀποκριθεὶς εἴπη); 13:8 (ἀποκριθεὶς λέγει; 13:25 (ἀποκριθεὶς ἐρεῖ); and 15:29 (ἀποκριθεὶς εἶπεν).

3. Καὶ ἰδού, *"and behold."* This idiom, common in the Septuagint, appears fifteen times in the voice of the narrator.[40] It is significant that while ἰδού without the καί appears frequently throughout the gospel, it so appears only once in the gospel's narration (Lk 22:47); and that outside of the narration of Luke, the formulaic καὶ ἰδού is frequent only in the speech of the angel (Lk 1:20, 31, 36).[41]

4. Ἐν τῷ *with infinitive, "when."* While the narrator uses this idiom thirty-one times in the gospel,[42] it appears only three times outside of his own speech (Lk 8:5; 10:35; 19:15). It is significant that twenty-four times the narrator's construction follows καὶ ἐγένετο[43]—which corresponds to the Septuagint's rendering of ‎ב‎ with infinitive. This joined construction appears only one time outside of the voice of the narrator in the gospel (Lk 19:15).

5. Δοξάζειν τὸν θεόν, *"praising God."* This phrase is used by the narrator eight times, but does not otherwise appear in the gospel.[44]

The constructions listed here are (a) highly formalized, and (b) almost exclusive to the narrator. The formalized δοξάζειν τὸν θεόν does not appear outside the gospel's narration; καὶ ἐγένετο with a following verb appears forty times in the voice of the narrator, and only once otherwise; ἐν τῷ with infinitive appears thirty-six times in his voice, and only four times otherwise; and καὶ ἰδού appears fifteen times in the voice of the narrator, and otherwise as a formula not frequently in the gospel. Clearly, there is a pattern linking these idioms to the narrator's voice.[45]

---

[40]Lk 2:25; 5:12, 18; 7:12, 37; 8:41; 9:30, 38; 10:25; 13:11; 14:2; 19:2; 23:50; 24:4, 13.

[41]The only place that the narrator uses ἰδού without the καί is at Lk 22:47. Angels use ἰδού four times. The one time that it appears in the angel's speech without καί is at Lk 2:10 where it is nonetheless formalized with γάρ.

[42]Lk 1:8, 21; 2:6, 27, 43; 3:21; 5:1, 12; 6:12; 7:11; 8:1, 40, 42; 9:18, 29, 33, 34, [36], 51; [10:38]; 11:1, 27, 37; 14:1; 17:11, 14; 18:35; 24:4, 15, 30, 51.

[43]Lk 1:8; 2:6; 3:21; 5:1, 12; 6:12; 7:11; 8:1; 9:18, 29, 33, [36], 51, [10:38]; 11:1, 27; 14:1; 17:11, 14; 18:35; 24:4, 15, 30, 51.

[44]Lk 2:20; 5:25, 26; 7:16; 13:13; 17:15; 18:43; 23:47.

[45]By applying the Chi-square test to the population of these idioms as a group and as entities one sees that the statistical evidence indicates an extremely high probability (at 99.5 percent level) of design.

But it is also significant that the constructions are all common formulas of the Septuagint. In fact, neither καὶ ἐγένετο or ἐγένετο δέ, followed by a resumptive καί, nor ἀποκριθεὶς εἶπεν seem to be in any other sense contemporary forms of the first century. They are not, for example, attested translations of contemporary Semitic speech. Rather, they are archaic Hebraic idioms that survived only in the language of the Septuagint.[46]

Three different explanations have been offered for the Septuagintalisms in Luke. Charles Cutler Torrey understood them to indicate that the gospel was translated from a Semitic original.[47] His main evidence consisted of several constructions in Luke that are written in very difficult Greek. According to Torrey these idioms could best be understood as literal translations of Aramaic or Hebrew.[48] But in spite of Torrey's readiness to identify Aramaic idioms behind difficult Greek expressions, few scholars have followed him. They have focused on Torrey's rather subjective definition of Semitisms as expressions in Greek that an interpreter, learned in Hebrew and Aramaic, recognizes as Semitic; the failure of Torrey and subsequent research to bring forth any hard evidence for the existence of Semitic originals for the gospels; and the difficulty of establishing a historical scenario to fit the Church's use of Aramaic Gospels.[49] To these difficulties can be added Matthew Black's contrary conclusion in *An Aramaic Approach to the Gospels and Acts* that there is evidence for an Aramaic tradition in Luke only in the sayings of Jesus—

---

[46]Horton, "Reflections on the Semitisms of Luke-Acts," 6. Blass, Debrunner, and Funk thought that ἀποκριθεὶς εἶπεν might indicate a translation from the Aramaic (*A Greek Grammar*, 3-4 n5). Eduard Schweizer concluded that ἐγένετο with a following finite verb, and ἐγένετο with a following καί, and ἐν τῷ with infinitive were Hebraisms and not Aramaicisms. To him, however, this indicated the probability of a Hebrew source underlying Luke ("Eine hebraisierende Sonderquelle des Lukas?" *Theologische Zeitschrift* 6 [1950]: 163-64).

[47]Charles Cutler Torrey, *Our Translated Gospels* (New York: Harper and Brothers, 1936).

[48]Ibid., chapter V.

[49]D. W. Riddle, "The Logic of the Theory of Translation Greek," *Journal of Biblical Literature* 51 (1932): 14.

but even these sayings, according to Black, are not literal translations into Greek, but rather Greek interpretations.[50]

A second explanation for Luke's Septuagintalisms has been offered by George Kennedy, H. F. D. Sparks, and others who have promoted a mimetic role for the author of the gospel.[51] According to this view, Luke attempted to carry on the literary tradition of the Septuagint by imitating it. But this explanation actually seems as difficult as the first, for Max Wilcox has pointed out that while many phrases in Luke-Acts are reminiscent of the Septuagint, the direct imitation of it is not very common.[52] Furthermore, this mimetic view seems to presuppose a misplaced modern notion of authorship and the reading public. This is readily seen, for instance, in John Drury's perception of Luke as a writer who on his first pages made a bid for the attention of his readers, and attempted to "hook them into his story."[53] The Septuagintalisms for Drury were literary devices, such "that a reader coming to the book freshly might easily suspect that he is hearing something from the old stories of the Jews—from Judges, Samuel, or Genesis."[54] But perhaps this tendency to view the gospels as literature meant for private reading, which the reader might come to "freshly," needs to be questioned. This would be especially true of a supposed imitation of the Septuagint, as one would then have to ask whether the author held some kind of canonical design for his book.

A third explanation has been suggested by Matthew Black, and more recently by Fred Horton, who have seen in the Lukan Septuagin-

---

[50]Matthew Black, *An Aramaic Approach to the Gospels and Acts,* 3rd ed. (Oxford: Clarendon Press, 1967) 275.

[51]George Kennedy, "Classical and Christian Source Criticism," *The Relationships Among the Gospels,* ed. William O. Walker, Jr. (San Antonio: Trinity University Press, 1978) 125-55; H. F. D. Sparks, "The Semitisms of St. Luke's Gospel," *Journal of Theological Studies* 54 (1943): 129-38.

[52]Max Wilcox, *The Semitisms of Acts.*

[53]Drury, *Tradition and Design in Luke's Gospel,* 46-66.

[54]Ibid., 46-47. Drury follows Sparks, "The Semitisms of St. Luke's Gospel," 136.

talisms an indication of a specialized language of worship.[55] Their suggestion is actually a refinement of Henry S. Gehman's contention that Hellenistic Jews used a Greek that was influenced by Hebrew for religious discourse.[56] Nigel Turner had supported this view with a study showing that ἐκεῖνος, ἕνεκα and πᾶς were used differently in the Septuagint than in the papyri of Greek-speaking Jews.[57] It was by adding this discovery that Hellenistic Jews used both koine and Septuagintal Greek to Wilcox's finding that there are actually two types of Septuagintalisms in Acts—direct reproductions, and a second class that only has an appearance of being Septuagintal—that Horton then concluded that the Semitisms of Luke-Acts are best explained as a type of "Synagogue Greek"—that is, a specialized language used for religious purposes only, paralleling the "mixed style of Hebrew" discovered by C. Rabin for the religious vernacular at Qumran.[58]

This third solution is especially appealing in light of two other peculiarities of the gospel's narration. One concerns the way that the author introduced Old Testament Scripture into the gospel. Although scriptural references are frequent in Luke, only three times do quotations appear in the voice of the narrator (Lk 2:23, 24; 3:4-6)[59] In each

---

[55]Matthew Black, "Second Thoughts IX: The Semitic Element in the New Testament," *Expository Times* 77 (1965): 20-3; Horton, "Reflections on the Semitisms of Luke-Acts."

[56]Henry S. Gehman, "The Hebraic Character of LXX Greek," *Vetus Testamentum* 1 (1951): 81-90.

[57]Nigel Turner, "The Unique Character of Biblical Greek," *Vetus Testamentum* 5 (1955): 208-13. Turner also pointed this way in "The Relation of Luke I and II to Hebraic Sources and to the Rest of Luke-Acts," *New Testament Studies* 2 (1955): 100-109. But see Paul Winter's answer in "On Luke and Lucan Sources," *Zeitschrift für die Neutestamentliche Wissenschaft* (1956): 217-42.

[58]C. Rabin, "Hebrew and Aramaic in the First Century," *The Jewish People in the First Century*, ed. S. Safrai and M. Stern in cooperation with D. Flusser and W. C. van Unnik (Assen: Van Gorcum, 1974) 2:1007-1039.

[59]In all, references to Scripture appear twenty-four times in Luke: sixteen in the speech of Jesus (Lk 4:4; 4:8; 4:12; 4:18-19; 7:27; 8:10; 18:20; 19:46; 20:17, 20:37; 20:42-43; 21:27; 22:37; 22:69; 23:30; 23:46); twice in the speech of the devil (Lk 4:10; 4:11); once in the speech of a lawyer (Lk 10:27), the crowd (Lk 19:38), and the Sadducees (Lk 20:28); and three times in the speech of the narrator.

case, however, the narrator introduces the scriptural saying in a way consonant with a formal setting in worship. In Lk 2:23, 24, the law of Moses is reiterated as the "law of the Lord," and Lk 3:4-6 is preceded by the formal heading, "As it is written in a book of the works of Isaiah the prophet."[60] But in contrast to this formal type of introduction, the other characters of the narrative often offer no introduction at all for Scripture (compare Lk 4:18-19; 8:10; 19:38; 21:27; 22:69; 23:30; 23:46). Five times a character simply says "it is written" and assumes the authority of the Word and the concurrence of the audience (Lk 4:4, 8, 10; 7:27; 19:46). To these occurrences can be added Lk 4:11 (introduced by the γέγραπται of Lk 4:10); Lk 20:17 (introduced by γεγραμμένον τοῦτο); and Lk 4:12 (introduced by εἴρηται). Likewise, the other diverse forms used by the narrative characters to introduce Scripture simply assume a common understanding of its authority (compare Lk 10:27; 18:20; 20:28, 37, 42-43; 22:37).

The second peculiarity of the narrator's voice that might support Horton's suggestion of a special language of worship is the narrator's use of three formulas that are not to be found in the Septuagint.

1. *The periphrastic construction of the verb "to be" with a participle.* Out of forty occurrences in the gospel, all but two appear in the narration of Luke.[61]

2. Ἄρχομαι *in a weak sense without emphasis on the idea of beginning (Lk 4:21; 5:21; 7:49; 11:29; 12:1; 20:9; 22:23).* It is significant that all seven cases are formulaic; Lk 4:21; 11:29; 12:1; and 20:9 (ἤρξατο

---

[60]One notes the same type of close definition of Scripture by the narrator at Lk 4:17, where he introduces a Scripture reference that is actually spoken by Jesus. It seems significant that this formal introduction for Scripture is also used by Jesus in the Temple (Lk 20:42, ἐν βίβλῳ ψαλμῶν); by Peter, speaking in Acts to a large gathering of the brethren (Acts 1:20, ἐν βίβλῳ ψαλμῶν); and by Stephen when preaching to the council (Acts 7:42, ἐν βίβλῳ τῶν προφητῶν).

[61]In proper Greek usage the periphrastic construction of the verb "to be" with a participle is found only when there is a definite intention to emphasize continuity of action (cf. Lk 4:38, 44; 6:12). Aramaic uses the construction frequently, often as an equivalent for the imperfect (cf. Lk 9:53; 11:14; 13:10, 11; 14:1). Outside of the speech of the narrator, the idiom appears in Lk 15:24; 24:32. Cf. Creed, *The Gospel According to St. Luke,* lxxx.

λέγειν) "he started to say," introducing speech by Jesus, and Lk 5:21, 7:49, and 22:23 introducing speech that purposefully excludes Jesus.[62]

3. (Ἐν) αὐτῇ τῇ ὥρᾳ, *"in that hour" in the sense of "forthwith."* Out of seven occurrences in the gospel, six appear in the voice of the narrator.[63]

In the sense in which Luke uses it, the last idiom is unparalleled in the koine, but matches an Aramaic idiom.[64] The other two constructions are found occasionally in good Greek, but according to Horton the frequency of their occurrence in Luke shades them as Aramaic.[65] All three idioms are highly formalized and appear in the gospel almost exclusively in the voice of the narrator. But do they indicate, then, a natural tendency on his part toward Aramaic? Is the narrator to be characterized as a person whose native tongue is Aramaic and who is speaking a second language? The suggestion might have some merit as it would allow a ready explanation for the narrator's use of πόλις for "province" (compare Lk 1:39; 8:39) and "open country" (compare Lk 8:27; 9:10), and his use of πᾶσαν τὴν οἰκουμένην for "all the land (of Israel)" (Lk 2:1).[66] But in light of their formulaic nature, and also Matthew Black's conclusion that Luke's narration does not otherwise show traces of the Aramaic,[67] it seems much more likely that these idioms are part of that mixed style of Jewish Greek worship language suggested by Black and Horton.

But it is not necessary here to decide whether the author consciously attempted to imitate the language of the Septuagint or more simply appropriated a Jewish-Greek worship language for his narration. In either case, it seems clear that he wanted to evoke a proper narrative voice for the gospel. To recapitulate: the idioms that char-

---

[62]The narrator uses ἄρχω also at Lk 11:53; 19:37, 45 but with a clear emphasis on the idea of beginning.

[63]It appears in the narrator's speech at Lk 2:38; 7:21; 10:21; 13:31; 20:19; 24:33. The construction appears in Jesus' speech at Lk 12:12.

[64]Horton, "Reflections on the Semitisms of Luke-Acts," 4.

[65]Cf. Creed, *The Gospel According to St. Luke,* lxxx.

[66]Torrey, *Our Translated Gospels,* 82-87.

[67]Black, *An Aramaic Approach,* 272.

acterize the narrator's speech are not those of proper Greek, or of everyday speech that might have slipped inadvertently into his account. Through the coordination of clauses and use of idioms, the author affected a formalized language that stood out sharply against classical Greek, that koine not attested by the Septuagint, and contemporary Aramaic.[68] But it cannot be overemphasized that this formalized language is the language of the narrator only, and also contrasts sharply with the speech of the other characters in the narrative and the Attic literary style of his own prologue. It does not contrast, however, with his narrative position as indicated by the titles that he applies to Jesus. To him, Jesus is Lord, and the story that he relates is the opening of the mind to understand all Scripture (compare Lk 24:45). The narrator believes, and as he does, participates in the meaning of Scripture that he tells through his story.

Conclusion

In sum, what can be said about Luke's narration? Three statements seem especially noteworthy. First, the narrator's voice is an affected voice. That is, the style of the third person narration is different from that of the first person prologue and from the other voices in the gospel, in part because the author wanted it to be different. He characterized his narration by repeating certain Septuagintal formulas. Second, as inhabitants of a modern society, we must remind ourselves that the narrator's voice is of an oral type. By no means was this simply a case of oral tradition influencing the style of literature. The author characterized the voice in this way. Proper sound, harmony, and rhythm were considered by the author to be important aspects of the narration. The narration was intended to be heard—rather than to be read silently. Third, the narrator's language has as its locus the community of faith. The narrator assumes in the story that the Christian community is the proper context for hearing the gospel. The story that he relates belongs to and is directed to those who worship Christ.

---

[68]Excluding the Septuagintal or "worship" formulas, the narrator's voice is generally of a proper Hellenistic style. For a complete discussion see Appendix B.

Jesus' Voice

Chapter 2

With some characteristics of the gospel's narration in mind, let me now ask some questions about Jesus' voice. Is Jesus' language really demonstrably different from the narrator's language? What are some of the important characteristics of Jesus' voice in Luke? Which of these characteristics show the influence of tradition? How much of Jesus' voice do we owe to the author's attempt at characterization? And, finally, is Jesus' language in any way unique in Luke?

The Distinctiveness of Jesus' Voice

I will attempt to illustrate the distinctiveness of Jesus' language first by showing how Luke has handled the Markan εὐθύς, "immediately." Luke's use of εὐθύς, εὐθέως, and παραχρῆμα, all different ways of saying "immediately," can seem very puzzling when perceived apart from the characters in the story. Εὐθύς appears more than forty times in Mark. John Hawkins declared it to be a characteristic word of the gospel,[1] and one notices, in fact, that it seems overused, appearing

---

[1]John C. Hawkins, *Horae Synopticae* (Oxford: Clarendon, 1909) 12.

eleven times in the first chapter alone. Often εὐθύς in Mark is joined with καί at the beginning of a clause, and stands apart from the verb. Nigel Turner has suggested that these instances are reminiscent of the Hebrew consecutive and for the most part should be interpreted with weak adverbial force: "and so."[2]

Given the repetitiveness and consecutive Hebraic use of the adverb in Mark, it is not unexpected that Matthew has reduced its appearance in his text, and has taken it over only six (seven) times.[3] It is somewhat unusual, however, that Luke has completely removed Mark's εὐθύς from his text. In one place he modified it to εὐθέως (Lk 5:13‖Mk 1:42), and five times he changed it to παραχρῆμα (Lk 5:25‖Mk 2:12; Lk 8:44‖Mk 5:29; Lk 8:55‖Mk 5:42; Lk 18:43‖Mk 10:52; Lk 22:60‖Mk 14:72). But not one of the instances of εὐθύς in Mark remains in Luke.

At this point, it has been argued that the author of the Third Gospel held some stylistic or personal bias against the word and simply removed it from his source, often substituting his own favorite, παραχρῆμα.[4] This argument, however, is not convincing, because Luke does use εὐθύς at Lk 6:49, either inserting it into or appropriating it from Q.[5] One is then placed in the peculiar position of affirming that εὐθύς was so distasteful to the author of Luke that he thoroughly removed it from Mark—redacting his source 40-50 times—while at the same time he either inserted the term into some Q material, or allowed its one occurrence in Q to slip by his editing pen. Such an explanation is not persuasive.

---

[2]J. H. Moulton, R. Howard, and N. Turner, *A Grammar of New Testament Greek*, 4 vols. (Edinburgh: T. and T. Clark, 1908-) 3:229.

[3]Cf. Mt 3:16‖Mk 1:10; Mt 13:20‖Mk. 4:16; Mt 13:21‖Mk 4:17; Mt 14:27‖Mk 6:50; Mt 21:2‖Mk 11:2; Mt 21:3‖Mk 11:3; Mt 26:74‖Mk 14:72. Matthew has modified εὐθύς to εὐθέως another six to eight times.

[4]Walter Grundmann, *Das Evangelium nach Lukas* (Berlin: Evangelische Verlagsanstalt, 1962) 183.

[5]Although no final answer can be given, Adolf von Harnack as argued that Lk 6:46-49 does not parallel Q as closely as does Mt 7:21, 24-27. If this is so, the probability is increased that εὐθύς was added to the text of Q by Luke; cf. A. Harnack, *The Sayings of Jesus: The Second Source of St. Matthew and St. Luke,* trans. J. R. Wilkinson (New York: G. P. Putnam's Sons, 1908) 70-74.

But what makes such an argument entirely untenable is the realization that the author never placed his favored παραχρῆμα in the mouth of Jesus. Only the narrator in the story uses παραχρῆμα.[6] When Jesus speaks, he uses εὐθύς (Lk 6:49) and εὐθέως (Lk 12:36, 54; 14:5; 17:7; 21:9). Moreover, not one of these instances in Jesus' speech is traceable to a source, and Lk 21:9 shows in fact that the author purposefully inserted εὐθέως into the Markan source (Lk 21:9‖Mk 13:7‖Mt 24:6).

Generally, then, the author of the gospel so redacted his sources as to have the narrator use παραχρῆμα and Jesus use εὐθέως. But why? What could have motivated such a narrational distinction? In his study of the two words, David Daube concluded that παραχρῆμα has a definite place in Lukan theology. It always appears in a pregnant sense indicating the fulfillment that resulted from divine activity. It is, in the narration, the immediate compliance with a divine command or prediction.[7] Very clearly παραχρῆμα fits with the language of the worshiping community used by the narrator. Εὐθέως, on the other hand, in the speech of Jesus seems to be a secular term. It never describes the immediate response to and fulfillment of a divine order.[8] Its meaning is nontheological—simply "at once."

Daube's conclusions fit nicely with the findings of the preceding chapter. The author of the gospel dramatized his story by providing a special language for his narrator. But this insight can be carried a little further. It has already been noted that the author of Luke almost completely removed εὐθύς from the speech of Jesus, replacing it with εὐθέως. While both terms were commonly used in the first century, there is some indication that εὐθέως was at that time considered somewhat less archaic than εὐθύς.[9] Thus the author's preference for

---

[6]Lk 1:64; 4:39; 5:25; 8:44, 47, 55; 13:13; 18:43; 19:11; 22:60. On the other hand, it seems that the author exercised as much care in editing the Markan εὐθύς out of Jesus' speech as he did in editing it out of the narrator's speech (cf. Mk 4:5‖Lk 8:6; Mk 4:15‖Lk 8:12; Mk 4:16‖Lk 8:13; Mk 4:17‖Lk 8:13; Mk 11:2‖Lk 19:30; Mk 11:3‖Lk 19:31).

[7]David Daube, *The Sudden in the Scriptures* (Leiden: E. J. Brill, 1964) 65.

[8]Ibid.

[9]Henry G. Liddell, Henry S. Jones, and Robert Scott, *A Greek-English Lexicon,* 2 vols. (Oxford: Clarendon Press, 1951) 1:716.

εὐθέως in the speech of Jesus might have been occasioned by a desire to make the language of Mark more contemporary. Nevertheless, it seems significant that while εὐθύς appears often in the Septuagint, εὐθέως does so rarely and certainly would not have had in Luke's community the "biblical" connotations of the former word. Εὐθέως was a more secular term, and the contrast between παραχρῆμα and εὐθέως was perhaps greater than would have been the contrast between πα-ραχρῆμα and εὐθύς. Thus the author might well have placed the more secular term into the speech of Jesus in order to heighten its contrast with παραχρῆμα. The one εὐθύς used by Jesus (Lk 6:49) could have been an oversight—but probably not, as it is dramatically fitting that in a sermon at the foot of a mountain Jesus should speak in a way that would remind his hearers of the Old Sinai covenant, and so employ the language of Scripture.

Certainly one should not discount sources, idiosyncracies, and happenstance when dealing with the variety of Luke. But in this case the evidence does suggest that the author wrote as if hearing his characters speak. Jesus uses the secular εὐθέως, except where it is dramatically propitious that he should use εὐθύς. The narrator, on the other hand, prefers the more reverential παραχρῆμα. The lone appearance of εὐθέως in the narrator's voice is important in that it indicates that the author's effort was spontaneous. The author did not set out to characterize his narrator by placing in his mouth a special word. Rather, the author listened with his mind's ear to his characters speaking, and the word that he most often heard from his narrator was παραχρῆμα and from Jesus εὐθέως.

The Style of Jesus' Speech

In addition to its contrast with παραχρῆμα, Jesus' use of εὐθέως is perhaps indicative of the popular style of his speech: In Luke, Jesus speaks the language of the people.[10] It is significant that approximately two-thirds of the instances that I note in Appendix C as indicating the popular standard of Jesus' speech cannot be attributed to any known sources. Out of the 212 instances of the popular standard of Jesus' speech in the gospel that I list in the appendix, forty-seven come from material that parallels

---

[10]For a complete discussion, see Appendix C.

either Mark or Matthew, but they are not in Mark or Matthew, while eighty-seven are in material peculiar to Luke. Certainly it is not demonstrable that the popular style of Jesus' speech in Luke is the result of slovenly editorial work on Mark and Q.[11] Rather, Jesus' speech characterizes him in the narrative. He does not speak as the narrator speaks. His language is the common language of the people.

While the standard of Jesus' language is that of the common man, the style of his speech is quite unusual.[12] His questions are most often rhetorical devices, either assuming a particular answer or assuming that no answer can be given. So, Jesus forms certain interrogatives with οὐ expecting an affirmative answer (Lk 2:49; 13:15, 16; 17:17, 18); others with οὐχί (Lk 6:39; 12:6; 14:28, 31; 15:8; 17:8, 17; 22:27; 24:26); others with μή expecting a negative answer (Lk 5:34; 10:15; 11:11, 12; 17:9: 22:35); and another with μήτι (Lk 6:39). Also, one notices double interrogatives joined by ἤ used rhetorically by Jesus (Lk 5:23; 6:9, 9; 14:3; 20:4; 22:27). Other questions used primarily as didactic or argumentative devices are found in Jesus' speech at Lk 6:32, 34, 42; 7:24, 25, 26, 31, 42, 44; 8:25; 9:41; 10:26 (twice), 36; 11:5-7, 18, 19; 12:14, 20, 25, 26, 42, 56, 57; 13:2, 4, 7, 18 (twice), 20; 14:5, 34; 15:4; 16:2, 11, 12; 17:7; 18:7 (twice), 8, 19; 19:22, 23, 31; 20:13, 15, 17, 24, 44; 22:46, 48, 52; 24:38.[13] There are approximately eighty such questions in the speech of Jesus in Luke. Outside of his speech, rhetorical questions are very infrequent and appear only at Lk 3:7, 5:21 (twice); 22:49; 24:32. Nonrhetorical questions, on the other hand, are not frequent with Jesus and appear only at Lk. 8:30, 45; 9:18, 20; 18:41; 24:17, 19, 41.

It is evident that the interrogative form of Jesus' language is peculiar to Jesus in the narrative.[14] It is equally clear that the main purpose

---

[11]This was the view of Wilfred L. Knox (*Some Hellenistic Elements in Primitive Christianity* [London: Oxford University Press, 1944]). But H. F. D. Sparks showed many Semitic additions to Jesus' speech in Luke in "The Semitisms of St. Luke's Gospel," *Journal of Theological Studies* 44 (1943): 129ff.

[12]Important rhetorical studies include Amos N. Wilder, *The Language of the Gospel: Early Christian Rhetoric* (New York: Harper and Row, 1964) and John D. Crossan, *In Fragments* (San Francisco: Harper and Row, 1983).

[13]One could possibly also include questions at Lk 6:41; 7:24, 25, 26.

[14]But this is not a recent discovery. A. T. Robertson was keenly aware of

of his questioning is not to gather information, create intimacy with his audience, or draw explicit points of contact with opponents. Thus, for example, after Jesus asks, "If you love those who love you, what credit is that to you?" (Lk 6:32), he does not pause to listen to an answer, but rather pushes ahead with the real point of his teaching: "Love your enemies, and do good, and lend, expecting nothing in return, and your reward will be great" (Lk 6:35-36). This is characteristic of Luke's Jesus. The general function of Jesus' questions is to vindicate his teaching by giving it a rational appearance.[15]

In analyzing argumentation, Ch. Perelman and L. Olbrechts-Tyteca identified this type of technique as the kind utilized when trying to es-

---

the peculiarity of Jesus' speech in Luke; see "Luke's Method of Research," *Biblical Review* 5 (1920): 195. The rhetorical form of Jesus' questions in Luke also contrasts sharply with the form of Jesus' speech in the Gospel of John. In John, Jesus uses such questions with less frequency than in Luke. On the other hand the other characters in John use a proportionately greater number of rhetorical questions than does Jesus.

[15]Ch. Perelman and L. Olbrechts-Tyteca, *The New Rhetoric: Treatise on Argumentation,* trans. John Wilkinson and Purcell Weaver (Notre Dame IN: University of Notre Dame Press, 1971) 305ff., 160. It is possible that the Lukan Jesus sometimes uses the "diatribe" form. Cadbury pointed to the accumulation of short precepts in Lk 6:27-28, 35, 36-38, the interruptive objections "you fool!" (Lk 12:20) and "you fools!" (Lk 11:40), and the emphatic "I will show you" (Lk 6:47; 12:5), "know this" (Lk 10:11), "make up your mind" (Lk 21:14); and "put these words in your ears" (Lk 9:44) as possible instances (*The Making of Luke-Acts* [London: SPCK, 1968] 152, 218 n8). While Jesus' rhetorical questions also show affinity with the diatribe form, the exact relationship of Jesus' extensive use of rhetorical questions with the Hellenistic diatribe is difficult to establish. Cadbury himself was very hesitant to stress the possible connection and emphasized rather how far the author of the gospel was "from adopting the style of prose, not to say the style of Hellenistic rhetoric and philosophy" (*The Making of Luke-Acts,* 153). One must, in fact, be very hesitant when attempting to establish the influence of the Hellenistic diatribe on the characterization of Jesus in Luke, because the rhetorical question is a form of popular argumentation in general, and is not peculiar to the Hellenistic diatribe. For some of the difficulties in establishing the diatribe form apart from other forms of popular speech, see Stanley Kent Stowers, *The Diatribe and Paul's Letter to the Romans* (Ann Arbor MI: Scholars Press, 1981) 7-78.

tablish some kind of solidarity between accepted judgments and others that are being promoted but are actually based on a different structure of reality.[16] In spite of their rational appearance, such arguments are only quasi-logical. Certainly in Jesus' case his teachings are almost always "arguments from authority." That is, it makes a difference that Jesus is the speaker. In the example above, the initial validation for the truth of the statement, "love your enemies, and your reward will be great," is that Jesus said it.[17] This is so, even though Jesus' words bring the hearer into a world where it makes sense to love one's enemies.

For the most part, Jesus' sayings are pronouncements. Even his parables are pronouncements in that they initially appeal to Jesus' own authority for their truth claims. In this sense, Jesus' speech in Luke is more prophetic than didactic. This is strikingly illustrated by the fact that Jesus, in the narrative, does not seem overly concerned with persuading his audience to his own point of view—as is perhaps the case in the Fourth Gospel, where Jesus often asks concerning the belief of his hearers.[18]

The form of Jesus' speech has been studied extensively through form criticism, and it is not necessary here to rehearse what others have shown: its form is Semitic.[19] By way of characterization, however, it is

---

[16]Perelman and Olbrechts-Tyteca, *The New Rhetoric*, 261ff.

[17]Bo Ivar Reicke, *La tradition chrétienne*, (Paris: J. Gabalda, 1950) 195-206.

[18]Cf. Jn 1:50; 3:12; 5:44; 47; 8:46; 9:35; 11:26, 40; 14:10; 16:31; 20:29.

[19]In *The History of the Synoptic Tradition* (trans. John Marsh [New York: Harper and Row, 1963]) Rudolf Bultmann sorted out three main groups of Jesus' sayings in Luke: (1) Wisdom sayings (cf. Lk 4:23; 5:31-32, 34, 36-38, 39; 6:27-28, 29-30, 31, 32-36, 39, 40, 43-44, 45a; 8:16, 17, 18b, 24, 25; 9:24, 25, 58, 62; 10:7b; 11:9-13, 17-18, 23, 28, 33, 34-36; 12:2, 3, 4-5, 6-7a, 22-24, 25, 27-31, 33-34, 47-48; 13:24; 30; 14:8-10, 11, 12-14, 34-35; 16:9, 10-12, 13, 15b; 17:3-4, 6, 33; 19:26; 22:25-26), which forms are those of the Old Testament and Jewish mashal; (2) Prophetic and apocalyptic sayings (cf. Lk 4:25-27; 6:20-23, 24-26, 46; 7:22-23; 9:26; 10:13-15, 18, 23; 11:29-30, 31-32, 42, 43, 44, 46, 47, 49-51, 52; 12:8-9, 35-38, 39-40, 42-46, 47-48; 13:26-27, 28-29, 30, 34-35; 17:20-21, 23-24, 26-27, 34-35; 18:29b-30; 19:42-44; 21:6, 8-28, 29-31, 32, 33, 34-36; 23:28-31), which forms are those of Old Testament and Jewish prophecy; and (3)

useful to note some of the prophetic elements in Jesus' speech: (1) the plural Μακάριοι, "blessed" (Lk 6:20, 21 (twice), 22; 10:23; 11:28; 12:37, 38); (2) οὐαί, "woe" (Lk 6:24, 25, 26; 10:13 (twice); 11:42, 43, 44, 46, 47, 52; 17:1; 21:23; 22:22); and (3) πλήν, "but" (Lk 6:24, 35; 10:11, 14, 20; 11:41; 12:31; 13:33; 17:1; 18:8; 19:27; 22:21, 22, 42,; 23:28).[20] It is quite meaningful that in the gospel these elements are found only in the speech of Jesus.

Through these and other such elements Jesus is characterized in the narrative as a prophet sent by God at the decisive hour. He is conscious of his prophetic role (Lk 6:22-23), and he also stands within and appeals to the tradition of Judaism (compare Lk 5:14; 6:9; 10:28, 37; 16:17; 17:14; 22:8). He quotes Scripture twice as often as all of the other speakers combined, including the third person narrator (Lk 4:4, 8, 12, 18-19; 7:27; 8:10; 18:29; 19:46; 20:17, 37, 42-43; 21:27; 22:37, 69; 23:30, 46);[21] that he understands his mission to be one of proclaiming the

---

Legal sayings (cf. Lk. 5:34; 6:3-4, 9; 8:21; 9:48; 10:2-12, 16, 26-28; 11:39-41, 42; 12:10; 14:5; 16:17; 17:1-2, 3-4; 20:33-35, 37-38, 41-44; 22:25-27), which (a) often appeal to Jewish law but include also (b) an exclusive principle separating Jesus from the practices or attitudes of his hearers. The other two groupings of Jesus' speech indicated by Bultmann are the similitudes and similar forms (cf. Lk 6:47-49; 7:31-35, 41-43; 8:5-8; 10:30-37; 11:5-8; 12:16-21, 39-40, 42-46, 54-56, 57-59; 13:6-9, 18-19, 20-21; 14:7-11, 12-14, 16-24, 28-33; 15:4-10, 11-32; 16:1-8, 19-31; 18:1-8, 10-14; 19:12-27; 20:9-16; 21:29-31), which form is the figurative and comparative language of Old Testament and Rabbinic Judaism, and the "I" sayings (Lk 4:43; 7:9, 33-34; 8:21; 10:3, 16, 18, 19-20, 21-22; 11:19, 20; 12:49-50, 51-53; 14:26, 27; 19:10; 22:28-30, 32; 23:43; 24:49).

[20]F. Blass and A. Debrunner, *A Greek Grammar of the New Testament and Other Early Christian Literature,* trans. Robert W. Funk (Chicago: University of Chicago Press, 1961) 3. Especially significant is the formal construction οὐαὶ ὑμῖν (Lk 6:24, 25; 11:42, 43, 44, [46], 47, 52); see F. Blass, *Grammar,* 268-69; Henry Cadbury, *The Style and Literary Method of Luke* (Cambridge MA: Harvard University Press, 1920) 147; J. Dupont, *Les beatitudes* (Paris: J. Gabalda, 1969) 3:324-28; F. Hauck and C. Bertram in *Theological Dictionary of the New Testament,* 10 vols. (Grand Rapids MI: William B. Eerdmans, 1964-1976) 4:362-70. P. L. Bernadicou, "Programmatic Texts of Joy in Luke's Gospel," *Biblical Theology* 44 (December 1969): 3102-3105.

[21]Otherwise Scripture is quoted at Lk 2:23, 24; 3:4-6; 4:10, 11; 10:27; 19:38; 20:28.

Word of God, which he does from necessity (Lk 4:43); that he is interested in those who listen to and follow his words (compare Lk 6:46-47; 8:21; 11:28-29); that he sees himself dying in Jerusalem as a prophet (Lk 13:33); and he preaches repentance (compare Lk 13:8), judgment (compare Lk 10:10ff.), and the resurrection of the just (compare Lk 14:14).

Conclusion

So what can be said about Jesus' voice in Luke? First, it is distinctive. In Luke, Jesus speaks in a very different way than does the narrator. Second, we can acknowledge that the characterization of Jesus' voice was intentional. I do not mean by this that the author broke with tradition when he related how Jesus spoke. What I do mean is that the author's hand can be traced as he redacted the tradition in order to emphasize certain patterns of speech. The author seems to have been as careful when characterizing Jesus as he was when characterizing his narrator. Third, we can say that the Lukan Jesus speaks the simple language of common people. Jesus speaks in a popular style, consonant, by the way, with his message in Lk 4:16ff. And fourth, we can reaffirm the prophetic form of Jesus' speech. While the narrator speaks a language of worship, Jesus speaks a language of prophecy.

Jesus' View

Chapter 3

The real issue is not to classify Jesus, but to understand him in the narrative.[1] In this chapter, I will move beyond matters of language and style, and listen more closely to Jesus' voice in Luke. I have already concluded that the form of Jesus' speech was prophetic. What does it mean to the story that Jesus' language is prophetic? I now turn to Jesus' perception of his time and of his own person. Is Jesus, in Luke, conscious of being the messiah? If so, in what way? What is Jesus' view of the kingdom? What does Jesus think of the age in which he lives? What is his concept of ministry? And how does he understand his role in God's history?

Jesus as Prophet and Christ

It is possible that the category of "prophet" has more to say to us than at first appearance. In 1946 F. W. Young wrote an insightful article in which he argued that the Jews of Jesus' day understood "prophet"

---

[1]Cf. Henry J. Cadbury, "Jesus and the Prophets," *Journal of Religion* 5 (1925): 608.

to be an eschatological term.[2] According to Young, the pervasive Jewish understanding was that prophecy had ceased in Israel, and would only return in messianic times. Then all the people would be supplied with the holy spirit of prophecy, Elijah would return, and the messiah would come. That Jesus appeared as a prophet, therefore, did not simply mean that Jesus was another Jeremiah, Isaiah, or Amos, but that he heralded the time of messianic salvation. For Jesus to accept the prophetic role was tantamount to claiming to be either Elijah or the messiah.

Young's conclusions have found some more recent support in two dissertations: T. R. Carruth's "The Jesus-As-Prophet Motif in Luke-Acts" (1973) and G. Greene's "The Portrayal of Jesus as Prophet in Luke-Acts" (1975).[3] Both have discovered eschatological significance in the prophetic designation of Jesus. That the Lukan prophet, Jesus, was in some way aware of his own eschatological significance, however, was perhaps best shown by Hans Conzelmann, who recognized that in Luke "the necessity of the Passion is fully brought out" by Jesus' perception of himself as an agent bringing to fruition the promises of Scripture (compare Lk 4:21; 17:25; 18:31; 22:37; 24:25; 24:44-45).[4] This theme is redacted into Luke and is an intended part of the author's characterization of Jesus.[5]

But there is an aspect of this characterization that is puzzling. It concerns that variety of details grouped in more traditional studies under the heading of the "messianic secret." If Young was right, and if the rubric "prophet" was in Jesus' day equally eschatological and dangerous, why does Luke's Jesus camouflage his messianic identity? Why

---

[2]F. W. Young, "Jesus the Prophet: A Reexamination," *Journal of Biblical Literature* 68 (1949): 285-99.

[3]T. R. Carruth, "The Jesus-As-Prophet Motif in Luke-Acts" (Ph.D. dissertation, Baylor University, 1973); G. Greene, "The Portrayal of Jesus as Prophet in Luke-Acts" (Ph.D. dissertation, Southern Baptist Theological Seminary, 1975).

[4]Hans Conzelmann, *The Theology of St. Luke,* trans. Geoffrey Buswell (New York: Harper and Row, 1961) 163-64 n3. Paul E. Davies also has argued for a special consciousness on the part of Jesus in "Jesus and the Role of the Prophet," *Journal of Biblical Literature* 64 (1945): 252-53.

[5]All of the instances mentioned above are additions by the author.

does Jesus in Luke seem ready to claim that he is a prophet and yet reluctant to claim that he is the messiah? This is all the more baffling since the Lukan Jesus seems anxious not to be mistaken for Elijah, the other prophet of the messianic age (compare Lk 7:26-28; 9:51-62; 16:16).

Conzelmann explained the secrecy motif in Luke in terms of the necessity of the Passion: If Jesus were recognized as the messiah, the support of the people might interrupt the divine plan.[6] But to facilitate this interpretation Conzelmann found it necessary to remove all eschatological connotations from the title "prophet." To this effect he proposed that by the time the Third Gospel was written, the titles of Jesus had become traditional and were often used interchangeably.[7] But my quick review of some of the other titles of Jesus in the introduction suggests that this was not the case. In Luke, the titles of Jesus seem to have been used with dramatic consciousness.

Moreover, there is direct narrative evidence that Jesus in Luke was not concerned with hiding the Passion. According to the story line of Luke, Herod sought to kill Jesus (Lk 13:31) exactly because he understood Jesus' messianic pretensions. As J. M. Creed pointed out, the ἐν αὐτῇ τῇ ὥρᾳ "at that very hour" of 13:31 connects Herod's desire to kill Jesus to the eschatological sayings of Lk 13:22-30.[8] According to the dramatic flow of events, it is because Herod fully understands himself to be identified as "one of the first who will be last" (13:30b) that he seeks to kill Jesus.[9] In turn, the message that Jesus sends with the Pharisees to Herod intentionally discloses the Passion.

---

[6]Conzelmann, *The Theology of St. Luke*, 76-77.

[7]Ibid., 170-71; cf. K. Berger, "Die königlichen Messiastraditionen des Neuen Testaments," *New Testament Studies* 20 (1974): 40.

[8]J. M. Creed, *The Gospel According to St. Luke* (London: Macmillan, 1957) 186.

[9]A. Denaux ("L'hypocrisie des Pharisiens et le dessein de Dieu. Analyse de Lc., xiii, 31-33," in F. Neirynck, ed., *L'évangile de Luc* [Gembloux: Editions J. Duculet, 1973] 245-85) argues that the assertion on the part of the Pharisees is hypocritical. According to Denaux, the Pharisees misrepresent Herod. See however, M. Rese, "Einige Überlegungen zu Lukas xiii, 31-33," in J. Dupont, et al., *Jesus aux origines de la christologie* (Louvain: Louvain University Press, 1975) 201-25.

> Behold, I cast out demons and perform cures today and tomorrow, and the third day I finish my course. Nevertheless I must go on my way today and tomorrow and the day following; for it cannot be that a prophet should perish away from Jerusalem. (Lk 13:32-33)

Here we can readily see that Conzelmann's explanation of the Lukan messianic secret does not fit with Jesus' view of events in the narrative.

But if Young was right about the eschatological connotations of "prophet," why then does Jesus not claim his messiahship with the same vigor that he claims to be a prophet? The answer might lie in a possible pattern in Luke concerning Jesus' self-appropriation of the titles "Prophet" and "Christ." Jesus calls himself a prophet only before his crucifixion (Lk 4:24; 13:33, 34). He appropriates the title Christ only after his resurrection (Lk 24:26, 46). Could it be, then, that Jesus, in the narrative, only thinks of himself as becoming the Christ after the crucifixion?

If so, we should not try to trace a developing consciousness on the part of Jesus in Luke, as if he first thought of himself as a prophet like other prophets, and only gradually came to realize that he was the messiah. It is clear in the narrative that even before the crucifixion Jesus is conscious of his special role.[10] From the very beginning of his ministry he heals the sick (Lk 5:24), raises the dead (Lk 7:14), forgives sins (Lk 5:20, 24), and commands demons (Lk 4:35). Likewise his concept of mission goes beyond that of a spokesperson: He calls himself "Lord of the Sabbath" (Lk 6:5) and directly and purposefully connects himself with the judging Son of man who will come on the clouds of heaven (Lk 9:26). Oftentimes in his speech he points to himself as an active ingredient in his own message (compare Lk 10:16; 12:8). He couples the announcement that the kingdom of God has come with his activity of casting out demons (Lk 11:20), and answers John's inquiry into his true identity (Lk 7:20) by referring to the blind who receive their sight, the lame who walk, lepers who are cleansed, the deaf who hear, the dead who are raised up, the poor who have good news preached to them, and "blessed is he who takes no offense at me" (Lk 7:22-23).

What can be demonstrated, therefore, by Jesus' speech in Luke is that Jesus perhaps drew a distinction between the concepts of prophet

---

[10]Cf. David L. Tiede, *Prophecy and History in Luke-Acts* (Philadelphia: Fortress Press, 1980) 70-78.

and Christ, that he did not purposefully confuse the two categories in order to combine in his one person the double expectation of the prophet of the end time and the messiah, and that his messianic consciousness was not late blooming, occurring at the resurrection after Jesus' prophetic ministry. But why does Jesus in the narrative wait until after the resurrection to claim openly to be the messiah?

The answer seems to lie in a concept of consummation through suffering. Joachim Jeremias pointed the way toward this answer when he observed (1) that "the allegorical representation of the messiah as a bridegroom is completely foreign to the whole of the Old Testament and to the literature of late Judaism," and (2) that the connection was first made in the early church in the Pauline writings at 2 Cor 11:2 and in the gospels at Mk 2:20‖Mt 9:15b‖Lk 5:34.[11] Yet Luke's Jesus does not refer to himself as the messiah until after the resurrection. It is dramatically misleading, therefore, to equate Jesus' perception of himself as the bridegroom (Lk 5:34-35) directly with his perception of himself as the messiah. Jesus' own understanding of the relation seems more complex in Luke.

C. H. Dodd indicated that the metaphor of the bridegroom is extended later in Jesus' speech (Lk 12:35-40) when he tells his disciples that they should expect the Son of man in the same way as would men expecting the return of their master from the marriage feast.[12] The figurative language sets up the allegorical relation: Jesus before the crucifixion = a bridegroom; the Son of man when he comes − a master returning from a marriage feast. Only certain elements of the figure overlap: a change is to occur; the bridegroom is to go away and then come back as the master (κύριος, Lk 12:36) who will serve at table the servants whom he finds waiting for him. There is a sharp distinction between an unconsummated state and a future consummation

---

[11]Joachim Jeremias, *The Parables of Jesus,* trans. S. H. Hooke (New York: Charles Scribner's Sons, 1963) 52 n14.

[12]Charles H. Dodd, *The Parables of the Kingdom* (New York: Charles Scribner's Sons, 1961) 128. Dodd speaks of the passage as a nucleus that is expanded.

connoted by the metaphor of the bridegroom.[13] This same distinction is also connoted by the figure of the returning master. The event of the feast has reached its end, which in turn has led to a new situation.[14]

Dodd also noticed that in the same context of the marriage feast Jesus draws upon another metaphor that maintains the same dialectic (Lk 12:50): "I have a baptism to be baptized with; and how I am constrained (συνέχομαι)until it is accomplished (τελεσθῇ)."[15] It is this allegorical concept of consummation that mediates in Jesus' speech between his self-perception as prophet and as Christ. Each time that Jesus refers to himself as the Christ, his words are couched in a framework of consummation.

> Was it not necessary that the Christ should suffer these things and enter into his glory? (Lk 24:26)
> Thus it is written, that the Christ should suffer and on the third day rise from the dead. . . . (Lk 24:46)

This same framework also structures his speech following Peter's confession (Lk 9:20-22)—which, by the way, is the only time that Jesus directly responds to the title in the narrative. Without the narrator's commentary, the notion of secrecy disappears, and Jesus' answer becomes strictly causal.[16]

> Jesus: "But who do you say that I am?"
> Peter: "The Christ of God."
> Jesus: "The Son of man must suffer many things, and be rejected by the elders and chief priests and scribes, and be killed, and on the third day be raised."

---

[13]Joachim Jeremias in *Theological Dictionary of the New Testament,* 10 vols. (Grand Rapids MI: William B. Eerdmans, 1964-1976) 4:1099-1106; cf. E. Stauffer, *TDNT* 1:653-57; Bo Reicke, "Die Fastenfrage nach Lk. 5:33-39," *Theologische Zeitschrift* 30 (1974): 323.

[14]Cf. I. H. Marshall, *The Gospel of Luke* (Grand Rapids MI: William B. Eerdmans, 1978) 532-39.

[15]C. H. Dodd, *The Parables,* 49-52.

[16]Heinz Schürmann, *Das Lukasevangelium,* (Freiburg: Herder, 1969) 1:533-34. Jesus' use of the first person present indicative passive τελειοῦμαι (Lk 13:32) is very instructive in this regard. The consummation of Jesus' true nature is directly related to his Passion; cf. D. L. Tiede, *Prophecy,* 72.

Both concepts, that of the Christ and that of the Son of man's suffering, rejection, death, and resurrection, are interdependent and only become whole (that is, consummated) in each other. J. A. T. Robinson pointed out that this same scheme is also present in the speeches of Peter and Paul in Acts (compare Acts 2:36; 13:33-34).[17] The Christ is not the Christ until he dies on the cross and is raised from the dead. Until such a time he is a prophet. From this, one sees also that in Luke the Son of man title might be Jesus' preferred way of referring to himself exactly because it incorporates the images of Jesus' perceived present and future self. Like Ezekiel, but also like the figure mentioned in Enoch, he is the Son of man—present before the crucifixion as a prophet, but potentially also present as his future manifestation, the judge who takes his kingdom for himself (Lk 21:27; 22:29-30).[18]

Jesus' Perception of the Kingdom

One of the elements of Jesus' point of view, made more complicated by the figures of the bridegroom who is taken away and the master who returns from the marriage feast, is the time frame of events. In the first instance, the marriage feast is an event symbolically paralleled in the life of Jesus.[19] The disciples are invited guests who participate in the feast with the bridegroom. In the second instance, the feast is symbolically referred to that period when the master is away.[20] The disciples are servants who wait for the master's return and then are served by him. It is the second of these that pinpoints the source of confusion by relating the master's return from the feast to the gift of the kingdom (Lk 12:32). By this figure the kingdom of God is placed in the

---

[17]J. A. T. Robinson, "Elijah, John and Jesus," *New Testament Studies* 4 (1958): 280. See also G. W. H. Lampe, "The Lucan Portrait of Christ," *New Testament Studies* 2 (1955-56): 173-74.

[18]Oscar Cullmann, *The Christology of the New Testament*, trans. Shirley C. Guthrie and Charles A. M. Hall (Philadelphia: Westminster Press, 1963) 137-92.

[19]Tim Schramm, *Der Markus-Stoff bei Lukas* (Cambridge: Cambridge University Press, 1971) 105-11.

[20]Marshall, *The Gospel of Luke,* 536.

future.[21] And yet undeniably in the gospel there are passages in which Jesus' perception of the kingdom is present-oriented (compare Lk 11:20).[22] But how can Jesus view the kingdom as both future and present? Is Jesus simply confused in the narrative about the time frame of events? Or does his speech imply a change of mind or a development in his thought? Or again, is there a consistent view underlying only seemingly disparate concepts?

It is this difficult juxtaposition of present and future that lends strength to Conzelmann's view that Luke thought in terms of a salvation history in which Jesus marked the center of time.[23] Jesus' time was a time in which salvation "appeared." It was because of this manifestation of salvation that the Church, then, could look forward to the future kingdom with certainty. But Conzelmann's tendency to minimize overall patterns in the text and to heavily weight the redactional changes in a select few passages has provoked an intense debate,[24] and it is well to look again at Jesus' language concerning the kingdom.

---

[21]Conzelmann (*The Theology of St. Luke*, 232) follows Jeremias's suggestion that the parable reflects the delay of the parousia; cf. Jeremias, *The Parables*, 53ff.

[22]J. Y. Campbell, "The Kingdom of God has Come," *Expository Times* 48 (1936-1937): 91-94, and K. W. Clark, "Realized Eschatology," *Journal of Biblical Literature* 59 (1940): 367-83, have argued that the aorist ἔφθασεν actually has a future meaning. This is a very difficult position, however; cf. Dodd, *The Parables*, 28-30, and "The Kingdom of God has Come," *Expository Times* 48 (1936-1937): 138-42; W. G. Kümmel, *Promise and Fulfillment* (Naperville IL: A. R. Allenson, 1957) 105-109; F. Blass and A. Debrunner, *A Greek Grammar of the New Testament and Other Early Christian Literature*, trans. Robert W. Funk (Chicago: University of Chicago Press, 1961) 101.

[23]Conzelmann, *The Theology of St. Luke*.

[24]This type of thinking comes through clearly in Robert H. Stein, "What is Redaktionsgeschichte?" *Journal of Biblical Literature* (1969): 45-56. But see Henry J. Cadbury, Review of Hans Conzelmann's *Theology of St. Luke*, *Journal of Biblical Literature* 80 (1961): 304-305; Leander Keck, "Jesus' Entrance Upon His Mission," *Review and Expositor* 64 (Fall 1967): 465-83; N. B. Stonehouse, Review of Hans Conzelmann's *Theology of St. Luke*, *Westminister Theological Journal*, 24 (1961): 65-70. Richard A. Edwards's call for a balance between "emendation criticism" and "composition criticism" seems well founded; cf. "The Redaction of Luke," *Journal of Religion* 49 (1969): 392-405.

Especially important is the pattern of the moods and tenses of verbs Jesus associates with the kingdom in Luke. Out of forty times that ἡ βασιλεία (τοῦ θεοῦ), "the kingdom (of God)," appears in the gospel, thirty-one are in the mouth of Jesus.[25] Seldom is the concept linked by Jesus with future verb tenses—only in Lk 13:28 (ἔσται), Lk 13:29 (ἥξουσιν, ἀνακλιθήσονται), Lk 17:21 (οὐδὲ ἐροῦσιν), and Lk 22:30 (καθήσεσθε). In no instance, moreover, is the future tense used as a reference point for the "coming" of the kingdom. In Lk 13:28, the future tense specifies a time when the workers of iniquity will weep and gnash their teeth; in Lk 13:29, a time when men will come from east, west, north, and south to sit at table in the kingdom of God; and in Lk 22:30, a time when the disciples will sit on thrones judging the twelve tribes of Israel. This last case is very interesting since the future indicative (καθήσεσθε) is found beside the present subjunctive (ἔσθητε, πίνητε); they follow a present indicative (διατίθεμαι) and an aorist indicative (διέθετο).

> [A]s my Father appointed a kingdom for me, so do I appoint for you that you may eat and drink at my table in my kingdom, and sit on thrones judging the twelve tribes of Israel. (Lk 22:29-30)

The Father assigned in the punctiliar past a kingdom to Jesus; so Jesus is assigning in the ongoing present to the apostles that they might eat and drink (ἵνα with present subjunctive) at Jesus' table in Jesus' kingdom. Sometime in the future the disciples will sit on thrones judging the twelve tribes of Israel. It is significant that the purpose clause joins the kingdom with the present indicative of the apostles' appointment and not with the future indicative of their manifestation as the judges of Israel. The grammar of the sentence implies that the kingdom of God and the judgment of Israel are not interchangeable concepts.[26] One

---

[25]Jesus uses (ἡ βασιλεία (τοῦ θεοῦ)) in Lk 4:43; 6:20; 7:28; 8:10; 9:27, 60, 62; 10:9; 11:2, 20; 12:31, 32; 13:18, 20, 28, 29; 16:16; 17:20, 21; 18:16, 17, 24, 25, 29; 19:12, 15; 21:31; 22:16, 18, 29, 30. Otherwise it is used by the narrator in Lk 8:1; 9:2, 11; 17:20; 19:11; 23:51; by the angel in Lk 1:33; by an indefinite speaker in Lk 14:15; and by one of the criminals crucified with Jesus in Lk 23:42.

[26]Jacob Jervell (*Luke and the People of God* [Minneapolis: Augsburg Publishing House, 1972] 75-112) toned down the distinction by suggesting that

notices this also in the source alteration in Jesus' speech at Lk 9:27‖Mk 9:1.

Mk 9:1	Lk 9:27
Truly, I say to you, there are some standing here who will not taste death before they see the kingdom of God come with power.	But I tell you truly, there are some standing here who will not taste death before they see the kingdom of God.

Here the idea of coming with power, ἐληλυθυῖαν (perfect participle) ἐν δυνάμει, is removed from the concept of the kingdom.

Certainly there is a sense for future time in Lk 9:27 as in Mk 9:1, supplied by ἕως ἄν with subjunctive.[27] In fact, it is the indefinite subjunctive that in the speech of Jesus most often indicates the future aspect of the kingdom of God: μὴ βλέπωσιν, μὴ συνιῶσιν (Lk 8:10); ἴδωσιν (Lk 9:27); ὄψεσθε (Lk 13:28); δέξηται, εἰσέλθῃ (Lk 18:17); λάβῃ (Lk 18:30); ἴδητε (Lk 21:31); φάγω, πληρωθῇ (Lk 22:16); πίω, ἔλθῃ (Lk 22:18); ἔσθητε, πίνητε (Lk 22:30). It is significant, however, that in all but one (Lk 22:18) of these cases, the subject of the verb is not the kingdom of God. Rather, it is a person whose potential future actions are in some way associated with the kingdom.[28]

As the subject of a verb, the kingdom (of God) appears once with the aorist subjunctive (Lk 22:18), once with a perfect indicative (ἤγγι-κεν, Lk 10:9), once with an aorist imperative (ἐλθέτω, Lk 11:2), once

---

βασιλεία (Lk 22:29-30) has the meaning of "reign" and not "kingdom." See also R. Tannehill, "A Study in the Theology of Luke-Acts," *Anglican Theological Review* 43 (1961): 200-201.

[27]Blass, Debrunner, and Funk, *A Greek Grammar,* 192.

[28]Conzelmann saw the source alteration Lk 8:9ff.‖Mk 4:10ff. as an important indication that Luke's "main emphasis is no longer on the coming of the kingdom" (*The Theology of St. Luke,* 103-104). Although he interpreted this shift in emphasis to be connected with the delay of the parousia, one in fact can interpret it in a radically different way to indicate that the kingdom was already present with the disciples. The Lukan addition of γνῶναι (Lk 8:10) to the Markan source could be taken in the sense of "recognition": "To you has been given to recognize the secrets of the kingdom of God." Cf. W. Bauer, F. W. Gingrich, and F. Danker, *A Greek-English Lexicon of the New Testament and Other Early Christian Literature* (Chicago: University of Chicago Press, 1979) 160-62.

with an aorist indicative (ἔφθασεν, Lk 11:20), and seven times with a present indicative (ἐστίν, Lk 6:20; 13:18; 17:21; 18:16; 21:31; εὐαγ-γελίζεται, Lk 16:16; ἔρχεται, Lk 17:20).

What the forms of these verbs show is that the matter of indefinite-ness is associated in Jesus' speech with the attributes and actions of people, and not (but for the possible exception of Lk 22:18) with the existence of the kingdom itself.[29] The kingdom is not only potentially real. In Jesus' view, the kingdom is not "a kingdom that is going to come into being, but does not yet exist." It exists "now" as a present entity.

Thus, the present indicative is used often by Jesus when referring to the kingdom of God,[30] to indicate, among other things, that the king-dom belongs (now) to the poor (Lk 6:20); that the kingdom is not (in the process of) coming with signs (Lk 17:20); that the kingdom is (now) in the midst (ἐντός) of you (Lk 17:21); that the kingdom belongs (now) to those who are like children (Lk 17:21); and that it is hard for those with riches to be (in the process of) entering the kingdom (Lk 18:24). With the last example, the design on the part of the author becomes clear, as he changed Mark's future indicative "they will enter" (εἰσε-λεύσονται, Mk 10:23) to the present indicative "they are entering" (εἰσπορεύονται, Lk 18:24).[31]

---

[29]Since ἔρχομαι often has the sense of "appear," "make an appearance," "come before the public," it is not necessary to assume that ἔλθῃ (Lk 22:18) indicates an indefinite existence of the kingdom (cf. Bauer, Gingrich, and Danker, A Greek-English Lexicon, 310-11). The difference between Lk 22:18 and Mk 14:25 might also be significant. Lk 22:18 stands parallel to Lk 22:16, which uses a language of fulfillment in regard to the kingdom. It is the length of time before the passover is consummated that is indefinite. If this paral-lelism were redacted into Luke's sources, then Lk 22:18 would actually take on the character of toning down Mark's statement that the kingdom of God belongs completely to the future. Concerning Lk 22:18's relation to Mark see Barry S. Crawford, "Near Expectation in the Sayings of Jesus" (Ph.D. disser-tation, Vanderbilt University, 1978) 211-36.

[30]Lk 6:20; 7:28; 9:62; 13:18, 20-21; 16:16; 17:20, 21; 18:16, 24; 21:31; 22:29.

[31]I. H. Marshall (The Gospel of Luke, 687) thinks that the variation is only literary and does not indicate a theological nuance. But the overall pattern of verbal forms used with the kingdom indicates otherwise.

Since the character, Jesus, demonstrates by the grammar of his speech in Luke that he views the kingdom to be an existing, actual entity (as opposed to a potential, conceptual entity), the here-not-here dialectic of his speech must be seen as spatial rather than temporal.[32] The question of the kingdom then becomes one of location: Where is the kingdom of God present? In heaven with God, but not on earth? On earth, but only present in the person of Jesus?[33] On earth, among human beings?

One thing that is evident about Luke's Jesus is that he does not employ Matthew's spatial schematization: the kingdom that is in heaven has moved close to earth. A couple of examples comparing Matthew's "the kingdom of heaven" with the Lukan "the kingdom of God" should make this clear.

Mt 10:7	Lk 10:8-9
	Whenever you enter a town and they receive you, eat what is set before you; heal the sick in it
And preach as you go, saying the kingdom of heaven has drawn near (ἤγγικεν ἡ βασιλεία τῶν οὐρανῶν).	and say to them, the kingdom of God has drawn upon you (ἤγγικεν ἐφ' ὑμᾶς ἡ βασιλεία τοῦ θεοῦ).
Mt 6:9ff.	Lk 11:2ff.
Pray then like this: Our Father who art in heaven, Hallowed be thy name.	When you pray, say Father, hallowed be thy name.
Thy kingdom come, Thy will be done on earth as it is in heaven.	Thy kingdom come.
Give us our daily bread. . . .	Give us our daily bread. . . .

---

[32]So also Helmut Flender, *St. Luke: Theologian of Redemptive History*, trans. Reginald and Ilse Fuller (London: SPCK, 1967); Fred O. Francis, "Eschatology and History in Luke-Acts," *Journal of the American Academy of Religion* 37 (1969): 49-63.

[33]J. Weiss and W. Bousset, *Die Schriften des Neuen Testaments*, (Göttingen: Vandenhoeck und Ruprecht, 1917) 1:493-94. M.-J. Lagrange, *Evangile selon St. Luc* (Paris: J. Gabalda, 1941) 666-69; Kümmel, *Promise and Fulfillment*, 32-35; E. E. Ellis, *The Gospel of Luke* (London: Nelson, 1966) 211.

The emphasis in Jesus' speech in Luke is placed on seeking, seeing, knowing, receiving, and entering the kingdom—an emphasis that cuts across time and incorporates the aorist indicative, the perfect indicative, the present indicative, and the futuristic subjunctive of the verbs employed.[34] Further, this emphasis, in places, clearly is edited into Luke. So "knowing" (Lk 8:10) is inserted into Mk 4:11; "seeing" is linked directly with the kingdom of God (Lk 9:27), rather than with the allied concepts of (a) the kingdom of God coming with power (Mk 9:1), or (b) the Son of man coming in his kingdom (Mt 16:28); "they are entering" (Lk 18:24) is inserted into Mk 10:23 in place of the future indicative "they will enter"; and the context of "leaving" in Lk 18:29 is changed in such a way that (a) the action becomes for the sake of the kingdom of God, and not for the sake of Jesus and for the gospel (compare Mk 10:29), and b) the "promise" of Lk 18:30 becomes directly related to the actions performed for the kingdom. Of special interest is the association of the present indicative ζητεῖτε (Lk 12:31) with the aorist indicative εὐδόκησεν (Lk 12:32). "But be seeking (ζητεῖτε) his kingdom and these things shall be granted to you. Do not be afraid, little flock, because it was your Father's good pleasure (εὐδόκησεν) to give you the kingdom." The focus of Jesus' view is on seeking a kingdom that has already been given.[35]

---

[34]Lk 8:10 (δέδοται, perf. ind. pass.; γνῶναι, aor. inf. act.; βλέποντες, part. pres. act.; μὴ βλέπωσιν, pres. subj.; ἀκούοντες, part. pres. act.; μὴ συνιῶσιν, pres. subj.); Lk 9:27 (ἴδωσιν, aor. subj.); Lk 12:31 (ζητεῖτε, pres. ind. act.); Lk 13:28 (ὄψεσθε, aor. subj.); Lk 16:16 (βιάζεται, pres. ind. pass. or middle); Lk 18:17 (μὴ δέξηται, aor. subj.; εἰσέλθῃ, aor. subj.); Lk 18:24 (εἰσπορεύονται, pres. ind. act.); Lk 18:25 (εἰσελθεῖν, aor. inf.); Lk 18:29-30 (ἀφῆκεν, aor. ind. act.; λάβῃ, aor. subj.); Lk 21:31 (ἴδητε, aor. subj.; γινόμενα, part. pres. ind., γινώσκετε, pres. imp. act.).

[35]Oftentimes the gift of the kingdom (Lk 12:32) is placed in the future (cf. Creed, *The Gospel According to St. Luke,* 175). Thus, the aorist εὐδόκησεν is taken in the sense of "resolve": "Your father resolved to give you the kingdom in the past. It has not come yet, so be seeking it. When it comes all the things that you need will be added unto you." Cf. Bauer, Gingrich, and Danker, *A Greek-English Lexicon,* 319. This interpretation is very difficult, however, because it postpones the gift of "all the things that you need" until a future coming of the kingdom. The phrase redacted (μὴ φοβοῦ, τὸ μικρὸν ποίμνιον,

The Judgment and the Kingdom

The verbal forms employed by Jesus when speaking of the kingdom emphasize a present kingdom that not all are able to see. There is great similarity with C. H. Dodd's position of "realized eschatology": The kingdom has been inaugurated and is in the process of becoming.[36] Helpful in this regard is Luke's Parable of the Mustard Seed. If the passage is not part of the Q material, then Mk. 4:30-32 was so edited by Luke (Lk 13:18-19) as to omit the comparatives qualifying the mustard seed as "the smallest of all" (Mk 4:31) and the grown bush as "the greatest of all" (Mk 4:32).[37]

Mk 4:30-32	Lk 13:18-19
With what can we compare the kingdom of God or what parable shall we use for it?	What is the kingdom of God like? And to what shall I compare it?
It is like a grain of mustard seed, which, when sown upon the ground, is the smallest of all the seeds on earth; yet when it is sown	It is like a grain of mustard seed which a man took and sowed in his garden;
it grows up and becomes the greatest of all shrubs, and puts forth large branches,	it grew and became a tree,
so that the birds of the air can make nests in its shade.	and the birds of the air made nests in its branches.

As J. Dupont pointed out, the concept of a qualitative, mysterious transformation that dominates the view of Mark's Jesus gives way in

---

Lk 12:32) rather indicates that the necessary clothes, food and drink (Lk 12:27-30) would be provided immediately. This radically colors the meaning of εὐδόκησεν, which takes on the sense of "delighted": "Your father delighted in giving you the kingdom." See also Otto Betz, "The Kerygma of Luke," *Interpretation* 22 (1968): 131-46; and Klaus Baltzer, "The Meaning of the Temple in the Lukan Writings," *Harvard Theological Review* (1965): 273-74.

[36]Cf. W. G. Kümmel, *The New Testament: The History of the Investigation of Its Problems,* trans. S. McLean Gilmour and Howard C. Kee (Nashville: Abingdon Press, 1972) 384-85.

[37]Dodd, *The Parables,* 152-54.

Luke to a quantitative, developmental transformation.[38] Moreover, the futuristic subjunctive ὅταν σπαρῇ, "when sown," of Mk 4:31 was changed in Luke to an aorist indicative (ἔβαλεν, "he sowed," Lk 13:19). In Luke, the metaphor points towards a past event. The mustard seed has already been sown.[39]

Most of all, however, the dialectic of Jesus' speech in Luke seems to be of a kingdom that already exists, but that has not been fully revealed. Following the similitude of the mustard seed, Jesus adds the similitude of the hidden leaven, which makes exactly this point (Lk 13:20-21): "To what shall I compare the kingdom of God? It is like leaven which a woman took and hid in three measures of meal, till it was all leavened." Although C. H. Dodd understood the parable to emphasize the "infectious influence" of Jesus' ministry, it is more likely that the parable is one of contrast. Joachim Jeremias has pointed to the way that the Oriental mind would see the parable: Out of "a mere nothing to the human eye, God creates his mighty kingdom."[40] Certainly, the most striking element of the parable is the hiddenness of the leaven. The kingdom is like leaven that was hidden. One notes that this is the natural meaning of Luke's κρύπτω (different from Matthew's ἐγκρύπτω).[41] Also in this regard it seems significant that the analogy is between the kingdom and leaven (ζύμη) which a woman hid (ἔκρυψεν), rather than between the kingdom and dough that a woman leavened. The author could have written ὁμοία ἐστὶν ἀλεύρῳ ὃν γυνὴ ἐζύμωσεν.[42]

---

[38]J. Dupont, "Les parables du sénève et du levain, *Nouvelle revue théologique* 80 (1967): 899ff.; G. W. H. Lampe, "The Lucan Portrait of Christ," 173-74; Dodd, *The Parables,* 153.

[39]For the eschatological connotations of κατεσκήνωσεν (Lk 13:19) see Jeremias, *The Parables,* 147.

[40]Ibid.

[41]A. Oepke, *TDNT,* 3:957-1000.

[42]This in fact seems to be the emphasis of Jeremias's interpretation: "We are shown a tiny morsel of leaven, absurdly small in comparison with the great mass of more than a bushel of meal. The housewife mixes it, covers it with a cloth, leaves the mass to stand overnight, and when she returns to it in the morning the whole mass of dough is leavened" (*The Parables,* 148).

In Lk. 17:20-24 Jesus employs a similar relation.

(a) The kingdom now = present, but hidden.
    The kingdom of God is not coming with signs to be observed; nor
    will they say, "Lo, here it is!" or "There!" for behold, the kingdom
    of God is in the midst of you. (Lk 17:20-21)

(b) The Son of man then = revealed for all to see.
    For as the lightning flashes and lights up the sky from one side to
    the other, so will the Son of man be in his day. (Lk 17:24)

Conzelmann correctly identified the exegetical problem of this passage in the juxtaposition of ἐντός, "in the midst" (Lk 17:21), and the
account of the Last Things that immediately follows (Lk 17:22ff.).[43]
However, he took a step that I cannot take. Because of what he called
"the analogous passage, Lk. 19:11," he resolved that Lk 17:20ff. also
must indicate that the kingdom is a future entity.[44] Thus, he gave a special interpretation to "the kingdom of God" in Lk 17:21b. According to
Conzelmann, it is not the kingdom itself, but rather the "preaching" of
the kingdom and the "manifestation" (that is, clear evidence) of the
kingdom that is present in Jesus' ministry.[45] But for my purposes the
difficulty arises in that Lk 19:11 is part of the narrator's voice. What I
seek is an understanding of Jesus' words separate from the narrator's
commentary.

    In his exegesis of the passage, Rudolf Bultmann drew attention to
the importance of correctly grasping the meaning of μετὰ παρα-
τηρήσεως, "with signs to be observed" (Lk 17:20b).[46] Bultmann
understood the phrase to have a future orientation, with the literal sense
of "being on the lookout for" the kingdom.[47] Thus, "when the kingdom

---

[43]Conzelmann, *The Theology of St. Luke,* 122.

[44]Ibid., also "Zur Lukasanalyse," *Zeitschrift für Theologie und Kirche* 49
(1952): 26.

[45]Conzelmann, *The Theology of St. Luke,* 106.

[46]Bultmann, *The History of the Synoptic Tradition,* trans. John Marsh (New
York: Harper and Row, 1963) 121.

[47]W. G. Kümmel, *Promise and Fulfillment,* 132; Norman Perrin, *The Kingdom of God in the Teaching of Jesus* (Philadelphia: Westminster Press, 1963)
175.

comes, no one will ask and search for it any more, but it will be there on a sudden in the midst of the foolish ones who will still want to calculate its arrival."[48] This interpretation of παρατήρησις has been challenged, however, by Richard Sneed, who after a thorough examination of the biblical and nonbiblical use of the substantive and verbal forms of the word concluded that the phrase in Luke must refer to a present reality. The object observed is present to the observer.[49] Sneed's conclusion seems well founded in that he discovered only one instance in which παρατηρέω was used with some sense of a future orientation (Diodorus Siculus 5.31, 3). It is significant that "no Biblical or Jewish author employs παρατήρειν or παρατήρησις to mean the observation of the future by present signs."[50]

H. K. Farrell has strengthened Sneed's case for a "present" interpretation of Lk 17:20-21 significantly by pointing out the chiastic construction of Lk 17:20-18:14.

> Luke 17:20-21 (A) is a word addressed to the Pharisees concerning the presence of the kingdom. Luke 17:22-37 (B) is a word addressed to the disciples concerning the future of the Judgment. Then, Luke 18:1-8 (B′) is a parable addressed to the disciples encouraging them to persevere through the persecutions because God will vindicate them speedily. Then 18:9-14 (A′) is a parable addressed to the Pharisees warning them that it is the humble who will be exalted. In other words, Luke is warning the Pharisees to repent and receive the Kingdom now, because the future will bring Judgment.[51]

The structural relationship of Jesus' words stresses the presence of the kingdom in Lk 17:20-21 and the future of the judgment in Lk 17:22-37. Although there is some connotation of suddenness in the metaphor of the lightning (Lk 17:24),[52] the analogy most emphasizes the clear vis-

---

[48]Bultmann, *The History of the Synoptic Tradition*, 121; H. W. Bartsch, "Early Christian Eschatology in the Synoptic Gospels," *New Testament Studies* 11 (1964-1965): 397.

[49]Richard J. Sneed, "The Kingdom's Coming: Luke, 17, 20-21" (S.T.D. dissertation, Catholic University of America, 1962) 58.

[50]Ibid., 364 n4.

[51]Farrell, "The Eschatological Perspective of Luke-Acts," 65.

[52]Creed, *The Gospel According to St. Luke*, 220.

ibility of the Son of man in his day.[53] At that time, the Son of man will be clearly visible.

Two points are especially striking about the relation of kingdom and judgment in Lk 17:20-21, 24: (a) the kingdom now = present, but hidden; (b) the Son of man then = revealed for all to see. The revelation of the Son of man is directly tied in with his consummation as the messiah. In this regard, W. Foerster and J. Zimijewsky have pointed out the theophanic elements of Lk 17:24.[54] The use of lightning in general and especially the construction ἀστραπὴ ἀστράπουσα indicates not only the visibility, but the glory of the Son of man. Again, there is a framework of consummation governing Jesus' perception of events. The Son of man will be revealed in his day for all to see, "But first he must suffer many things and be rejected by this generation" (Lk 17:25). The passage assumes Jesus' identity as the Son of man. And again, it is evident that one should not think in terms of a Jesus in Luke who knew that he was the messiah but who tried to maintain his true identity a secret. True, there is a secrecy motif with Luke's Jesus, but it does not pertain to his messiahship. Rather, it pertains to the presence of the kingdom. The kingdom of God has come, but not all see it. The disciples are blessed because their eyes are seeing (βλέπετε, present indicative) and their ears hearing (ἀκούετε, present indicative) what many prophets and kings desired to see and hear, but did not (Lk 10:23-24). Others, however, are seeing (βλέποντες, present participle), but not seeing, and hearing (ἀκούοντες, present participle) but not perceiving (Lk 8:10). It is the Father who has hidden (ἀπέκρυψας, aorist indicative) these things from the wise and understanding," and "revealed (ἀπεκάλυψας, aorist indicative) them to babes" (Lk 10:21). "Whoever does not receive (δέξηται, aorist subjunctive) the kingdom of God

---

[53]Marshall, *The Gospel of Luke*, 661. C. H. Talbert, "The Redaction Critical Quest for Luke the Theologian," *Jesus and Man's Hope*, 2 vols. (Pittsburgh: Pittsburgh Theological Seminary, 1970) 1:179; R. H. Hiers, The Problem of the Delay of the Parousia in Luke-Acts," *New Testament Studies* 20 (1974): 154.

[54]W. Foerster, *TDNT* 1: 505; J. Zmijewski, *Die Eschatologiereden des Lukas-Evangeliums* (Bonn: P. Haustein, 1972) 404-406.

like a child shall not enter it (εἰσέλθῃ, aorist subjunctive)" (Lk 18:17).[55]

The second point that is striking about the relation—(a) the kingdom now = present, but hidden; (b) the Son of man then = revealed for all to see—is that the full revelation of the Son of man is directly tied in with the consummation of the kingdom. The day that the Son of man is revealed for all to see is also a day of judgment (Lk 17:26-30): "but on the day when Lot went out from Sodom, fire and brimstone rained from heaven and destroyed them all—so will it be on the day when the Son of man is revealed."[56] The Christ is of the age to come, and not of this age. This perhaps explains the otherwise very difficult saying,

> How can they say that the Christ is David's son? For David himself says in the Book of Psalms,
>> The Lord said to my Lord,
>> Sit at my right hand,
>> Till I make enemies a stool for thy feet.
> David thus calls him Lord; so how is he his son? (Lk 20:41-44)

David is of this age. The Christ is of the age to come.[57] But regardless of the interpretation given to this passage, it is clear that when the

---

[55]With the modification that God's reign is breaking in, but not already present, this seems to be a "Q" emphasis that might go back to Jesus; cf. Rudolf Bultmann, *Theology of the New Testament*, trans. Kendrick Grobel, 2 vols. (New York: Charles Scribner's Sons, 1951-1955) 1:6. Nevertheless, as the story of the ten lepers illustrates, it is fully appropriated by Luke. It is the Samaritan who "sees" that he is healed who turns back to thank Jesus; cf. H. D. Betz, "The Cleansing of the Ten Lepers (Lk. 17:11-19)," *Journal of Biblical Literature* 90 (1971): 319, 325.

[56]J. Schlosser, "Les jours de Noé et de Lot. A propos de Luc xvii, 26-30," *Revue Biblique* 80 (1973): 13-36.

[57]The Davidic descent of Jesus is not questioned anywhere in the New Testament, and in fact is emphasized in Luke. Consequently, the denial of Davidic sonship indicates a denial of certain messianic preconceptions; cf. Eduard Schweizer, *The Good News According to Mark*, trans. Donald H. Madvig (Richmond VA: John Knox Press, 1970) 254-58. Given the division of aeons in Luke, it is natural to distinguish David (before John the Baptist) from Christ (after John the Baptist); cf. Lk 16:16; 7:28.

master returns from the marriage feast, the kingdom will be consummated.

In Jesus' view, the concept of the full revelation of the Son of man is paralleled with the judgment.[58] It is when people shall see (ὄψον-ται, future indicative) the Son of man coming in a cloud with power and great glory, that they will know that their redemption is drawing near (ἐγγίζει, present indicative, Lk 21:27-28). The emphasis is on the clear revelation of something now taking place.[59] The separation of the ages becomes complete at the time of judgment. So, while the kingdom of God cuts through time, its consummation marks the division of time. While the kingdom of God, as a concept, is not defined in Jesus' speech with the future indicative, the judgment and the resurrection of the just are consistently so defined (compare ἔσται, Lk 10:12; 13:28; ἐκζητηθήσεται, Lk 11:51; ἥξει, Lk 12:46; δαρήσεται, Lk 12:47, 48; ἀπολεῖσθε, Lk 13:3, 5; ἔσονται, [παρα]λημφθήσεται, ἀφεθήσεται, Lk 17:34, 35; ἐπισυναχθήσονται, Lk 17:37; ὄψονται, Lk 21:27; ἐπεισελεύσεται, Lk 21:35; κατισχύσητε, Lk 21:36; ἄρξ-ονται, Lk 23:30).[60]

Jesus' Perception of His Own Age

According to Jesus' scheme of time, there are two aeons: The end of the first was marked by John the Baptist. "The law and the prophets were until John; since (ἀπό) then the good news of the kingdom of God is preached . . . " (Lk 16:16). John appeared immediately before the dawn of the new age, and belonged wholly to the past age.[61] The beginning of

---

[58]Farrell, "The Eschatological Perspective of Luke-Acts," 93-101.

[59]Cf. Talbert, "The Redaction Critical Quest for Luke the Theologian," 179; Dodd, *The Parables,* 64; O. Betz, "The Kerygma of Luke," 131-46; W. G. Kümmel "Current Theological Accusations Against Luke," *Andover-Newton Quarterly* 16 (1975): 137.

[60]Cf. W. G. Kümmel, *The Theology of the New Testament,* trans. John E. Steely (Nashville: Abingdon Press, 1973) 32-33, 39-43.

[61]Cullmann, *The Christology of the New Testament,* 23ff. Some have argued that Lk 16:16 includes John in the new age; cf. Walter Wink, *John the Baptist in the Gospel Tradition* (Cambridge: Cambridge University Press, 1968) 51-55; David Daube, *The New Testament and Rabbinic Judaism* (London: Athlone Press, 1956) 285-86. But in light of Lk 7:28, it is best to include John's proclamation in the old age; so Betz, "The Kerygma of Luke," 133.

the second aeon shall be marked by judgment and the full revelation of the Son of man.

> [S]o will it be on the day when the Son of man is revealed. On that day, let him who is on the housetop, with his goods in the house, not come down to take them away; and likewise let him who is in the field not turn back. . . . I tell you, in that night there will be two men in one bed; one will be taken and the other left. There will be two women grinding together; one will be taken and the other left (Lk 17:30-35).

Intersecting the two ages lies the present in-between-time in which the kingdom exists as a hidden, unconsummated realm. Certainly Jesus sees a particular program of events governing the in-between-time. It has been suggested that Jesus' appearance in Nazareth (Lk 4:16-30) is of programmatic significance.[62] Dibelius, Bultmann, and others have understood the scene to be patterned after Mk 6:1-6.[63] Luke then rearranged the order of Mark and placed an enlarged account of the rejection scene at the beginning of Jesus' ministry in order to signal Jesus' mission.[64]

Thomas Hoyt has been helpful in emphasizing the significance of the messianic prophecy at Lk 4:18-19. As he put it, "the point of the Lukan pericope is no longer simply the rejection at Nazareth; it has been expanded to introduce what Jesus' ministry is all about."[65] Conzelmann also had emphasized the importance of the introduction of Isaiah's prophecy at the beginning of the Nazareth account. In light of Lk 4:21—"And he began to say to them, 'Today (σήμερον) this Scripture has been fulfilled (πεπλήρωται) in your hearing' "—Conzelmann placed the significance of the quotation in Jesus' claim that he is bringing in the time of salvation.[66] He contended, however, that the σήμερον of Lk 4:21 located the

---

[62]F. W. Beare, *The Earliest Records of Jesus,* (Nashville: Abingdon Press, 1962) 44; E. E. Ellis, *The Gospel of Luke,* 95; Marshall, *The Gospel of Luke,* 177.

[63]Bultmann, *The History of the Synoptic Tradition,* 31-32; Martin Dibelius, *From Tradition to Gospel,* trans. Bertram L. Woolf (New York: Charles Scribner's Sons, 1935) 386-87.

[64]Marshall, *The Gospel of Luke,* 178.

[65]Thomas Hoyt, Jr., "The Poor in Luke-Acts" (Ph.D. dissertation, Duke University, 1975) 133.

[66]Conzelmann, *The Theology of St. Luke,* 36.

fulfillment of the prophecy exclusively in Jesus' time,[67] and so distinguished the "appearance of salvation" in Jesus' ministry from the kingdom of God that was to come in the future.[68] But as I have already indicated, the verbal forms used by Jesus in his language of the kingdom make this reading very difficult. Consistently in Jesus' speech, the kingdom is a present entity. Moreover, Conzelmann's position has met with extensive resistance at exactly this point.[69]

Conzelmann was helpful, however, in his suggestion that the introduction of the quotation (Lk 4:18-19) might have been occasioned by Jesus' description of his ministry in his reply to John the Baptist, Lk 7:22.[70]

Lk 7:22-23	Lk 4:18-19
Go and tell John what you have seen and heard; the blind receive their sight, the lame walk, lepers are cleansed, and the deaf hear, the dead are raised up, the poor have good news preached to them. And blessed is he who takes no offense at me.	The Spirit of the Lord is upon me, because he has anointed me to preach good news to the poor. He has sent me to proclaim release to the captives and recovering of sight to the blind, to set at liberty those who are oppressed to proclaim the acceptable year of the Lord.

There was, in fact, an attempt to emphasize the Q saying of Lk 7:22 in Luke, as it was also redacted into Lk 7:21.[71]

The same general categories of people—the poor, maimed, blind, and lame—also appear in the parable of the Great Banquet (Lk 14:15-29). Commentators readily agree that this parable refers to the messianic feast. Hahn suggested that it was in its original form an inter-

---

[67]Ibid., 103.

[68]Ibid., 113.

[69]Cf. Flender, *St. Luke: Theologian of Redemptive History,* 147; Paul Minear, "Luke's Use of the Birth Stories," *Studies in Luke-Acts,* ed. L. Keck and J. L. Martyn (Philadelphia: Fortress Press, 1980) 123; Hoyt, Jr., "The Poor in Luke-Acts," 133; Kümmel, "Current Theological Accusations against Luke," 138.

[70]Conzelmann, *The Theology of St. Luke,* 191.

[71]John F. Craghan, "A Redactional Study of Lk 7:21 in the light of DT. 19:15," *Catholic Biblical Quarterly* 29 (July 1967): 47-61.

pretation of Jesus' behavior of eating with tax collectors and sinners.[72] Luke then allegorized the original in an attempt to include new guests. Vögtle has rightly added the necessity of stressing the temporal sense of the parable.[73] Noting that Lk 14:21 was edited into the pericope, Vögtle concluded in the manner of Jeremias that the original version threatened Jews who paid no heed to Jesus' message with the possibility of being replaced by the gentiles.[74] Jesus' threat became a reality in the experience of the Church, which then allegorized the parable by contrasting the poor gentiles (Lk 14:21) to the rich Jews (Lk 14:18-20).

It is not exactly correct to view the parable of the Great Banquet as an allegory, because Jesus' intention in telling the parable is not to emphasize a scheme of salvation history, but rather to confront those at table with him with the new reality of the kingdom. This is why Jesus spends half of the parable detailing the excuses made by those who were first invited. Jesus' use of the parables in Luke is very consistent with his prophetic language. He uses the parables to confront his audience with a new reality. The kingdom is different than expected.

But at the same time Jesus introduces allegorical features into the parable of the Great Banquet, so that Vögtle was correct in emphasizing the intended contrast between the first and second invitations. The difficulty of Vögtle's view rests in his identification of the poor of Lk 14:21 with the gentiles. There is no evidence to indicate such a correlation. The real correlation is between the servant's commission in Lk 14:21 and Jesus' definition of his own ministry in Lk 7:22.

The Servant's Second Commission Lk 14: 21-22	Jesus' Ministry Lk 7:22
Then the homeholder in anger said to his servant, "Go out quickly to the streets and lanes of the city, and bring in the poor and maimed and blind and lame."	. . . the blind receive their sight, the lame walk, lepers are cleansed, and the deaf hear, the dead are raised up, the poor have good news preached to them.

---

[72]Ferdinand Hahn, "Das Gleichnis von der Einladung zum Festmahl," *Verborum Veritas. Festschrift für Gustav Stählin*, ed. O. Böcher, et al. (Wuppertal: Rolf Brockhaus, 1970) 51-82.

[73]A. Vögtle, *Das Evangelium und die Evangelien* (Düsseldorf: Patmos-Verlag, 1971) 171-218.

[74]Ibid., 194ff.; Jeremias, *The Parables,* 176ff.

The parallel is too exact to be ignored.[75] Moreover, it must be stressed that this phase of bringing the downtrodden into the kingdom is not part of Matthew's parable of the marriage feast (Mt 22:1-10) and gives every indication of being an emphasis edited into the thought of Luke's Jesus.[76]

Given the connection of Jesus's definition of his own ministry with the servant's commission in the parable, the redacted nature of Lk 14:21 and Lk 4:18-19, and the temporal aspects of the pericope, the parable of the messianic banquet takes on a framework of salvation history.[77]

a. A man invited many to a great banquet.

b. At the time for the banquet he sent his servant to tell the invited guests that the banquet was prepared.

c. But those invited made excuses and sent the servant back to his master alone.

d. The master then in anger sent his servant to the streets and lanes of the city to bring in to his banquet the unfortunates of society.

e. This, the servant did, but still there was room.

f. The master then sent the servant outside the city to the highways and hedges in order to compel people to come and fill the master's house.

g. At this point the master took back his first invitation.

It is not difficult to interpret the underlying chronological framework. The key to its decipherment rests in the discovery that Jesus sees himself at the beginning of his ministry as the servant sent "to preach good news to the poor, . . . proclaim release to the captives and the recovering of sight to the blind, to set at liberty those who are oppressed . . .

---

[75]Πτωχούς (Lk 14:21) = πτωχοί (Lk 7:22); ἀναπείρους (Lk 14:21) = λεπροί, κωφοί, νεκροί (Lk 7:22); τυφλούς (Lk 14:21) = τυφλοί (Lk 7:22); χωλούς (Lk 14:21) = χωλοί (Lk 7:22).

[76]Cf. Bultmann, *The History of the Synoptic Tradition*, 175.

[77]Contrary to Hoyt, "The Poor in Luke-Acts," 122; and H. Palmer, "Just Married, Cannot Come," *Novum Testamentum* 18 (1976): 253.

" (Lk 4:18-19)—that is, at step "d" above.[78] Events a, b, and c have preceded Jesus' ministry.

Certainly the allegorical elements of the parable should not be overemphasized. There is a problem, for example, in saying that the servant of Lk 14:17 is a different allegorical servant than the servant of Lk 14:21. Perhaps the fact that the parable is set up in such a way as to contrast "the Lord" from "the servant" helps in that the distinction between servants is subsidiary to the main point that Jesus is trying to express. Moreover, one notices a looseness in the boundaries that Jesus draws around the times of the commissions: While he sees his own mission as symbolically parallel to the second commission, Jesus simultaneously continues also the work of the first commission and previews the work of the third commission. It can be added that Matthew's parable of the marriage feast also does not explicitly distinguish between the servants of Mt 22:3 (that is, the prophets who preceded John and Jesus) and the servants of Mt 22:8 (that is, the Christians who followed John and Jesus), although that distinction is certainly intended.

But in spite of the problem of associating more than one figure with "the servant" of the parable, it is clear that in Jesus' perception, event "b" pertains foremost to the past proclamation of John the Baptist. It is John who was, in Jesus' view, the servant sent to tell the invited guests that the banquet was ready.[79] Not only is this consistent with Jesus' announcement of the kingdom to the unfortunates of society (Lk 4:18-19), but it is also consistent with his view that John was the prophet of

---

[78]This explains the great emphasis given to John the Baptist in Lk 1-2. He also plays a significant role in salvation history by announcing that the banquet is prepared and by being rejected.

[79]Cf. Lk 7:33; F. Mussner, "Der Nicht erkannte Kairos (Mt. 11, 16-19 = Lk 7, 31-35)," *Biblica* 40 (1959): 612. Otto Betz ("The Kerygma of Luke," 137-38) also sees John as the last prophet before the end. This is consistent with Luke's redaction of the Baptist material. The report of John's imprisonment (Lk 3:19-20) is inserted immediately before the story of Jesus' baptism and the beginning of his ministry; cf. J. Kodell, "The Theology of Luke in Recent Study," *Biblical Theology Bulletin* 1 (1971): 130. It also allows for the portrayal of a first period of salvation history in Lk 1-2, See W. D. Tatum, "The Epoch of Israel: Luke i-ii and the Theological Plan of Luke-Acts," *New Testament Studies* 13 (1967): 184-95.

the end time (Lk 7:27-28). Moreover, it makes the popular style of Jesus' language entirely understandable. His speech fits his message. The posture assumed by Jesus at the very start of his ministry becomes understandable.[80] John came, but his message was rejected (event "c"). In Jesus' words, "For John the Baptist has come eating no bread and drinking no wine; and you [the men of this generation] say, 'He has a demon' " (Lk 7:33).

It was because the rejection of God's invitation as delivered through John was already a past event that Jesus then should begin his ministry as he does. In line with the servant of Lk 14:21, Jesus voices in Nazareth the anger of God, the master. Although he was well received (Lk 4:22),[81] Jesus suddenly and without cause (were it not supplied by the parable's explanation that the first message had already been re-

---

[80]For some of the literary difficulties in Lk 4:22-23 see David Hill, "The Rejection of Jesus at Nazareth (Lk iv 18-30)," *Novum Testamentum* 13 (1971): 162-70.

[81]Luke's redaction of Mark is informative at this point.

Mk 6:2b-3	Lk 4:22
	And all spoke well (ἐμαρτύ-
. . . and many who heard him were	ρουν) of him, and wondered
astonished (ἐξεπλήσσοντο),	(ἐθαύμαζον) at the gracious
	words (τοῖς λόγοις τῆς χάρι-
	τος) which proceeded out of his
	mouth;
saying, "Where did this man get all	and they said,
this? What is the wisdom given to	
him? What mighty works are	
wrought by his hands!	
Is not this the carpenter, the son of	"Is not this Joseph's son?"
Mary and brother of James and	
Joses and Judas and Simon, and	
are not his sisters here with us?"	
And they took offense at him	
(ἐσκανδαλίζοντο ἐν αὐτῷ).	

For my position, see Leander Keck, "Jesus' Entrance Upon His Mission," *Review and Expositor* 64 (Fall 1967): 465-83. For a discussion of the problems see H. Anderson, "Broadening Horizons: the Rejection at Nazareth Pericope of Luke 4:16-30 in Light of Recent Critical Trends," *Interpretation* 18 (1964): 259-75.

jected) turned on his own countrymen and previewed his own rejection by Israel (Lk 4:24), and Israel's rejection by God (Lk 4:25-27).[82]

That from the very beginning Jesus is conscious of God's rejection of Israel is one of the striking differences between the Jesus in Luke and the Jesus in Matthew. According to the Matthean Jesus (Mt 22:1-10), he and John were sent exclusively "to call those who were invited," that is, the just, and only after their predicted deaths were the servants to be sent out to gather "all whom they found, both good and bad."[83] Luke's Jesus, on the other hand, starts his ministry by acknowledging that the just had refused their invitation. His statement in Lk 5:31-32, "Those who are well have no need of a physician, but those who are sick; I have not come to call the righteous, but sinners to repentance," is in 5:31 laden with irony (compare Lk 4:23), and in 5:32 programmatic of his mission.[84]

Although events a, b, c, and d are seen in the parable as past events, it is incorrect to think that Luke's Jesus sees them as closed events at the time that he tells the parable. Rather, Jesus in the narrative seems to hold that while these events of the parable had taken place, they had not yet been completed—at least not in the sense that the possibility of entering the kingdom had been foreclosed to his hearers. So even on the cross (that is, after the telling of the parable) Jesus continues to bring the outcasts of society into the kingdom (Lk 23:43); and even though John the Baptist had been rejected by the "men of this generation" (compare Lk 7:33), and Jesus came with God's second commission, Jesus continues also the work of the first commission until his rejection on the cross. There is a certain liquidity to Jesus' thought as the old missions are extended past the beginning of each new mission. In this last case, the collapsing of categories is perhaps explained by Jesus' parable of the vinedresser who asks the owner of the

---

[82]Conzelmann pointed to the importance of Luke's use of the future tense ἐρεῖτε; his redaction is not careless, but purposeful (*The Theology of St. Luke*, 34-35). See also E. E. Ellis, *The Gospel of Luke*, 98; and E. M. Prevallet, "The Rejection at Nazareth. Lk. 4:14-20," *Scripture* 20 (1968): 5-9.

[83]J. C. Fenton, *Saint Matthew* (London: SCM Press, 1970) 348ff.

[84]R. Pesch, "Das Zöllnergastmahl (Mk 2, 15-17)," *Mélanges biblique*, ed. A. Descamps, et al. (Gembloux: J. Ducolot, 1970) 81-82.

vineyard for one more year to put manure and dig around a fruitless fig tree before cutting it down (Lk 13:6-9).[85] One also gets a sense for the pathos of Jesus' situation in Lk 13:34): "O Jerusalem, Jerusalem, killing the prophets and stoning those who are sent to you! How often would I have gathered your children together as a hen gathers her brood under her wings, and you would not!" The best explanation for this general collapsing of categories, however, is that while the parable of the feast is oriented to societal groups—Israel, in the first case; the poor, in the second case; and the gentiles, in the third case—Jesus, in his ministry appeals to individuals. Entrance into the kingdom is not a corporate endeavor, but an individual acceptance or rejection of the invitation extended.[86]

In the same way that the old mission of calling those first invited is extended with Jesus past John the Baptist, so also the third commission is previewed from the start of Jesus's ministry. The phrase εἰς τὰς ὁδοὺς καὶ φραγμούς, "into the highways and hedges" (Lk 14:23), is by its construction paralleled in the allegory to the phrase εἰς τὰς πλατείας καὶ ῥύμας τῆς πόλεως, "to the streets and lanes of the city" (Lk 14:21). The symbolic contrast set up by the omission of ἡ πόλις, "the city" in the third commission is important, especially in that both ὁδός and φραγμός carry strong overtones of an inside-outside relation. There can be little doubt that the third mission in the allegory is to be toward the gentiles—especially in light of God's final rejection of Israel, which significantly does not come until the last verse of the parable.[87] Also, there can be little doubt that while Jesus previews the third mission (compare Lk 4:25-27; 7:9; 17:18-19; 20:9-18), it is the apostles who are to carry it out (Lk 24:46-48).[88]

---

[85]Cf. J. Jeremias, *The Parables*, 170-71.

[86]Conzelmann, *The Theology of St. Luke*, 225-31.

[87]So Peder Borgen, "From Paul to Luke," *Catholic Biblical Quarterly* 31 (1969): 171 and Bultmann, *The History of the Synoptic Tradition*, 175. But see Eta Linnemann, *Jesus of the Parables*, trans. John Sturdy (New York: Harper and Row, 1964) 159 n6.

[88]G. W. H. Lampe, *St. Luke and the Church of Jerusalem* (London: University of London, 1969) 5-6.

Conclusion

Before proceeding, let me reemphasize two of the more significant elements of Jesus' view. First, Luke's Jesus emphasizes his own time. And second, his view is cast in terms of "consummation." To his own way of thinking in the story, Jesus must suffer and die before he can become the Christ. "Prophet" is an eschatological title. The present age is an in-between-time in which the kingdom is present but, at the same time, hidden. At "the judgment" everyone will see the kingdom. At that time everyone will also recognize the Christ. Jesus' ministry consists of bringing the dispossessed of society into the kingdom. Israel has already rejected its call. It will be the work of the church to bring the gentiles into the kingdom.

The Narrator's Interpretation of Jesus

Chapter 4

I now propose two tasks. I will attempt to broaden our study of the author's method of dressing characters with appropriate language, hoping to show that the enterprise was truly comprehensive. I will also begin to explore the way that the narrator of the gospel adapted Jesus' view into a view about Jesus. In what way did Jesus' message become with the narrator a message about Jesus?

Characterization

In the introduction I noted how the author was careful to match certain titles for Jesus with certain voices in the narrative. Thus, the "unearthly beings" refer to Jesus as the "Son of God," and Jesus uses the self-designation "Son of man." The narrator does not use these, but prefers the title "Lord."

I further noted in the first and second chapters how the author dressed his narrator and Jesus with appropriate styles of speech. He did this also with the other characters in the narrative. For instance, I. H. Marshall has pointed out that "the King of Israel" of Mk 15:32 was changed in Lk 23:37 to "the King of the Jews," because the latter is more appropriate in the mouth of the gentile soldiers who are speaking in Luke.[1] "Jews," in fact, otherwise appears in the gospel only in the speech of Pilate (Lk 23:3) and of the narrator (Lk 7:3; 23:51), and on the inscription over the crucified Jesus (Lk 23:38)—that is, in a context suited to foreigners. "Israel" appears in the speech of the angel (Lk 1:16), Mary (Lk 1:54), Zechariah (Lk 1:68), the narrator (Lk 1:80; 2:25), Simeon (Lk 2:32, 34), Jesus (Lk 4:25, 27; 7:9; 22:30), and Cleopas and his companion (Lk 24:21).

In contrast to the Semitic speech of many narrative characters, Pilate uses a more Attic standard of speech. By appropriating Cadbury's listing of the significant vocabulary, one notices that Pilate uses three "Common Attic words, or words occurring in several Attic writers": αἴτιον (Lk 23:4, 14, 22); ἀνακρίνω (Lk 23:14); and ἀποστρέφω (Lk 23:14).[2] Pilate's use of the dative agent αὐτῷ (Lk 23:15) in the classical construction with the perfect passive participle πεπραγμένον conforms to this standard.[3] Certain phrases perhaps reflecting legal terminology characterize Pilate. Such phrases include ὁ ἄνθρωπος οὗτος, "this man," which is repeated in a formalized way (Lk 23:14 twice); οὐδὲν ἄξιον θανάτου, "nothing deserving death," which appears otherwise in Paul's defenses before Festus (Acts 25:11) and before Agrippa (Acts 25:25), and in Agrippa's verdict (Acts 26:31);[4] παιδεύω, "chastise," which is repeated as a proposed punishment by Pilate (Lk 23:16, 22), and which probably indicates a less severe punishment than

---

[1] I. H. Marshall, *The Gospel of Luke* (Grands Rapids MI: William B. Eerdmans, 1978) 870.

[2] Henry J. Cadbury, *The Style and Literary Method of Luke* (Cambridge MA: Harvard University Press, 1920) 10-17. It is interesting that Luke's Pilate uses no words (α-ε) from Cadbury's other divisions.

[3] J. H. Moulton, R. Howard, and N. Turner, *Grammar of New Testament Greek,* 4 vols. (Edinburgh: T. and T. Clark, 1908-) 2:459; F. Blass and A. Debrunner, *A Greek Grammar of the New Testament and Other Early Christian Literature,* trans. Robert Funk (Chicago: University of Chicago Press, 1961) 102, 191.

[4] The same construction is used by Plutarch, *Plutarch's Lives,* ed. T. E. Page and W. H. D. Rouse (New York: MacMillan, 1914) 349.

φραγελλόω, "scourge" (compare Mk 15:15);[5] ἐνώπιον ὑμῶν ἀνακρί-
νας, "examining before you."

But others in the narrative are likewise characterized by appropriate idioms. Thus, for instance, one notices that the Latin phrase ἄξιός
ἐστιν ᾧ παρέξῃ τοῦτο (dignus est cui hoc praestes) appears in the
mouth of those who speak for the centurion (Lk 7:4).[6] The double
question form in the speech of the chief priests, scribes, and elders,
"Tell us by what authority you do these things, or who it is that gave
you this authority" (Lk. 20:2), is Jewish. Also, the quasi-adverbial καθ'
ὅλης τῆς 'Ιουδαίας, "throughout all of Judea" (Lk 23:5), in the
speech of the whole company is properly Semitic, and the whole company's διαστρέφω, "mislead" (Lk 23:2), and ἀνασείω, "stir up" (Lk
23:5), are very much the fitting language of the Jewish accusation.

Examples of this type of characterization could be multiplied. The
crowd, which accompanies Jesus and which is by and large Jewish,
uses the Semitic υἱὸς 'Ιωσήφ without the article (Lk 4:22). One also
notes in the typically Jewish form of Lk 11:27 and 14:15 the Palestinian
situation presupposed in the formulation of Lk 12:13, "Teacher, bid my
brother divide the inheritance with me," and the Semitic construction,
introducing a direct question (Lk 13:23).

The Narrator's Interpretation

Obviously the author was an accomplished artist who could con-
trol the language of his characters. It is also a credit to his ability as a
storyteller that the author allowed his narrator and Jesus to hold different views concerning some elements of the story. A place where the
different views crystallize and perhaps can be easily seen is with the
author's use of the words γενεά, "generation," and λαός, "people."
The first occurs fourteen times in the gospel, eleven times in the speech

---

[5]A. N. Sherwin-White, "Roman Society and Roman Law," *Novum Testamentum* (1963): 27-28; G. Bertram in *Theological Dictionary of the New Testament,*10 vols. (Grand Rapids MI: William B. Eerdmans, 1964-1976) 5:597-625.

[6]C. F. D. Moule, *Idiom Book of New Testament Greek* (Cambridge: Cambridge University Press, 1959) 192.

of Jesus but never in the voice of the narrator.[7] The second term occurs thirty-seven times in the gospel, twenty-four times in the narrator's voice but only once in the speech of Jesus.[8] Lk 7:29 and 31 are instructive because they show the author using the two terms in an overlapping manner to characterize the same audience, but in the mouth of the two different speakers.

Scene (Lk 7:24a):
When the messengers of John had gone, he [that is, Jesus] began to speak to the *crowds* (ὄχλους) concerning John.

Jesus (Lk 7:24b-28):
What did you go out into the wilderness to behold? A reed shaken by the wind? What then did you go out to see? A man clothed in soft raiment? Behold, those who are gorgeously appareled and live in luxury are kings' courts. What then did you go out to see? A prophet? Yes, I tell you, and more than a prophet. This is he of whom it is written, "Behold, I send my messenger before thy face, who shall prepare thy way before thee." I tell you, among those born of women none is greater than John; yet he who is least in the kingdom of God is greater than he.

Narrator (Lk 7:29-30):
When they heard this *all the people* (πᾶξ ὁ λαός) and the tax collectors justified God, having been baptized with the baptism of John; but the Pharisees and lawyers rejected the purpose of God for themselves, not having been baptized by him.

---

[7]Γενεά appears in the speech of Jesus at Lk 7:31; 9:41; 11:29, 30, 31, 32, 50, 51; 16:8; 17:25; 21:32. It also appears in the speech of Mary at Lk 1:48, 50 (twice).

[8]Λαός appears in the speech of the narrator at Lk 1:10, 21; 3:15, 18, 21; 6:17; 7:1, 29; 8:47; 11:53; 18:43; 19:47, 48; 20:1, 9, 19, 26, 45; 21:38; 22:2, 66; 23:13, 27, 35. It appears in Jesus' speech at Lk 21:23.

Jesus, continued (Lk 7:31-35):
To what then shall I compare *the men of this generation* (τοὺς ἀνθρώπους τῆς γενεᾶς ταύτης), and what are they like? They are like children sitting in the market place and calling to one another, "we piped to you, and you did not dance; we wailed, and you did not weep." For John the Baptist has come eating no bread and drinking no wine; and *you* say, (λέγετε) "He has a demon." The Son of man has come eating and drinking; and *you* say, (λέγετε) "Behold, a glutton and a drunkard, a friend of tax collectors and sinners!" Yet wisdom is justified by all her children.

Jesus' sense of rejection is obvious: "You are saying" (λέγετε, second person plural present indicative) that John has a demon, and that I am a glutton and a drunkard, a friend of tax collectors and sinners. To Jesus, most of the people, that is, "the men of this generation," reject him. To the narrator however, Jesus is accepted by most of the people. The position of the majority of people toward Jesus is reversed. The crowd is composed of Pharisees, lawyers, tax collectors and "all the people," and only the Pharisees and lawyers reject "the purpose of God for themselves."[9]

According to Paul Minear, the author of the gospel used the term λαός so often because it connoted a specific historical community that had been set apart by the covenant God had sealed with it.[10] To Luke, πᾶς ὁ λαός signified the "whole" people of God. It meant the elect nation of Israel, or Israel minus its leaders. Therefore λαός was the proper term by which the narrator distinguished Israel, and then the church, from other nations, and it was also the proper term by which

---

[9]Although their original relationship to the tradition is unclear, verses 29, 30 in their present position "cannot be anything other than a comment by the narrator" (Marshall, *The Gospel of Luke*, 297).

[10]Paul S. Minear, "Jesus' Audiences, According to Luke," *Novum Testamentum* 16 (1974): 81-109.

he distinguished the people of Israel who followed Jesus from their leaders who persecuted him.

This understanding of λαός seems quite correct and does indeed fit nicely with the narrator's interpretation of his story. The messiah is surrounded by the "people of God" who "glorify God" as they see Jesus working out God's will on earth. This is why the narrator (and only the narrator) uses the Septuagintal phrase "they glorified God" to describe the response of the "people" in general (compare Lk 5:26; 7:16), and of certain individual characters in the narrative to the deeds of Jesus.[11] As during the exodus, the proper answer of God's chosen community to His saving activity is to glorify Him.

> Then sang Moses and the children of Israel this song to God, and spoke, saying, Let us sing to the Lord, for he is very greatly glorified. Horse and rider he has thrown into the sea. He was to me a helper and protector for salvation: This is my God and I will glorify him.[12]

"This generation which rejected Jesus," then gives way in the view of the narrator to the "whole people of God who supported Jesus." It should be pointed out, however, that the theme of rejection, which is so central to Jesus' self-perception in Luke—and also in the source, Mark[13]—is not completely done away with by the narrator. To a great

---

[11]According to the narrator, those who praise, justify, or bless God are Zechariah (Lk 1:64); a multitude of heavenly host (Lk 2:13); the shepherds (Lk 2:20); Simeon (Lk 2:28); Anna (Lk 2:38); the man who was paralyzed (Lk 5:25); all who saw Jesus heal the paralyzed man (Lk 5:26); all who saw Jesus resuscitate the young man at Nain (Lk 7:16); all the people and the tax collectors (Lk 7:29); the woman who had had a spirit of infirmity for eighteen years (Lk 13:13); one of the ten lepers (Lk 17:15); the blind man near Jericho (Lk 18:43); the centurion who witnessed the crucifixion (Lk 23:47); and those who witnessed the ascension (Lk 24:53).

[12]Ex 15:1-2. This is the beginning of Moses' victory hymn, whose place in the tradition was clearly liturgical. Cf. Frank Moore Cross, *Canaanite Myth and Hebrew Epic* (Cambridge MA: Harvard University Press, 1973) 112-44; Brevard S. Childs, *The Book of Exodus* (Philadelphia: Westminster Press, 1974) 240-53.

[13]Cf. Eduard Schweizer, *The Good News According to Mark* (Richmond VA: John Knox Press, 1970).

extent, it is simply toned down into a well-intentioned lack of understanding. If one were to pay attention only to the narrator's comments, apart from the direct discourse of the characters, his interpretation of the story would be this: Many people recognize that something out of the ordinary is happening with the event of Jesus.[14] Only a few, however, perceive the true significance of events,[15] and even his closest

[14]As interpreted by the narrator, those who are amazed include those who witnessed Zechariah name John (Lk 1:63); Joseph and Mary (Lk 2:33, 48); all who heard the boy Jesus in the temple (Lk 2:47); all who heard Jesus in Nazareth (Lk 4:22); those in Capernaum (Lk 4:32, 36); Simon Peter, James, and John (Lk 5:9); all who witnessed the healing of the paralytic (Lk 5:26); Jesus (Lk 7:9); the disciples in the boat with Jesus (Lk 8:25); the parents of the child whom Jesus resuscitated (Lk 8:56); all who saw Jesus heal the boy with a demon (Lk 9:43); the people who witnessed the casting out of the dumb demon (Lk 11:14); the Pharisees (Lk 11:38); and the spies who pretended to be sincere (Lk 20:26).

Likewise, there are some who are afraid. In the view of the narrator they include Zechariah, when he saw the angel (Lk 1:12); Zechariah's neighbors, when his tongue was loosed (Lk 1:65); the shepherds, when they saw the angel (Lk 2:9); all who witnessed the resuscitation of the young man at Nain (Lk 7:16); the disciples close to Jesus (Lk 8:25; 9:34, 45; 24:37); the people who saw sitting at the feet of Jesus the man from whom the demons had gone (Lk 8:35, 37); Peter, John, and James (Lk 9:34); some of the scribes (Lk 20:40); the women who did not find Jesus' body in the tomb (Lk 24:5); the eleven and those with them (Lk 24:37).

[15]There are a variety of characters in the narrator's commentary who recognize Jesus or otherwise understand the meaning of events. They include the multitude of the people who perceived that Zechariah had seen a vision (Lk 1:22); John the Baptist, who leaped in the womb (Lk 1:41); Zechariah and Elizabeth, who name their son John (Lk 1:59, 64); the shepherds (Lk 2:20) and all those who praise, justify or bless God (see n11); Simeon (Lk 2:25-27); Anna (Lk 2:38); Jesus (Lk 2:40, 47, 52; 5:20; 9:47; 11:17; 20:23; 24:27; 45); all who heard Jesus in the synagogues (Lk 4:15); demons (Lk 4:41); multitudes (Lk 5:15; 6:18, 19; 18:43; 19:37, 48; 23:48); the sinners (Lk 15:1); the disciples who realize that Jesus is going to die (Lk 22:49); Peter, who remembers the words of Jesus (Lk 22:61-62); one of the criminals on the cross (Lk 23:40); the two disciples who went to Emmaus (Lk 24:31); the eleven and those about them (Lk 24:45, 52).

followers do not fully understand the true meaning and identity of Jesus until the very end of the narrative when Jesus opens their minds to understand the Scriptures (Lk 24:45). Demons recognize Jesus for who he is, but Jesus does not allow them to speak. He purposefully keeps his true identity a secret (Lk 4:41; 5:14; 7:37ff.; 8:37ff.; 9:7, 45; 11:14ff.; 18:34; 20:26). Although the narrator does not quite understand the reason for Jesus' reticence he nonetheless believes that in some way his secrecy is part of the divine plan.[16]

Jesus begins his ministry by preaching to the people in Galilee (Lk 4:14ff.; 7:1; 8:1), but soon turns to Jerusalem (Lk 9:51, 53). In fact, Jerusalem is of thematic importance to the narrator (compare Lk 2:38; 4:9; 9:51, 53; 10:38; 13:22; 17:11; 19:1, 11, 28, 41), who sees it as the place where the Scriptures are fulfilled (Lk 2:22, 24; 24:27, 45). Opposition to Jesus begins with the devil who tests Jesus, and culminates with Satan who enters Judas. During his ministry Jesus is opposed by various narrative characters and for a variety of reasons.[17] Most often,

---

[16]Hans Conzelmann claims that the command of secrecy in Luke "rests on the necessity of the Passion"; see *The Theology of St. Luke,* trans. Geoffrey Buswell (New York: Harper and Row, 1961) 76-77 n3. This is in keeping with Jesus' use of titles, as he only called himself "the messiah" after his resurrection. But to the narrator, Jesus was the messiah from the very beginning of his ministry.

[17]Many characters are placed in opposition to Jesus by the narrator's comments. Definitely opposed to Jesus are the devil, who tempted Jesus (Lk 4:2, 13); all the people who heard Jesus in the synagogue of Nazareth and were filled with wrath (Lk 4:28-29); the scribes and the Pharisees, who watched Jesus so that they might find an accusation against him (Lk 6:7, 11; 11:53-54); the people of Samaria, who would not receive Jesus (Lk 9:53); a lawyer who tried to test Jesus (Lk 10:25); others who tried to test Jesus (Lk 11:16); the ruler of the synagogue who was indignant because Jesus healed on the sabbath (Lk 13:14, 17); those who dined with Jesus at the house of the ruler who was a Pharisee (Lk 14:1); the chief priests and the scribes and the principal men of the people, who sought to destroy Jesus (Lk 19:47-48); the scribes and chief priests, who tried to lay hands on Jesus (Lk 20:19; 22:2; 23:10); Satan, who entered Judas (Lk 22:3); the chief priests and captains, who were glad that Judas might betray Jesus (Lk 22:5); Judas, who betrayed Jesus (Lk 22:6); and the whole company of the assembly of elders and their council, who accused

opposition is caused by disputes over the law (see Lk 6:7ff.; 13:14ff.; Lk. 14:1ff.); always it is initiated by Jesus' opponents.[18] Opposition to Jesus grows and is centered on his teachings (Lk 11:53-54; 19:47; 20:19). Gradually the principal opponents of Jesus are stylized into the chief priests and the scribes and the principal men of the people (Lk 19:47-48; 20:19; 22:2, 5; 23:10).[19] Jesus is surrounded by supporting crowds and since his opponents are few and afraid of the crowds (Lk 20:19) they cannot take him. They try to entrap him, but cannot (Lk 13:17; 19:47-48). They send spies (Lk 20:20) but to no avail (Lk 20:26, 40). Satan, who has been waiting for an opportune time (Lk 4:13) enters Judas (Lk 22:3) who then plots with the chief priests and captains (Lk 22:5) and betrays Jesus (Lk 22:6). Jesus is mocked (Lk 22:63, 65; 23:11, 35-36, 39) and accused before Pilate. He refuses to defend himself and is reluctantly handed over to the will of his accusers (Lk 23:23ff.). Jesus dies, and the multitudes mourn (Lk 23:48). But he rises

---

Jesus before Pilate (Lk 23:2, 10). With these perhaps belong also the Pharisees and the lawyers who rejected the purpose of God for themselves (Lk 7:30); Pilate who delivered Jesus to the will of his accusers (Lk 23:25); and several characters who scoffed at Jesus: those who were weeping over the death of the ruler's daughter (Lk 8:53); the Pharisees (Lk 16:14); the men who were holding Jesus (Lk 22:63, 65); Herod with his soldiers (Lk 23:11); the rulers (Lk 23:35); the soldiers (Lk 23:36); and one of the criminals (Lk 23:39).

[18]There is a striking contrast between Jesus' view and the narrator's view concerning the origin of disputes. Often in Luke Jesus presents himself in the prophetic mold as one denouncing his hearers. The narrator reverses the roles of the antagonists, however, and credits the cause of conflict to Jesus' "accusers."

[19]Instead of a growing opposition to Jesus, Conzelmann regarded the active hostility against Jesus as "isolated motifs, which are not linked together according to an overall plan" (*The Theology of St. Luke*, 194 n1). He understood the real hostility in the gospel to be governed by the expression συντελέσας πάντα πειρασμόν of Lk 4:13. Temptation was removed from Jesus and did not return until Lk 23:11. It does seem, however, that the leaders of the temple actively plot well in advance of the reappearance of Satan. Their plans simply do not succeed (cf. Lk 19:47-48; 20:19). Cf. Schuyler Brown, *Apostasy and Perseverance in the Theology of Luke* (Rome: Pontifical Biblical Institute, 1969).

from the dead and appears to some of his disciples and interprets to them in all the Scriptures the things concerning himself (Lk 24:27, 45).

In this near-caricature of the narrator's view, Jesus is the misunderstood but well-liked messiah, who dies innocently. What "rejection" of "the Lord" there is in the story is placed to the credit of the leaders of the Jews, who along with Satan fabricate the evil.

But even had the narrator agreed whole-heartedly with Jesus' view of himself as fully rejected by his own generation, he still would not have been able to appropriate the designation of Jesus' audience as "the men of this generation." The aorist παρέδοσαν of the prologue (Lk 1:2) indicates that the generation of eyewitnesses had passed (or was quickly passing) away, so that the message of Jesus could not have continued to be vital to the community of faith had it not been stretched beyond that first generation. The narrator's choice of λαός was doubly useful, then, because it at once allowed the universal Church, both Jews and Gentiles, a part in the story of salvation and provided that necessary temporal extension of Jesus' message.

A further illustration of the contrast between the points of view of the narrator and Jesus is found in the way in which Jesus' acts of salvation are reinterpreted by the narrator as moments of power.[20] One can see this very clearly in the gospel's description of the healing miracles of Jesus. Three verbs of healing are used by the gospel's characters: ἰάομαι, θεραπεύω, and σῴζω. Jesus never uses ἰάομαι, and he uses θεραπεύω only when referring to some indefinite situation (compare Lk 4:23; 10:9; 14:3).[21] When he actually heals someone and

---

[20]The narrator refers to Jesus' miracles exclusively by the metonymy, δύναμις (Lk 4:14; 5:17; 6:19; 9:1; 19:37). He does not use τέρας or ἔργον, and when he uses σημεῖον (Lk 11:16; 23:8) he does so with negative implications. The δύναμις of Jesus' miracles refers to the power that causes the miracles. The power is linked in the gospel with the Holy Spirit (Lk 4:14), which provides the connection with the worship of the early Church. "It was that same power that caused Jesus' miracles that was also present in the narrator's Church" (so S. V. McCasland, "Miracle," Interpreter's Dictionary of the Bible [Nashville: Abingdon Press, 1962] 3:394).

[21]Lk 4:23: "Doubtless you will quote to me this proverb, 'Physician, heal (θεράπευσον) yourself.' " Lk 10:8-9: "Whenever you enter a town and they receive you, eat what is set before you; heal (θεραπεύετε) the sick in it. . . . " Lk 14:3: "Is it lawful to heal (θεραπεῦσαι) on the sabbath, or not?"

mentions it, he always uses σῴζω (see Lk 8:48; 17:19; 18:42).[22] The narrator, on the other hand, never uses σῴζω in reference to Jesus' healing miracles. He always refers to them with either ἰάομαι or θεραπεύω.[23] A comparison of the narrator's speech at Lk 8:47 and Lk 17:15 with Jesus' speech at Lk 8:48 and Lk 17:19 is especially enlightening.[24] What the narrator describes with ἰάομαι Jesus describes with σῴζω.

This was a purposeful concern of the author, and one that he was careful to edit into his sources. In numerous instances he described Jesus' miracles by adding ἰάομαι and θεραπεύω to his main source, Mark—but not once did he so insert either term into the speech of Jesus. On the other hand, wherever σῴζω was used in Mark to describe "healing," and was not in the speech of Jesus, the author of Luke omitted it (compare Mk 5:23, 28; 6:56).

The reason for the author's redaction was clearly that he wrote his gospel as if listening to the different voices of the story characters. But, of course, he was not at this point interested in idiosyncrasies of vocabulary, as if ἰάομαι and σῴζω were simple synonyms, one preferred by the narrator and the other by Jesus in the same manner as were οὖν

---

[22]At Lk 8:48 Jesus heals the woman who had had a flow of blood for twelve years; at Lk 17:19, the Samaritan leper; and at Lk 18:42, the blind beggar of Jericho.

[23]The narrator uses ἰάομαι at Lk 5:17; 6:18, 19; 8:47; 9:2, 11, 42; 14:4; 17:15; 22:51. He uses θεραπεύω at Lk 4:40; 5:15; 6:7, 18; 7:21; 8:2, 43; 9:1, 6; 13:14.

[24]Lk 8:47-48:
Narrator: And when the woman saw that she was not hidden, she came trembling, and falling down before him [Jesus] declared in the presence of all the people why she had touched him, and how she had been immediately healed (ἰάθη).
Jesus: "Daughter, your faith has made you well (σέσωκεν); go in peace."
It is noteworthy that Luke omits the third phrase from his source (Mk 5:34) where Jesus adds, καὶ ἴσθι ὑγιὴς ἀπὸ τῆς μάστιγός σου.
Lk 17:15, 19:
Narrator: Then one of them, when he saw that he was healed (ἰάθη), turned back praising God with a loud voice.
Jesus: "Rise and go your way; your faith has made you well (σέσωκεν)."
It is noteworthy that both the narrator and Jesus distinguish the cleansing of the leprosy (ἐκαθαρίσθησαις, Lk 17:14, 17) from the healing that occurs.

and μετά with genitive.[25] Rather, what controlled the choice of the different words for healing in the gospel was the double meaning of σώζω for "healing" and "salvation." The narrator's choice of ἰάομαι draws attention only to the miraculous healing of the sick people.[26] The connotation of Jesus' σώζω, however, especially since he uses it in the perfect tense, is that those who were infirm were not only healed, but were also incorporated into the divine kingdom.[27] Through their faith, the woman who had a flow of blood for twelve years, the Samaritan leper, and the blind beggar had been saved from eternal death. Forcefully, Jesus' phrase ἡ πίστις σου σέσωκέν σε, "your faith has made you well/has saved you," placed his time as the time of salvation.

The difference in the vocabulary used by Jesus and the narrator, then, at this point is related to the worship of the community of believers: the narrator transferred to his own time that emphasis that Jesus had placed on his time. The Lukan narrator emphasizes the miraculous power that caused the miracles rather than the original recipients of salvation. In his eyes the miracles are not so much signs of the in-breaking kingdom, or even signs that Jesus was the Christ, but moments of that power that through the Holy Spirit is still present in the community of believers. In this way, he appropriates Jesus' saving activity from the past into the present people of God. Like the λαός in the story, God's people in the narrator's community can also then witness the power of God and "glorify Him."

Lukan scholarship has recognized that the narrator reworked the eschatological expectation of Jesus and extended the appearance of the kingdom into the future (compare Lk 19:11).[28] And usually schol-

---

[25]See Appendixes B and C.

[26]Cf. Albrecht Oepke, "ἰάομαι," *TDNT* 3:194-215.

[27]Cf. Werner Foerster, "σώζω," *TDNT* 7:989-1003; H. D. Betz, "The Cleaning of the Ten Lepers (Lk. 17:11-19)," *Journal of Biblical Literature* 90 (1971): 315-16, 321.

[28]Peder J. Borgen, "The Eschatology and 'Heilsgeschichte' in Luke-Acts" (Ph.D. dissertation, Drew University, 1956); Conzelmann, *The Theology of St. Luke;* H. Flender, *St. Luke: Theologian of Redemptive History,* trans. Reginald and Ilse Fuller (London: SPCK, 1967); W. C. Robinson, Jr., *Der Weg des Herrn: Studien zur Geschichte und Eschatologie im Lukas-Evangelium* (Hamburg: Bergstadt, 1964).

arship has seen in the narrator's interpretation also the position of the author of the gospel. This might well be the case, but it is interesting that the author of the gospel actually highlighted the difference between the narrator's and Jesus' end-time expectations by adding to his main source, Mark, several passages in the mouth of Jesus that stress the nearness of the kingdom (for example, Lk 10:9, 11; 12:38-40, 41-48; 12:54-13:9; 18:7-8).[29]

Thus the author also highlighted the contrast in views concerning John the Baptist. While Jesus perceives the Baptist to be an end-time Elijah figure, the narrator interprets him to be an Elijah figure who preceded Jesus and not the coming of God's kingdom. This distinction in the points of view of Jesus and the narrator has been convincingly demonstrated by J. A. T. Robinson's article "Elijah, John, and Jesus: An Essay in Detection."[30] According to Robinson, John's prophecy concerning the "coming one who will baptize with the Holy Spirit and with fire" (Lk 3:16) indicates that John did not think of himself as Elijah, but rather expected the coming of Elijah. Therefore, when John sent his disciples to ask Jesus if he were the one who was to come (Lk 7:19-20) he was really asking, "Are you Elijah?" That Robinson is correct at this point is clear in Luke, since the author found the motive for John's question in a report concerning a miracle performed by Jesus that was reminiscent of Elijah's resuscitation of the widow's son at Zarepath (Lk 7:11-17).[31] As Robinson has pointed out, Jesus, in the story,

---

[29]It was with these passages that Conzelmann had his greatest difficulties. He was forced to admit that Lk 10:11 is "an assertion of the nearness of the Kingdom" (Conzelmann, *The Theology of St. Luke*, 107). Why would an author who redacted his sources with the theological intention of delaying the parousia purposefully insert such a passage into his gospel?

[30]J. A. T. Robinson, "Elijah, John and Jesus: An Essay in Detection," *New Testament Studies* 4 (1957-1958): 263-81. See also Howard M. Teeple, *The Mosaic Eschatological Prophet* (Philadelphia: Society of Biblical Literature, 1957) 4, 8, 9.

[31]John Drury, *Tradition and Design in Luke's Gospel* (Atlanta: John Knox Press, 1977) 71-72; A. Feuillet, "Le récit lucanien de l'agonie de Gethsemani (Lc.XXII. 39-49)," *New Testament Studies* 22 (1975-1976): 409; see also L. C. Crockett, "Lk. 4:25-27 and Jewish-Gentile Relations in Luke-Acts," *Journal of Biblical Literature* 88 (1969): 182.

does not give an open and positive answer to John's question (Lk 7:21-23) until John's messengers depart. Then he says openly that John and not he is the messenger prophesied by Malachi (Lk 7:26-28).[32] Jesus' view of John is that he is the Elijah, foretold by Malachi, and it is significant that Jesus never in Luke redefines this figure as a forerunner of the messiah.[33] It is the narrator who modifies the expected figure of Elijah by placing him before Jesus instead of before the coming of God's kingdom. For this reason the narrator changes Isaiah's prophecy (Lk 3:4-6‖Is 40:3-5), omitting the phrase ὅτι κύριος ἐλάλησε (Is 40:5) from his quotation, and replacing Isaiah's τοῦ θεοῦ ἐμῶν (Is 40:3) with αὐτοῦ. Thus the narrator allows a longer time before the appearance of the kingdom.

But although there is an explanation for the delay of the kingdom in the narrator's reworking of the story's eschatology, the narrator himself betrays no consciousness of a crisis in the community.[34] The author did not have his narrator appear as a problem-solving scholar or theologian, but as a believing participant in the cult who is repeating the story of Jesus. Any reinterpretation on the narrator's part, therefore, is closely tied to the community's attempt to experience its own salvation in the story of Jesus. In its narration the story becomes alive to a new community, and its events transcend the past and move into the time of the participating congregation.

---

[32]The singular σου of Lk 7:27 presents a difficult exegetical question. Does the σου refer to the "people of Israel"? See F. W. Danker, *Jesus and the New Age* (St. Louis: Clayton Publishing House, 1972) 97. Or does it refer to Jesus (as messiah)? See H. Schürmann, *Das Lukasevangelium* (Freiburg: Herder, 1969) 1:417. Robinson gave strength to the former reading when he pointed out that the first clear reference to the idea that Elijah was expected as the precursor of the messiah did not occur until Justin Martyr's *Dialogue with Trypho* ("Elijah, John and Jesus," 34, 36-37).

[33]Conzelmann's reading of Lk 16:16 emphasizing the separation of Jesus from John cannot be overlooked (*The Theology of St. Luke*, 20ff.). There is a sharp separation of Jesus and John also in Jesus' speech at Lk 7:28.

[34]Against Erich Grässer, *Das problem der Parusieverzögerung in den synoptischen Evangelien und in der Apostelgeschichte* (Berlin: Verlag Alfred Töpelmann, 1957).

The Narrator's
New View of Jesus

Chapter 5

I have just observed that the narrator of Luke shifts the focus of the narrative away from Jesus' "generation" to "all of the people," and how that change is accompanied by some significant reinterpretation on his part. In Jesus' speech, the comprehensive category, "men of this generation" is used to identify those who are rejecting the will of God. But in the narrator's speech, the comprehensive category, "all of the people" is used to identify those accepting God's purposes for themselves. While in the eyes of Jesus many reject and few accept his proclamation, in the eyes of the narrator many accept and few reject it.[1]

The Opposition

This is an important difference, because the narrator then finds it necessary to build up the betrayal theme and emphasize the complicity of Satan. According to the narrator, Jesus was surrounded by sup-

---

[1] The meaning of this contrast will be discussed in the last chapter.

porting crowds. Jesus' enemies, who are stylized into the chief priests and the scribes and the principal men of the people (Lk 19:47-48; 20:19; 22:2, 5; 23:10), were afraid of the crowds (Lk 20:19). They tried to entrap Jesus (Lk 13:17; 19:47-48) and sent spies (Lk 20:20), but did not succeed (Lk 20:26, 40) until Satan, who had been waiting for an opportune time (Lk 4:13) entered Judas (Lk 22:3). Judas then plotted with the chief priests and captains (Lk 22:5), and betrayed Jesus (Lk 22:6). When Jesus died, the multitudes mourned (Lk 23:48). What "rejection of the Lord" there is in the story is placed by the narrator to the credit of the leaders of the Jews, who along with Satan plotted the evil.

But Jesus presents a much dimmer view of the multitude. Not only are the leaders of the Jews evil, but Jesus' "generation" is evil (Lk 7:31ff.; 9:41; 11:29ff.; 17:25). Satan, on the other hand, is of much lesser consequence in Jesus' thought. His power has already been broken (Lk 10:18; 11:18ff.; 13:16; 22:31). The kingdom has dawned.

The Messiah

Jesus and the narrator, then, hold different views of the rejection of Jesus. And it is not as if this were an isolated occurrence in the narration of the gospel. Actually, the different views of the rejection of Jesus make part of a subtle complex of contrasting insights into the purpose of Jesus. As I have previously pointed out, Jesus' view of the messiah is governed by a concept of consummation. Throughout Luke, Jesus understands himself to be a special person, with unusual authority and a singular purpose. But Jesus also holds that it is only through a suffering death that he becomes the Christ. Thus, after the resurrection, Jesus calls himself the Christ, and before the crucifixion, he calls himself a prophet.

The narrator, however, does not call Jesus a prophet at all. To the narrator, from the beginning, Jesus was the Christ. For example, the narrator sets the stage for Simeon's joyful recognition of God's salvation by commenting that Simeon was expecting before death to see the Lord's Christ (Lk 2:26); he prefaces John the Baptist's statement about the one who is coming, mightier than himself, with the comment that all men were questioning whether John were the Christ (Lk 3:15); and he adds to the pericope of the healing of many with demons, the notice that the demons knew that Jesus was the Christ (Lk 4:41). The author's editing of Mark to emphasize the narrator's position is evident in the second example with the introduction of Lk 3:15 into the Markan text (see Mk 1:7-8‖Lk 3:15-16). The comment in Lk 4:41 (compare Mk 1:34) shows a more complex redaction, as both the cry of the demons, "You are the Son of God," and the narrator's interpretation that "they knew that he was the Christ" were inserted into the Markan framework.

This last example is also instructive, because it shows the narrator's use of the Markan theme of the messianic secret. As already mentioned, the Lukan Jesus makes no attempt to keep his identity a secret. True, he does not call himself the messiah until after his resurrection. But it is because his thinking is governed by that type of consummation Christology present in the old Philippian hymn (Phil 2:6-11)—not because his thinking is governed by any desire for concealment.

Jesus' understanding is very different from that of the narrator, who, holding throughout that Jesus was the Christ, appropriates the idea of secrecy into his account (compare Lk 4:41; 5:14; 8:56). William Wrede pointed out that this creates confusion in the narrative, for Jesus himself is anxious in Luke to announce his role in salvation history (see Lk 4:21).[2]

In Mark, of course, the secrecy motif makes part of a general theme of misconception that leads up to full rejection.[3] But that is not the case with the narrator in Luke, who locates the rejection of Jesus with a small band of authorities. This creates real tension in Luke between the narrator's notices of secrecy, on the one hand, and Jesus' open proclamation of his authority (compare Lk 6:46ff.) and the unmistaken perception of Jesus' identity by the disciples and the crowd (compare Lk 7:16), on the other.[4]

Wrede acknowledged that the views in Luke could not be reconciled, but tended to credit it to the author's use of his source. Thus he gingerly classified the author as one who could no longer come to

---

[2]William Wrede, *The Messianic Secret,* trans. J. G. Greig (Cambridge: James Clarke, 1971) 172-79.

[3]Cf. Eduard Schweizer, *The Good News According to Mark* (Richmond VA: John Knox Press, 1970) 54-56, 165-66, 190-91; T. J. Weeden, *Mark—Traditions in Conflict* (Philadelphia: Fortress Press, 1971) 52-59.

[4]H. Schürmann, *Das Lukasevangelium,* (Freiburg: Herder, 1969) 1: 402-403; Wrede, *The Messianic Secret,* 241.

terms with the Markan theme of secrecy but nevertheless adopted it.[5] At the same time Wrede cautioned against a glib acceptance of this, his own view, indicating that Luke often changed Mark's notices of secrecy.[6] For our purpose, it is worth noting that the demand for secrecy never occurs on the lips of Jesus in Luke.[7] In this respect, Luke's redaction of Mk 1:44 in Lk 5:14 might be significant, as the charge "to tell no one" was taken out of the speech of Jesus and placed into the commentary of the narrator.[8]

It is true that the distinction between direct and indirect discourse is not as clear in Hellenistic Greek as in modern English, and the shift in voice in Lk 5:14 might very well result from some sort of stylistic quality of the writer. I certainly do not want to overstate the significance of the redaction at this point. But neither do I want to minimize the pattern present in Luke's use of the secrecy motif. Take, for instance, the omission of the ugly scene between Peter and Jesus at the

---

[5]Wrede, *The Messianic Secret*, 178-79.

[6]Ibid., 164.

[7]A possible exception is Luke's appropriation of Jesus' command to the man with an unclean spirit, φιμώθητι καὶ ἔξελθε ἀπ' αὐτοῦ (Lk 4:35‖Mk 1:25). It is not clear, however, that Jesus' demand for silence is related to a desire to keep his identity a secret. This interpretation only comes to the fore in the commentary of the narrator in Lk 4:41.

[8]I. H. Marshall understood the author to be attempting unsuccessfully to shift into a more classical style of indirect discourse (*The Gospel of Luke* [Grand Rapids MI: William B. Eerdmans, 1978] 209). The mixture of direct and indirect discourse was not uncommon in classical Greek, however, and the characterization of the shift as a "relapse" is unwarranted; cf. F. Blass, and A. Debrunner, *A Greek Grammar of the New Testament and Other Early Christian Literature*, trans. Robert W. Funk (Chicago: University of Chicago Press, 1961) 247. Schürmann's insight that the cure and its attestation by the priest were to serve as evidence to the people of the messianic act of God in Jesus is helpful in ascertaining that Jesus in Luke is really not interested in maintaining his identity secret (*Das Lukasevangelium*, 1:277). Beare's perception of how Luke subdued Mark's view by having Jesus go into desert places in order to pray rather than to escape the throngs is also helpful (cf. Lk 5:16‖Mk 1:45); see F. W. Beare, *The Earliest Records of Jesus* (Nashville: Abingdon Press, 1962) 72.

time of the messianic confession at Caesarea Philippi/Bethsaida (Mk 8:27-33‖Lk 9:18-22). As the bitter dialogue makes clear in Mark, Jesus' command for secrecy is related to the mistaken comprehension of the disciples. But that is not the case in Luke, as the disciples do correctly understand Jesus' identity (see Lk 10:23-24; 22:28ff.; 24:21).[9] There-fore, the Lukan Peter adds the qualification "of God" to his assertion that Jesus is the Christ, and does not rebuke Jesus for his teaching on the necessity of a suffering death (Mk 8:32).

In fact, the command for silence (Lk 9:21) becomes extremely dif-ficult in Luke as in the very next chapter Jesus sends seventy disciples into every place where he is about to go (Lk 10:1) with the promise that "He who hears you hears me, and he who rejects you rejects me, and he who rejects me rejects him who sent me" (Lk 10:16); the seventy return saying, "Lord, even the demons are subject to us in your name" (Lk 10:17). Far from keeping Jesus' identity a secret, the seventy ap-peal to his authority at his own behest.

With this in mind, Conzelmann joined the command for secrecy in Lk 9:21 to the saying on the suffering death of Jesus that immediately follows: the "secret" concerns the necessity of the Passion, and not the identity of Jesus.[10] Following Wrede, Conzelmann pointed out that this fits well with the notices in Lk 9:45 and Lk 18:34, in which the dis-ciples do not understand the necessity of the Passion.[11]

And this does seem to be the narrator's view. The disciples under-stand everything except the suffering motif. But what is interesting at

---

[9]The use of the perfect participle διαμεμενηκότες in Lk 22:28 shows the past and continuing loyalty of the disciples. The reference to the third day in Lk 24:21 is an indication of the disciples' correct understanding of Jesus. The resurrection is not completely unexpected; cf. J. M. Creed, *The Gospel Ac-cording to St. Luke* (London: Macmillan, 1957) 296; Wrede, *The Messianic Se-cret*, 241-42.

[10]Hans Conzelmann, *The Theology of St. Luke*, trans. Geoffrey Buswell (New York: Harper and Row, 1963) 107-108, 76-77 n3.

[11]Ibid., 74. Conzelmann located the misunderstanding in the disciples' expectation of a quickly approaching parousia. To do this, however, he forced the application of Lk 19:11 to the disciples. Wrede also applied Lk 19:11 to the disciples, but with the accompanying expectation of a national, political messiah; see *The Messianic Secret*, 167-71.

this point is that the narrator has linked this lack of understanding with a divine plan for secrecy. The disciples do not understand because they are not supposed to understand.[12] This motif was clearly redacted into the voice of the narrator (compare Lk 9:45‖Mk 9:32; Lk 18:32ff.‖Mk 10:33-34).[13] Thus the narrator gives the reason for the disciples' misperception of the Passion: Jesus' sayings were concealed from them so that they should not perceive.[14]

It seems to me rather striking that Jesus, when seen through his own discourse, holds no such view of a divinely intended secret. To the contrary he expects the disciples to understand the indispensability of the Passion. No less than eight times he predicts that he must die (Lk 9:22, 44; 13:33-34; 18:31-32; 20:15; 22:15, 22, 37).[15] Not one of these predictions in the mouth of Jesus hints at a divine plan for secrecy. Furthermore, there are good indications that the author redacted his sources so as to make it clear that Jesus expected the disciples to understand what he was saying. Giving every sign of sincerity, the Lukan Jesus prefaces one of his statements about the demand of the Passion with the phrase "Let these words sink into your ears" (Lk 9:44‖Mk 9:31).[16] The prediction at Lk 13:32-33, which is peculiar to Luke but

---

[12]Cf. Marshall, *The Gospel of Luke,* 394; 691.

[13]Helmut Flender, *St. Luke, Theologian of Redemptive History,* trans. Reginald and Ilse Fuller (London: SPCK, 1967) 157-58; Alfred Loisy, *L'évangile selon Luc* (Paris: Emile Nourry, 1924) 280; Conzelmann, *The Theology of St. Luke,* 59 n2, 197-98.

[14]W. Grundmann, "δεῖ, . . . " in *Theological Dictionary of the New Testament,* 10 vols. (Grand Rapids MI: William B. Eerdmans, 1964-1976) 2:21-25.

[15]Marshall was aware of the tension between these predictions of the Passion and the narrator's view of a divine plan for secrecy. Referring to Jesus' prediction in Lk 18:31-34, Marshall wrote that Jesus' statement is so clear that it is difficult to see how they (that is, the disciples) could have been so blind" (cf. Lk 18:34; *The Gospel of Luke,* 691).

[16]The difficulty of the juxtaposed expectation that the disciples understand in Lk 9:44 and the narrator's view of a divinely intended secret in Lk 9:45 has led several commentators to attempt to apply the phrase θέσθε εἰς τὰ ὦτα . . . τούτους to preceding events. For a discussion see M.-J. Lagrange,

shows evidence of the author's hand, begins with an antithesis to secrecy: Jesus commands that the necessity of his death at Jerusalem be explained to Herod—"Go and tell that fox. . . . "[17] It is rather odd, in Conzelmann's terms of a plan to keep the Passion hidden, that the predictions at Lk 22:15, 22, 37 should have been partly understood by the disciples. Peter, at least, appears ready to follow Jesus to prison and death (see Lk 22:33)—and again one notices that Peter's speech has been changed in Luke to emphasize his correct understanding.[18] Finally, Jesus' words after his resurrection to the two persons traveling on the road to Emmaus are grounded in the expectation that the disciples should have understood: "O foolish men, and slow of heart to believe" (Lk 24:25). Cleopas and his friend are foolish and slow of heart because they should understand but do not.[19]

To recapitulate: While both Jesus and the narrator understand Jesus to be the Christ, different nuances are reflected in their thoughts. Jesus holds to a concept of consummation. He sees his own suffering

---

Evangile selon saint Luc (Paris: J. Gabalda, 1948) 279-80.

Mk 9:31-32	Lk 9:44-45
Jesus: The Son of man will be delivered into the hands of men, and they will kill him; and when he is killed, after three days he will rise. *Narrator:* But they did not understand the saying, and they were afraid to ask him.	*Jesus: Let these words sink into your ears;* for the Son of man is to be delivered into the hands of men. *Narrator:* But they did not understand this saying and *it was concealed from them, that they should not perceive it,* and they were afraid to ask him about this saying.

[17]Contra Alfred Loisy (*L'évangile selon Luc,* 374) Jesus' answer does not imply that the Pharisees are Herod's agents. Rather, the participle πορευθέντες indicates that they are being commissioned by Jesus.

[18]W. Ott, *Gebet und Heil* (München: Kösel-Verlag, 1965) 80.

[19]George R. Brunk III, "The Concept of the Resurrection According to the Emmaus Account in Luke's Gospel" (Th.D. dissertation, Union Theological Seminary in Virginia, 1975) 226-28; Marshall, *The Gospel of Luke,* 896; Lagrange, *Evangile selon saint Luc,* 606.

death as a necessary step toward becoming the messiah. Thus he emphasizes the necessity of the Passion, and does not call himself the Christ until after his resurrection. But from a different perspective the narrator perceives Jesus to be the messiah throughout his ministry. In order to explain Jesus' silence, he appropriates the Markan motif of the messianic secret, and sees Jesus valiantly, but without success, attempting to keep his identity a secret. This creates great tension in the story, as the idea of secrecy in no way corresponds to Jesus' open proclamation of who he is and what he is all about. Jesus' view of being rejected by "the men of this generation" presupposes an open annunciation. Fitting in with this open proclamation is Jesus' expectation that the disciples understand the necessity of the cross. Again the narrator has a different view as he makes the rulers of the people responsible for the rejection, and explains the disciples' incomprehension in terms of a divine plan for secrecy.

The Kingdom

While the narrator ties a motif of secrecy to Christology, Jesus appropriates a concept of secrecy for the kingdom of God. I have noted that Jesus holds the view of a present kingdom that not all can see. Someday, so his thinking goes, the kingdom will be fully revealed, but for now it is hidden. The emphasis is on knowing and receiving something that already exists, but that is for the most part unperceived.

I noted in the last chapter one subtle difference between this view and that of the narrator. While Jesus' σῴζω connotes incorporation into the kingdom, the narrator's ἰάομαι is a more limited term and draws attention to the physical miracles performed by Jesus.

More conspicuous, however, are the broad differences in subject matter. Jesus' speech shows much greater concern for the kingdom of God than does the narrator's. Only five times does the narrator mention the kingdom, and only one of these instances gives any real content to the term (Lk 19:11).[20] Nevertheless, this one occurrence has played a significant role in Lukan discussions, and it is well to study it more closely.[21]

---

[20]The narrator speaks of the kingdom in Lk 8:1; 9:2, 11; 19:11; 23:51.

[21]As already indicated, this passage played a key role in Conzelmann's view; cf. *The Theology of St. Luke*, 64, 72ff., 83, 113, 121, 139-40, 198; see also Flender, *St. Luke*, 28, 45n, 59, 60, 76n, 91, 150n.

The narrator prefaces Jesus' story of the pounds with the comment that Jesus told the parable "because he was near to Jerusalem, and because they [that is, the crowd][22] supposed that the kingdom of God was to appear immediately" (Lk 19:11). Since the parable refers to a nobleman who went away into a far country to receive a kingdom and then return, the narrator's comment serves as a caution against a false expectation that the kingdom was to appear with Jesus' entry into Jerusalem.[23] First Jesus must go away into a far place, and then return. When he does, the kingdom will appear.[24]

It is possible to draw some points of contact between the narrator's comment on the parable and Jesus' thinking on the kingdom. Like Jesus, the narrator does not think of a kingdom that becomes fully visible before Jesus' return from the "far country." Also, the narrator uses the verb ἀναφαίνω, "come in sight of," for the kingdom; although it does not otherwise appear in Luke, the verb fits with Jesus' emphasis on seeing the kingdom.[25] If S. Aalen is correct, the verb refers specifically to the Parousia, so that it is possible to match the narrator's comment with Jesus' idea of a present kingdom that will be consummated in the future.[26] In this respect, one could say that the narrator is emphasizing the delay of the consummation of the kingdom.

---

[22]Conzelmann linked the false expectation with the disciples (rather than the crowd), and this allowed him to think of the misunderstanding of Lk 9:45 and 18:34 in terms of redemptive history; see *The Theology of St. Luke*, 74. But this exegesis does considerable violence to the text, as the audience in Lk 19:11-27 is the same crowd that murmurs, "He has gone in to be the guest of a man who is a sinner" (Lk 19:3, 7) when Jesus visits Zacchaeus; cf. Marshall, *The Gospel of Luke*, 700. The disciples' misunderstanding concerns the suffering of Christ.

[23]Erich Klostermann, *Das Lukasevangelium*, 3rd ed. (Tübingen: J. C. B. Mohr [Paul Siebeck], 1975) 185.

[24]Joachim Jeremias, *The Parables of Jesus*, trans. S. H. Hooke (New York: Charles Scribner's Sons, 1963) 59.

[25]This is brought out by Marshall's exegesis: "although salvation has come *today* (19:9f.), the End, and the coming of the Son of man to judgment, still lie in the future" (*The Gospel of Luke*, 703).

[26]Sverre Aalen, " 'Reign' and 'House' in the Kingdom of God," *New Testament Studies* 8 (1961-1962): 221.

But immediately one must be wary, for there are great difficulties with this reading of the parable. For one, it seems that the purpose that the narrator attributes to Jesus for telling the parable does not match the content of the parable, which inherently has nothing at all to do with Jerusalem and little to do with a delay.[27] Jesus' interest in the story is fixed on what the servants did with the money entrusted to them. The dramatic climax occurs when the man entrusted with his master's money returned it without increase, so incurring the wrath of the king and losing his trust. Furthermore, the narrator's identification of Jesus with the nobleman is extremely tenuous.[28] If the journey "into a far country to receive a kingdom" allegorically refers to Jesus' exaltation, then how is it possible that an embassy of his enemies follows him to petition against his reign (Lk 19:14)? Similarly, if it is the exaltation that is being referred to, what sense is there in the claim that "his citizens hated him" (Lk 9:14)? How can the image of Jesus as a severe man who takes up what he did not lay down and reaps what he did not sow (Lk 19:21-22) be reconciled with Jesus' other teachings of the Good Samaritan and the Prodigal Son? How can the harsh saying in Lk 19:26, "I tell you that to every one who has, will more be given; but from him who has not, even what he has will be taken away," be reconciled with the parable of the Rich Man and Lazarus?[29] And how can the vengeful king of the parable (Lk 19:27) be the same Jesus who prays from the cross "Father, forgive them for they know not what they do" (Lk 23:34)?

The difficulties are so great that form critics have often suggested that the narrator, perhaps led astray by the various meanings of the word

---

[27]Jeremias, *The Parables*, 58-63.

[28]For a thorough discussion of the difficulties see Elton Trueblood, *The Humor of Christ* (San Francisco: Harper and Row, 1964) 110-15. Jeremias summed up the problems when he wrote, "it is hardly conceivable that Jesus would have compared himself, either with a man 'who drew out where he had not paid in, and reaped where he had not sown' (Lk 19:21), that is, a rapacious man, heedlessly intent on his own profit; or with a brutal oriental despot, gloating over the sight of his enemies slaughtered before his eyes (19:27: ἔμπροσθέν μου)"; *The Parables*, 59-60.

[29]This saying appears also in Lk 8:18—but hardly in reference to material possessions. The earlier passage concerns "understanding the good news of the kingdom" (cf. Lk 8:1, 21).

"Lord," misapplied the parable to Jesus.[30] The correctness of this suggestion is confirmed by the author's use of "ten servants" to describe those entrusted with the nobleman's money (Lk 19:13). The employment of ὁ ἕτερος, "the other" for the third servant (Lk 19:20) seems to indicate that the δέκα, "ten," of Lk 19:13 was not taken over from the tradition, but forced into the story.[31] But why would the author have redacted ten servants into the text when the traditional number of disciples was twelve?

Obviously, the author was not interested in identifying the servants with the disciples—or the nobleman with Jesus, for that matter. As is well known, the story resembles that of Archelaus, who on the death of Herod went to Rome to receive his kingdom, but was followed by a deputation of Jews who did not want him to rule. The slaughter at the end of the parable, while out of character for Jesus, is quite appropriate for Archelaus.[32] While the matter of redaction cannot be completely decided, none of these elements are in the Matthean parable.[33] Although the Herodian connection likewise cannot be proven, the strange introduction of the "ten servants" could find a ready explanation with the "ten sons of Herod."[34] If the kingdom of Herod were being used as a type for the parable, it would certainly fit that he had ten sons, but that his kingdom was divided among three.

There are some other elements in the parable that also seem to typecast it with the Herodians. Thus, the desire for revenge; the demand for profit and wealth; the fear of the third servant; the characterization of the Lord as a severe man; the concept of the rich becoming richer, and the poor, poorer; the idea of reaping what was not sown; and the disproportionate awards, especially the granting of authority over cities, connect easily with the Herodian kingdom.

---

[30]Jeremias, *The Parables*, 59.

[31]See also Marshall, *The Gospel of Luke*, 704.

[32]Josephus, *Jewish War* 2.80; *Antiquities* 17:299-300.

[33]Thus Jeremias thought that Matthew's version is the more original (*The Parables*, 58ff.).

[34]Cf. Samuel Sandmel, "Herod," *Interpreter's Dictionary of the Bible*, 5 vols. (Nashville: Abingdon Press, 1962, 1976) 2:585-94.

Many of the parable's characteristics are also reminiscent of taxation practices. For example, it is because of the servants' ability to raise money that they are placed over cities. With this, one must remember that in Luke it is while the crowd is hearing what Jesus says to Zacchaeus that Jesus also tells the parable of the pounds.[35]

Given these elements, it seems likely that the Lukan Jesus does not intend to identify himself with the nobleman, but rather intends to play the old kingdom to which Zacchaeus belonged off against the new kingdom to which Zacchaeus now belongs. If the narrator's comment (Lk 19:11) is removed from the story, Jesus' words set up an antithetical parallelism that locates the real point of the parable in the radical contrast between Zacchaeus's answer to the Lord, Jesus, "the half of my goods I give to the poor; and if I have defrauded any one of anything, I restore it fourfold" (Lk 19:8), and the demand of the severe Lord: "I tell you that to every one who has will more be given; but from him who has not, even what he has will be taken away."

There is also a sharp contrast offered by those who originally did not wish for the Lord's rule. In the case of the severe ruler, his enemies are killed. In the case of Zacchaeus, Jesus goes and eats at his house. The phrase that Jesus applies to Zacchaeus, "He also is a Son of Abraham" (Lk 19:9) is reminiscent of the teaching of John the Baptist: "I tell you, God is able from these stones to raise up children to Abraham" (Lk 3:8).[36]

Jesus told the parable to emphasize the contrast between two kingdoms: God's kingdom that brings salvation, but means giving, and the worldly kingdom that is unjust, built upon taking, and leads to death. And again there is a tremendous difference in the meaning of the par-

---

[35]Jeremias pointed out that the phrase αἴρεις ὅ οὐκ ἔθηκας (Lk 19:21) belonged to the vocabulary of banking (*The Parables,* 59 n40); cf. F. E. Brightman, "Six Notes," *Journal of Theological Studies* 29 (1928): 158.

[36]The meaning of Lk 19:9 has been debated. Some of the alternatives that have been offered are (1) Salvation must be extended to Zacchaeus, because even if he is a tax collector he is nevertheless still a Jew (cf. O. Michel, *TDNT* 8:104; E. Schweizer, *TDNT* 8:365); (2) a Jew, even though he has strayed, is nevertheless a part of Israel (cf. Jeremias, *TDNT* 4:500); and (3) Zacchaeus is in spite of everything, a "spiritual son" of God (Ellis, *The Gospel of Luke* [need publication information] 220-21).

able when seen through the eyes of Jesus and the meaning indicated by the narrator. In the narrator's perception of the parable, the nobleman only receives the kingdom when he travels to the far country. But this is not Jesus' view. For him, the kingdom is a present reality (compare Lk 11:20; 13:18ff.; 22:30), which comes, by the way, to Zacchaeus. Significantly, the emphasis of the narrator is different. The association of the kingdom with the exaltation leads the narrator to stress the future appearance instead of the present hiddenness of the kingdom. He is not so much concerned with perceiving and being part of the kingdom as with being ready for the day of reckoning. The focus is not on present salvation, but on delayed justice.

Judgment and the Kingdom

Conzelmann was quite right in his perception that Lk 19:11 presupposes a concern about the delay of the parousia.[37] The narrator does bend the natural meaning of the parable toward second-generation Christianity's concern for reward for faithfulness at the judgment day,[38] and does push the kingdom off into the indefinite future. This makes room for the suffering patience of later Christian generations, but stands in sharp contrast to Jesus' concern with his own generation detailed in the last two chapters, and to the immediacy of Jesus' call in such passages as Lk 10:9, 11; 18:7-8; 21:32—the last two examples being redacted into Luke.

In Jesus' thought the judgment signals the full revelation of the kingdom that is now present. The narrator's hardening of this concept into a day of justice when inequities are punished and faithfulness rewarded seems to be implicit, apart from his comment on the parable of the pounds, in his concept of proclaiming the gospel.

Εὐαγγελίζομαι, "to announce the good news," appears ten times in Luke.[39] Twice it is used by the angel (Lk 1:19; 2:10), once referring to the son that is to be born to Zechariah, and once referring to the

---

[37]Conzelmann, *The Theology of St. Luke*, 74.

[38]This same emphasis is present in the narrator's comment in Lk 18:1; cf. Conzelmann, *The Theology of St. Luke*, 128, 131.

[39]Cf. Lk 1:19; 2:10; 3:18; 4:18, 43, 7:22; 9:6; 16:16; 20:1.

birth of Jesus. Both times, the good news being announced refers to the present appearance of salvation.[40]

Four times εὐαγγελίζομαι is used by Jesus (Lk 4:18, 43; 7:22; 16:16). Two occurrences speak only of Jesus' annunciation of the kingdom of God without better defining what that means (Lk 4:43; 16:16),[41] but the other two occurrences tie the good news specifically to the poor (Lk 4:18; 7:22). Jesus saw himself as coming to call the poor and oppressed of society into the kingdom. His message of good news to the poor is that the long-awaited kingdom has arrived. It is theirs, not in the future but now in the present (compare Lk 6:20). As with the angel, the good news is that the time of salvation has dawned.

The narrator also uses εὐαγγελίζομαι four times (Lk 3:18; 8:1; 9:6; 20:1). Three times the verb appears with very indefinite meaning. But the meaning of the other occurrence is clear. After John's declaration that the coming one is going to clear his threshing floor, gathering the wheat into his granary while burning the chaff, the narrator comments, "So, with many other exhortations he preached good news to the people"(Lk 3:18). As with the parable of the pounds, the narrator throws his emphasis on a future time of salvation as the day of judgment when the wheat will be gathered into the granary and the chaff will be burned with unquenchable fire.

Bultmann indicated that εὐαγγελίζομαι in this context does not denote "good" news at all, but carries the more vague meaning of proclaiming the message of God.[42] Certainly, the close association with παρακαλέω, "to exhort," in the verse gives εὐαγγελίζομαι a quality of timelessness not present in Jesus' speech. This reading of the verb is also substantiated by the two occurrences in the narrator's speech where εὐαγγελίζομαι is used intransitively (Lk 9:6; 20:1). It is no

---

[40]Creed pointed out how the words of the angel agree with the language concerning the birth of Augustus (*The Gospel According to St. Luke*, 35).

[41]These passages do indicate, however, that the "good news" is something new. Jesus' good news of the kingdom of God should in no way be confused with a good news of impending judgment preached by John the Baptist (cf. Lk 3:18).

[42]Rudolf Bultmann, *Theology of the New Testament*, trans. Kendrick Grobel (New York: Charles Scribner's Sons, 1951) 1:87, 88.

longer the definite act of announcing the arrival of the kingdom, but rather the much more inclusive "preaching" that is signified. In this sense, εὐαγγελίζομαι has become in the mouth of the narrator completely synonymous with κηρύσσω. The parallel use of the two verbs in the narrator's speech at Lk 8:1 and the narrator's use of κηρύσσω to describe Jesus' claim that he "must preach the good news of the kingdom of God" (Lk 4:43-44) further illustrate the point.

Jesus' Time

Again, I do not want to overemphasize the distinctive way Jesus and the narrator use εὐαγγελίζομαι in Luke. Rather I draw attention to the pattern of narration. In contrast to the narrator, who is concerned with the delay of a kingdom that many await (Lk 19:11ff.), Jesus focuses attention on the presentness of an unconsummated realm that few see (Lk 6:20; 13:18ff.; 17:21; 18:16; 21:31). "Babes" see that Satan has been defeated, but the wise and understanding do not (Lk 10:21). The kingdom is hidden, but will be fully revealed on the day when the Son of man is fully revealed (Lk 13:20-21; 17:20-24). Jesus perceives his own age as lying in between two aeons (Lk 14:16ff.; 16:16; 17:30-35). The first encompasses the past history of Israel and ends with John the Baptist. The second begins with the judgment and the full revelation of the Son of man. Intersecting the two ages lies the present in-between-time in which the kingdom exists as a hidden, unconsummated realm. Jesus' mission, as he sees it, is to call the poor and oppressed into the kingdom. Since Israel rejected the invitation delivered by John, God rejected Israel and sends Jesus to gather the downtrodden of society into his banquet. It will be the mission of the church to bring in the Gentiles.

But the narrator tends to associate salvation with the future day of judgment instead of with Jesus' present. Thus the in-between time is redefined in his thinking. It is the time of the appearance of Jesus and the preaching of the kingdom.[43] This subtle change is made evident by the narrator's dulled use of εὐαγγελίζομαι. It also appears in the narrator's view of John the Baptist. While Jesus draws attention to the rejection of John's message (Lk 7:24ff.), the narrator emphasizes the

---

[43]Conzelmann seems correct at this point, but only insofar as the narrator is concerned. For his position see *The Theology of St. Luke*, 185-206.

people's acceptance of John's message (Lk 3:7, 15, 18, 21). This is an important distinction, for Jesus perceives John to be God's messenger who invited Israel to join in the messianic banquet. It is because John was rejected that God in turn rejects Israel and sends Jesus to gather the downtrodden of Galilee and Judea into the kingdom (Lk 4:16ff.; 14:16ff.). But the narrator perceives John's function in salvation history quite differently, and actually demotes him into a forerunner figure whose main purpose was to announce the coming of Jesus (Lk 3:4-6, 15).[44] In the narrator's thinking, everything points to Jesus—not to the kingdom of God.

Yet it is the exalted Lord Jesus that really colors the view of the narrator, whose tendency, then, is to associate the age of salvation with a future time, when the Lord will return. In consequence the categories by which Jesus understood his own age are collapsed in favor of the age of the exalted Lord. Jesus' message becomes broader. No longer does the narrator measure it in terms of its present proclamation to the oppressed of society. He is much more interested in "all of God's people." The presence of the kingdom gives way to a future kingdom that will come on the judgment day. The great importance in salvation history given to the proclamation of John is obliterated, and John becomes the forerunner figure who pointed to Jesus. Satan, on the other hand, remains a determinative force up until the resurrection, and plays an important role in bringing about Jesus' death. Jesus is recognized and followed by the masses, who do not fully understand only because of Jesus' attempt to keep his identity a secret. The idea of rejection is localized with the small band of rulers, who succeed because Jesus allows them to succeed, and because they get help from Satan. The crucifixion is not brought about by the people's rejection so much as by the powers of evil, which have scored a first-half victory.

---

[44]Bultmann was probably right in his view that Lk 3:15 was composed by the author; cf. *The History of the Synoptic Tradition*, trans. John Marsh (New York: Harper and Row, 1963) 361. Schürmann has argued otherwise, but without substantive evidence; cf. *Lukasevangelium* 1:170-71.

The Author's Purpose

Chapter 6

It bears emphasizing that Jesus' view, gleaned from his own speech, is entirely self-consistent. As a dramatic character, he is well defined and quite distinct. When heard through his own speech, he has a different view of events than when he is seen through the eyes of the narrator. Jesus is interested in his own generation; God's call to Israel has been rejected with John the Baptist and is again rejected with Jesus; the kingdom is present, but few see it; and so on. In part, Jesus' perception of events seems to hearken back to a very early theology. For example, his view of being rejected is much closer to Mark's view than it is to the narrator's view. Likewise, his view of messianic consummation at the cross seems very old. At the same time, however, Jesus' view in Luke is an authored view, and is not one that has simply been taken over from older sources. The extensive influence of the author is very clear in Jesus' concept of salvation history. "The kingdom is present, but not all see it. At the judgment, the Son of man will be fully revealed and the kingdom will be consummated. The first period of history ended with Israel's rejection of John. Jesus is the servant sent to the streets and lanes of the city to call the downtrodden of society to the messianic banquet." Luke has thoroughly edited his sources in order to give Jesus this concept of events.

The extensive nature of the redaction in the gospel raises several issues. Why did the author dramatize his gospel in this way? If only the narrator's view had been edited into the gospel, then the process of characterization could be understood readily as the attempt to transfer the message of Jesus into the present while keeping the original traditions of Jesus intact. But the double redaction of the narrator and Jesus presents a more complicated problem. Jesus and the narrator have been given not only distinct views of narrative events but in some ways contradictory views of narrative events. The author's characterization went beyond matters of appropriate dialect.

The Gospel's Prologue

Could it be that the author's concern was historical at this point? Might he have wanted to recapture and reproduce, as best he could, Jesus' own language and views, even though realizing that the message of Jesus had been modified by the Church?

Some support for this view can be found in the gospel's prologue, especially when read with rhetorical considerations in mind. Most often, Luke's use of the aorist impersonal ἔδοξε κἀμοὶ . . . σοι γράψαι in the prologue (Lk 1:3) has been explained (1) by hypothesizing that the author used the punctiliar past to refer to "his decision" to write,[1] or (2) by hypothesizing that the author actually wrote his preface after he had completed the narrative portion of the gospel.[2] Both suggestions are possible. They are nonetheless difficult, as in the first case one would rather expect something in the manner of δεδόκηκα δεῖν σοι γράψαι or some such use of the perfect tense, which in fact was the tense Josephus employed (ἐγκεχείρισμαι) when discussing his decision to write *The Antiquities,*[3] and as in the second case one would expect the aorist indicative

---

[1] I. H. Marshall, *The Gospel of Luke: A Commentary on the Greek Text* (Grand Rapids MI: William B. Eerdmans, 1978) 42.

[2] Henry J. Cadbury, "Commentary on the Preface of Luke," in *The Beginnings of Christianity,* ed. F. J. Foakes Jackson and Kirsopp Lake, 5 vols. (reprint, Grand Rapids MI: Baker Book House, 1979) 2:500-501.

[3] Flavius Josephus, *Jewish Antiquities,* ed. Page, E. Capps, W. H. D. Rouse (New York: G. P. Putnam's Sons, 1930) 4.

used directly of γράφω, in the manner of ἀνέγραψά σοι, as in fact was common in historical prefaces.[4]

What rhetorically occasioned the choice of the somewhat peculiar construction with δοκέω was the author's attempt to parallel the beginning of the sentence's apodosis with the protasis, ἔδοξε κἀμοί with ἐπειδήπερ πολλοί. Rightly this has been seen not only as a stylistic parallel, but as an attempt to unite the narrator to the "many" of the first clause.[5] As is well agreed, the use of ἐπιχειρέω intends no disparagement of what has gone before, and only points to the difficulty of the task.[6] The narrator joins himself to πολλοί, "the many," and participates in their enterprise.

But at this point the impersonal use of δοκέω becomes doubly peculiar, for its carefully purposed construction makes very clear just how different the narrator was from his history-writing contemporaries who stressed the uniqueness rather than the traditional nature of their histories. In fact, as best as we can discern, Polybius, Dionysius of Halicarnassus, Diodorus Siculus, Josephus, Arrian, Dio, Herodian, and Philostratus each gave as his dominant creative impulse the unfulfilled need to produce a correct narrative (a) where none existed before, or (b) where those that existed were in some way unsatisfactory. Neither need applied to Luke.[7]

---

[4]Cf. Arrian, *Anabasis of Alexander,* Loeb Classical Library (Cambridge MA: Harvard University Press, 1929) 1:2. Arrian is especially interesting because he uses both the present ἀναγράφω and the aorist ἀναγράψα.

[5]Cadbury, "Commentary on the Preface of Luke," 510; Marshall, *The Gospel of Luke,* 42.

[6]J. H. Moulton and G. Milligan, *The Vocabulary of the Greek New Testament* (London: Hodder and Stoughton, 1914-1929) 250-51.

[7]Polybius, *The Histories,* Loeb Classical Library (Cambridge MA: Harvard University Press, 1922) 1:10-11; Dionysius of Halicarnassus, *The Roman Antiquities,* Loeb Classical Library (Cambridge MA: Harvard University Press, 1937) 1:4-5; Diodorus of Sicily, *The Library of History,* Loeb Classical Library (Cambridge MA: Harvard University Press, 1933) 1:12-17; Josephus, *The Jewish War,* Books I-III, Loeb Classical Library (Cambridge MA: Harvard University Press, 1927) 2:2-11; Arrian, *Anabasis of Alexander,* 1:2-5; Cassius Dio Cocceianus, *Dio's Roman History,* Loeb Classical Library (Cambridge MA:

Thus there has been an attempt to moderate the stark contrast between Luke's and the Hellenistic historians' views of their predecessors by suggesting that the πολλοί, "many," of Lk 1:1 should be taken in close connection with διήγησιν, "narrative," as an indication of the author's "sources." It has been further suggested that "the many" was intended as a formal exaggeration that need not be taken literally.[8] This fits nicely with the historical understanding of Luke's redaction of Mark and Q (or, possibly, Matthew) and allows for the few sources actually used by Luke.

The author's stress, it is said, was not on the number of the πολλοί but on the justification that their writings offered for his own effort.[9] But when seen first in its rhetorical significance, the author's intention was indeed to stress the number of the πολλοί, for it is exactly this emphasis on "the many" that also emphasizes the κἀμοί of the apodosis, and offers the best explanation for the use of the impersonal construction with δοκέω. It was the dramatic effect of the combination πολλοὶ . . . κἀμοί that was uppermost in the mind of the author.

Indeed one notices that the historical reading of the first phrase of the prologue as if, except for literary convention, it were written ἐπειδήπερ ὀλίγοι συνέγραψαν διηγήσεις proves very difficult. Certainly the comparative evidence for understanding πολύς as a formal characteristic with practically no numerical force is more tenuous than it is often made out to be.[10] But (1) the number of διήγησιν is sin-

---

Harvard University Press, 1914) 2-3; Herodian, *The First Book of Herodian's History of the Empire from the Time of Marcus Aurelius,* ed. E. H. Warmington (Cambridge MA: Harvard University Press, 1969) 1:2-7; Flavius Philostratus, *The Life of Appollonius of Tyana,* trans. F. C. Conybeare (New York: Macmillan, 1912) 1:II, 6-9.

[8]W. G. Kümmel, *Introduction to the New Testament,* trans. Howard Clark Kee (Nashville: Abingdon Press, 1975) 90-91.

[9]Marshall, *The Gospel of Luke,* 41.

[10]The formal, constructive force of πολύς is well demonstrated in antiquity; cf. Cadbury, "Commentary on the Preface of Luke," 492-93. What is not clear, however, is the total loss of the numerical force of πολύς—if it is to stand for the one or two or three sources used by the author of Luke. In fact, it seems to be the dramatic emphasis on the number of πολύς that makes it

gular, and one must stretch the syntax of the sentence considerably to read the object in close association with the plural subject as indicating the "many (or few) narratives (or sources)" used by the author in composing his own work. The force of the language is that there was one διήγησιν περὶ τῶν πεπληροφορημένων ἐν ἡμῖν πραγμάτων that the many ἐπεχείρησαν ἀνατάξασθαι just as οἱ ἀπ' ἀρχῆς αὐτόπται καὶ ὑπηρέται γενόμενοι τοῦ λόγου παρέδοσαν (it) ἡμῖν.[11] (2) Also the lexical denotation of ἀνατάξασθαι διήγησιν must be stretched thin if one is to make it mean, as Cadbury suggested, "no more and no less" than καθεξῆς γράψαι.[12] The term διήγησις does not easily cover the miracle stories, the sayings of Jesus, and many other loose bits and pieces of tradition that form critics would at this point like to see behind Luke's gospel.[13] Moreover, the prepositional

---

a formal characteristic. According to Tertullus, it is exactly the πολλῆς εἰρήνης brought about by the governor that makes Paul's sedition of concern to the governor (Acts 24:2-6). Likewise it is exactly because Paul knows that the governor has been a judge ἐκ πολλῶν ἐτῶν that he feels confident of receiving a fair hearing (Acts 24:1-13). Certainly, historical questions about whether indeed there had been "great quietness" during the governorship of Felix or whether Felix had indeed judged the nation for many years are valid questions. Nevertheless, one must recognize that the rhetorical emphasis of the two statements falls exactly on the number of the πολλοί. Both statements are presented as postulates (with numerical force not to be questioned) that help ascertain the correctness of the arguments that follow; see Ch. Perelman and L. Olbrechts-Tyteca, *The New Rhetoric* (Notre Dame: University of Notre Dame Press, 1971) 63-114. But see also F. H. Colson's discussion of literary convention with αὐτοψία in "Notes on St. Luke's Preface," *Journal of Theological Studies* 24 (1923): 309. Also J. Bauer, "Polloi: Lukas 1:1," *Novum Testamentum* 4 (1960): 263-66.

[11]It is best to think of Luke as selecting and emphasizing elements already present. Cf. I. H. Marshall, "Recent Study of the Gospel According to St. Luke," *Expository Times* 80 (1968): 7. See also A. W. Mosley, "Historical Reporting in the Ancient World," *New Testament Studies* 12 (1965-1966): 10-24.

[12]Cadbury, "Commentary on the Preface of Luke," 495; U. Luck, "Kerygma Tradition und Geschichte Jesu bei Lukas," *Zeitschrift für Theologie und Kirche* 57 (1960): 66.

[13]Friedrich Büchsel, "διήγησις" in *Theological Dictionary of the New Testament*, 10 vols. (Grand Rapids MI: William B. Eerdmans, 1964-1976) 2:909.

force of ἀνατάξασθαι emphasizes the "reproduction" of tradition, rather than the "composition" of the tradition. True, it has been suggested that the verb's prefix was weak and that the author actually used ἀνατάξασθαι as a simple substitute for the συντάξασθαι of written compositions, so making an implicit distinction between the written attempts of "the many" and the oral account handed down by tradition.[14] But this reading of the passage, as if the author had intended ἐπειδήπερ πολλοί συντάξαντο διήγησεις . . . καθὼς ἔλεγον ἡμῖν οἱ ἀπ᾽ ἀρχῆς αὐτόπται καὶ ὑπηρέται γενόμενοι τοῦ λόγου is quite improbable since (a) the explicit contrast of οἱ πολλοί with οἱ ἀπ᾽ ἀρχῆς αὐτόπται καὶ ὑπηρέται γενόμενοι τοῦ λόγου downplays any implicit comparison in the same passage between the oral and written forms of the διήγησις, and (b) in its two clearest attestations in Greek literature, the rare middle ἀνατάξασθαι does in fact stress the sense of "repetition." Friedrich Blass was among those who attempted to show that ἀνατάξασθαι has the meaning of restoring (into writing) the oral tradition that was likely to pass into oblivion.[15] It is good to look at his very clear drawing of the evidence.

> Now, it [that is, ἀνατάξασθαι] occurs, as Grimm shows, only twice in the whole range of Greek literature,[16] once in Plutarch and once in Irenaeus, besides the passage in question [that is, Lk 1:1-4]. Plutarch, in his treatise de Sollertia Animalium, gives a curious narrative of an elephant, who was rather dull by nature, but at the same time very eager to learn. This elephant was being taught some tricks, in which he succeeded much more poorly than his comrades; but his ambition made him rise at night and repeat by himself those movements he was to learn. Now this is ἀνατάττεσθαι. The passage runs ὤφθη νυκτος αὐτος ἀφ᾽ ἑαυτου προς την σεληνην ἀνατατομενος τα μαθηματα και μελετων, "bringing together, repeating from memory," and we see therefore that in this compound the preposition had

---

[14]Cf. Walter Bauer, F. W. Gingrich, and F. Danker, *A Greek-English Lexicon of the New Testament and Other Early Christian Literature* (Chicago: The University of Chicago Press, 1979) 61.

[15]Friedrich Blass, *Philology of the Gospels*, (London: Macmillan, 1898; reprint, Chicago: Argonaut, 1969) 7-20.

[16]Gerhard Delling ("ἀνατάξασθαι," *TDNT* 8:32-33) adds to these the use of the middle by Hippiatrica Berolinensa, 1, 1.

by no means lost its sense of repetition. Again, Irenaeus gives the well-known Jewish tradition of Ezra's restoring the sacred books of the Old Testament, which had perished by the flames in the capture of Jerusalem. This is expressed by: τους των προγεγονοτων προφητων παντας ἀναταξασθαι λογους. Here we clearly see the wide difference between συνταξασθαι and ἀναταξασθαι : What those ancient writers had composed (συνεταξαντο) Ezra restored from memory, ἀνεταξατο.[17]

What is most certain from the evidence is not that ἀνατάξασθαι denotes a "reconstruction or restoration from memory," but rather that its force lies in the repetition of something already established. In Lk 1:1, the verb would have the intention of "retelling": "Inasmuch as many have attempted to tell a narrative . . . just as . . . . " If my understanding of the prologue is correct then, the "many" had placed themselves in "the service of the word" and had attempted to pass down the same story delivered to them by those who from the beginning were eyewitnesses and ministers of the word.[18] As historical figures they would have had much in common with the priests of Israel whose function it was to remember and repeat the tradition of the people, keeping alive that which had been passed down to them.

It was with these figures that the narrator identified himself. And the function of the "many" helps explain some of those characteristics that I observed earlier about the narrator's voice that connect it broadly with early Christian worship. In a sense the author characterized his narrator as one who retold the story of Jesus to a community of believers.

But in the prologue there is also a statement that the author intended to write καθεξῆς, that is, with proper concern to right sequence. The order that he had in mind might have been topical or chronological. But given the concern in the gospel for distinguishing between the voices of Jesus and the narrator, it might well be that καθεξῆς refers to the correct succession of views. Thus the author would have been interested in showing the stages of the Jesus tradi-

---

[17]Blass, *Philology of the Gospels,* 14-15.

[18]This view of repetition is common among Lukan scholars, cf. W. G. Kümmel, "Current Theological Accusations Against Luke," *Andover-Newton Quarterly* 16 (1975): 139-40; A. T. Robertson, "Luke's Method of Research," *Biblical Review* 5 (1920): 172.

tion. He would have been a historian in the best sense, one whose purpose was to recapture and preserve the past accurately.

The Structure of the Story

This view that the author was a historian interested in doing justice to the layers of the Jesus tradition is powerful but in my estimation not fully convincing. It is Jesus and not the narrator who is the intended mediator of the gospel to the believer. In a sense, the author sided with Jesus against his own narrator. In addition to a concern for history, the author seems to have had something else in mind in the play of the voices in Luke.

As already indicated, the gospel is closely tied to the believing community, and the narrator himself sees Jesus as Lord and Christ. Furthermore, the narrative's structure supports Jesus' view of events—not the narrator's. Two examples should suffice. This is important, for it seems to me that the structure of the narrative is the best indication of the author's purpose. Earlier, I showed how Jesus viewed himself as the messenger commissioned to bring the unfortunates of society into the kingdom, and how he presupposed that a first invitation to Israel delivered by John the Baptist had been rejected. This view of an earlier, rejected call to Israel preceding Jesus' own ministry is strongly supported by the special character of Lk 1-2.

Jesus' Point of View and Lk 1-2

There is a sharp break between Lk 1-2 and Lk 3-24. The change in language is well known.[19] There is also a shift in tone. John the Baptist begins his speech by calling his audience "a brood of vipers" and by threatening that God is able from stones "to raise up children to Abraham." This is quite in contrast with the tone of the spokespersons for God in Lk 1-2. They rejoice. The angel, Zechariah, and Simeon, speaking the language of worship, proclaim the salvation promised by God (Lk 2:11; 1:69, 77; 2:30-32); Zechariah and the heavenly host announce the arrival of peace (Lk 1:73, 79; 2:14); and the angel and Elizabeth speak of the great joy that accompanies their message (Lk 1:44;

---

[19]Cf. Harald Sahlin, *Der Messias und das Gottesvolk* (Uppsala: Almqvist und Wiksells, 1945); C. C. Torrey, *Our Translated Gospels* (New York: Harper and Brothers, 1930).

2:11). John, on the other hand, threatens the multitudes with the judgment of God. It is only the narrator who interprets the threats as "good news" (Lk 3:18).[20]

But it seems significant that other than these differences of language and tone, John and all of the spokespersons in Lk 1-2 are united in what J. Gresham Machen called "a genuinely Jewish religious ideal."[21] Thus, their language, message and expectation are oriented toward Israel and not toward specifically Christian dogma or later events in the life of Jesus.[22] The angel announces that Jesus will receive "the throne of his father David" and "reign over the house of Jacob for ever" (Lk 1:32-33);[23] Zechariah prophesies that the God of Israel has "redeemed his people" and "remembered his oath which he swore to (our) father Abraham" (Lk 1:68-73);[24] and Simeon speaks of "the fall

---

[20]For a clear delineation of the issue see Krister Stendahl, *Paul Among Jews and Gentiles* (Philadelphia: Fortress Press, 1976) 97-108; E. Klostermann, *Das Lukasevangelium* (Tübingen: J. C. B. Mohr, 1929) 54-55.

[21]J. G. Machen, "The Origin of the First Two Chapters of Luke," *Princeton Theological Review* 10 (1912): 260-61.

[22]Thus also John Drury, *Tradition and Design in Luke's Gospel* (Atlanta: John Knox Press, 1978) 46-66; Paul Winter, "The Cultural Background of the Narrative in Luke I and II," *Jewish Quarterly Review* 45 (1954-1955): 159-67, 230-42, 287; E. D. Burton, "The Purpose and Plan of the Gospel of Luke," *Biblical World* 16 (1900): 254; Augustin George, "Israel dans l'oeuvre de Luc," *Revue Biblique* 75 (1968): 486; H. L. MacNeill, "The Sitz im Leben of Lk 1:5-2:20," *Journal of Biblical Literature* 65 (1946): 126-28.

[23]J. A. Fitzmyer, "The Contribution of Qumran Aramaic to the Study of the New Testament," *New Testament Studies* 20 (1973-1974): 382-407; O. Schmitz, *TDNT* 3:160-67; E. Löhse, *TDNT* 8:478-88; C. Burger, *Jesus als Davidssohn* (Göttingen: Vandenhoeck und Ruprecht, 1970); H. Sasse, *TDNT* 1:197-208; Paul Winter, "The Main Literary Problem of the Lucan Infancy Story," *Anglican Theological Review* 40 (1958): 259-60.

[24]H. Schürmann, *Das Lukasevangelium* (Freiburg: Herder, 1969): 86-90; F. W. Beare, *The Earliest Records of Jesus* (Nashville: Abingdon Press, 1962) 34; P. Auffret, "Note sur la structure littéraire de Lc. 1.68-79," *New Testament Studies* 24 (1977-1978): 248-56; D. Jones, "The Background and Character of the Lukan Psalms," *Journal of Theological Studies* 19 (1968): 28-32.

and rising of many in Israel" (Lk 2:34) and recalls Isaiah's promise that Israel will be raised "as a light to the nations" (Lk 2:32; cf. Is 49:6).[25]

Without question the narrative up to the point of Jesus' baptism is strongly oriented toward Israel. There is a hint that the focus of the story will shift when John the Baptist threatens that "God is able from these stones to raise up children to Abraham" (Lk 3:8)—and, sure enough, it does, as soon as Jesus opens his ministry in Nazareth with a proclamation of good news to the poor and rejection to Israel (Lk 4:16ff.). But prior to the baptism the characters in Luke associate the good news exclusively with Israel. The structure of the gospel, then, accords with Jesus' view of an earlier call to Israel.

W. Barnes Tatum, focusing on the theme of the Holy Spirit, noticed the same thing and concluded that "St. Luke uses the birth stories to characterize that period in salvation history before the ministry of Jesus as the Epoch of Israel."[26] Perhaps this statement is a little broader than the gospel intends, as Lk 1-2 portrays only the time in which the salvation promised to Israel was being manifested to Israel.[27] Nevertheless the contrast that Tatum drew between the spontaneous outburst of the prophetic Spirit in Lk 1-2 and how the Holy Spirit is related to Jesus during the time of his ministry proves helpful. According to Tatum, the shift from the passive forms of πληρόω to describe the Spirit's relation to the characters of Lk 1-2 to the adjective πλήρης to describe the relation of the spirit to Jesus indicates a change from an epoch in which there is an intermittent association with the Spirit to one in which the association is permanently present in Jesus.[28] And

---

[25]J. Jeremias, *TDNT* 6:541-42; Marshall, *The Gospel of Luke*, 122-23; D. Jones, "The Background and Character of the Lukan Psalms," 42-43; W. Barnes Tatum, "The Epoch of Israel: Luke I and II and the Theological Plan of Luke-Acts," *New Testament Studies* 13 (1967): 194-95.

[26]W. Barnes Tatum, "The Epoch of Israel," 186.

[27]Tatum seemed to relate Lk 1-2 to a much broader span of time than the thirty years preceding Jesus' ministry. If so, his view agrees with Drury's (*Tradition and Design,* 46ff.).

[28]Tatum, "The Epoch of Israel," 190-93. Augustin George has similarly pointed out that whereas before Jesus the spirit is given to prophets, after Jesus he is the only possessor of the spirit in Luke ("Israel dans l'ouevre de Luc," 484-85).

again, this fits well with Jesus' view that the kingdom was announced to Israel, but rejected, becoming present only in his own ministry to the poor.

The paralleling of the births of John and Jesus also supports this view of events. René Laurentin has pointed out that the angel supports the birth announcements with signs. He makes Zechariah "unable to speak until the day these things come to pass" (Lk 1:19-21); he refers Mary to her kinswoman Elizabeth "who was called barren" (Lk 1:36); and he directs the shepherds to the manger, where they "will find a babe wrapped in swaddling clothes" (Lk 2:12).[29] With this, Raymond Brown has reminded us that in the faith of Israel, signs were not only indications of the truth of prophecy (cf. 1 Sam 2:34; 2 Kings 19:29; Is 7:14), but were also formal indications of the fidelity that accompanied covenant agreements (cf. Gen 9:12; 17:11; Ex 31:13).[30] One of the dominant themes, therefore, running through the angel's announcement is that God is actively keeping the promises that he made to his people.

It is also characteristic of the angel that (a) he begins each conversation with the phrase "do not be afraid" (μὴ φοβοῦ, Lk 1:13, 30; μὴ φοβεῖσθε, Lk 2:10); (b) he ordains the names to be given to John and Jesus with the same phrase (καὶ καλέσεις τὸ ὄνομα αὐτοῦ, Lk 1:13, 31); (c) he announces of each that "he will be great" (ἔσται γὰρ μέγας, Lk 1:15; οὗτος ἔσται μέγας, Lk 1:32); and (d) he indicates that joy will come to many people because of the birth of John and Jesus (καὶ πολλοὶ ἐπὶ τῇ γενέσει αὐτοῦ χαρήσονται, Lk 1:14; χαρὰν μεγάλην ἥτις ἔσται τῷ λαῷ, Lk 2:10).[31]

The parallel forms in Lk 1-2 make John into much more than the forerunner figure proposed by the narrator. The structure grants the Baptist an eminence consonant with Jesus' view of him. According to Jesus, he was the messenger entrusted with calling Israel to the king-

---

[29]René Laurentin, *Structure et theologie de Luc I-II* (Paris: J. Gabalda, 1964) 23-42.

[30]Raymond E. Brown, *The Birth of the Messiah* (New York: Doubleday, 1977) 420ff.

[31]Ibid., 270-98.

dom.[32] Also, as Conzelmann had indicated, Luke's otherwise strange reference to the imprisonment of John (Lk 3:19-20) before the baptism of Jesus (Lk 3:21) clearly functions to divide the ministry of John from the ministry of Jesus.[33] The ministry of John was toward Israel, and that of Jesus was toward the oppressed.

Jesus' Point of View and the Theme of Rejection

A second good example of how Jesus' view of events is supported by the gospel's narrative structure is to be found in the complex of elements that make up the motif of rejection. We have already noted how Jesus emphasizes his own rejection by the people of his generation. This is an important part of his thought, for it is only through rejection and death that Jesus sees himself becoming fully the Christ. We have also seen how the narrator has taken the sting out of the rejection— (1) by localizing it completely in the hands of a few authorities who want Jesus to die; (2) by emphasizing the outside involvement of a superpower, Satan; and (3) by making it all part of a history predetermined by God.

One can readily understand what would prompt the narrator to do this. It is very difficult for the believer to conceive of sensible people rejecting someone as compassionate and concerned about others as Jesus was. Moreover, Jesus appears in the narrative full of power. At almost every turn, he performs miracles and saves others.[34] To the believer, it is natural to think that if Jesus had really wanted to do so, he

---

[32]Paul L. Bernadicou interpreted the parallelism to mean that the missions of John and Jesus are not separate missions in Luke; see "Programmatic Texts of Joy in Luke's Gospel," *The Bible Today* 44 (December 1969): 3099. See also H. L. MacNeill, "The Sitz im Leben of Luke 1:5-2:20," 124-25. There is a sympathetic union of John and Jesus in Luke; cf. Augustin George, "Israel dans l'oeuvre de Luc," 488.

[33]Hans Conzelmann, *The Theology of St. Luke*, trans. Geoffrey Buswell (New York: Harper and Row, 1961) 21.

[34]Paul J. Achtemeier, in fact, saw an attempt in Luke to balance "Jesus' miraculous activity and his teaching in such a way as to give them equal weight" ("The Lukan Perspective on the Miracles of Jesus: a Preliminary Sketch," in *Perspectives on Luke-Acts,* ed. Charles H. Talbert [Edinburgh: T and T Clark, 1978; reprint, Macon GA: Mercer University Press, 1984] 156-57).

could have saved himself. It is also easy to turn this thought upside down and say that Jesus wished to die.[35] After all, he many times predicts the necessity of his death—and what sense can one make of rejection when Jesus stands mute before his accusers, failing to inform them of who he is and failing to demonstrate his power? Didn't Jesus remain silent at his trial, one asks, in order to conceal his true identity, knowing that if his accusers really understood who he was and what he was about, they would have glorified rather than killed him?

But this inclination demonstrated by the narrator to make the rejection into something less than full rejection, while understandable, does not accord with the structure of the narrative. Jesus does not want to die. At the Mount of Olives, he prays for God's intervention (Lk 22:39-46).[36] In this passage, the narrator himself indicates Jesus' desire to live. The redactional description of Jesus' agony and the introduction of an angel who strengthens Jesus show the personal struggle that Jesus faces in accepting the way to the cross.[37] This struggle also emphasizes the fallacy of Conzelmann's position that Jesus' journey to Jerusalem is prompted in Luke by his awareness that he must suffer.[38] The poignancy of the scene indicates more than last-second cold feet. Certainly Jesus is aware from Lk 9:22 on that he is to die, and there is a kind of inevitability assumed by Lk 13:33. But Jesus does not go to

---

[35]So often the commentaries regarding Jesus' saying in Lk 12:50; cf. E. E. Ellis, *The Gospel of Luke* (London: Nelson, 1966) 182; Marshall, *The Gospel of Luke*, 547. Alfred Loisy was more helpful, however, as he drew a parallel between Lk 12:50 and the scene at Gethsemane (*L'évangile selon Luc* [Paris: Emile Nourry, 1924] 356).

[36]A comparison with John's gospel highlights the difference between the suffering Jesus and the glorious Jesus (cf. Jn 17), and shows the problem that the motif of rejection posed to the developing Church.

[37]Marshall, *The Gospel of Luke*, 828. For a discussion of the textual problems, see A. Feuillet, "Le recit lucanien de l'agonie de Gethsemani (Lc. XXII. 39-46)," *New Testament Studies* 22 (1975-1976): 397-98. Feuillet drew attention to the intensity of Jesus' emotion (401, 403), and also to the humble nature of his submission (400).

[38]Conzelmann, *The Theology of St. Luke*, 68, 133, 139, 197.

Jerusalem seeking martyrdom. He goes for the festival, and to take back God's temple for God.[39]

Likewise, the structure of the narrative does not indicate that it was God's will that Jesus die. It is true that the motif of fulfilling Scripture has often been read to show that the progress of Jesus' career in Luke is governed by divine necessity.[40] But Luke is not so much interested in the value of Scripture in prescribing history as in interpreting and understanding Scripture in terms of Jesus' life and death (cf. Lk 22:37; 24:27, 32, 44).[41] The governing agent in Luke is Jesus and not the Scrip-

---

[39]Conzelmann (*The Theology of St. Luke*, 75-76, 199) has demonstrated how, by the omission of Mark's episode of the fig tree, Luke has made the cleansing of the temple the goal of Jesus' so-called journey toward Jerusalem (Lk 19:28-48). René Laurentin (*Jesus au temple* [Paris: J. Gabalda, 1966] 90-91) has seen something similar in the allusions in Lk 1-2 to Malachi's oracle concerning the Lord who comes to his temple to purify the sons of Levi (Mal 3:1ff.). According to Laurentin, Jesus' enigmatic statement as a boy at the temple, οὐκ ἤδειτε ὅτι ἐν τοῖς τοῦ πατρός μου δεῖ εἶναί με (Lk 2:49), previews his function as an adult: Jesus comes as the Son of God, who takes back and purifies God's temple (ibid., 37-76). This dovetails rather nicely with the narrator's view that opposition to Jesus is centered at the temple, and sets the stage for the death of Jesus at the hands of the chief priests and scribes, who ironically do not recognize the Son of God who is teaching daily in the temple.

[40]Walter E. Pilgrim, "The Death of Christ in Lukan Soteriology" (Th.D. dissertation, Princeton Theological Seminary, 1971) 365ff.; W. C. Robinson, Jr., "The Theological Context for Interpreting Luke's Travel Narrative (Lk 9:51ff.)," *Journal of Biblical Literature* 79 (1960): 24-25; Robert Tannehill, "A Study in the Theology of Luke-Acts," *Anglican Theological Review* 43 (1961): 197; Bo Reicke, *The Gospel of Luke*, trans. R. MacKenzie (Richmond VA: John Knox Press, 1964) 50.

[41]See the very fine chapter in David L. Tiede, *Prophecy and History in Luke-Acts* (Philadelphia: Fortress Press, 1980) 97-125. G. W. H. Lampe quoted Augustine to good effect: "In the Old Testament the New Testament lies hid; in the New Testament the meaning of the Old becomes clear" ("The Reasonableness of Typology," in *Essays on Typology* [London: SCM Press, 1957] 13); it is only through Christ that the full meaning of God's dealing with Israel can be understood (25ff.). See also Leander E. Keck, *A Future for the Historical*

tures. Again, Jesus' prayer on the Mount of Olives has been misread in that way, as if God appointed Jesus' path of suffering.[42] But Jesus does not accuse God of wishing his death. Rather, he asks whether God is willing to stop the killing.[43] According to Jesus, the Passion is not God's doing, but the doing of men. "This is your [that is, Jesus' enemies from the temple] hour," he says, "and the power of darkness" ἡ ἐξουσία τοῦ σκότους, Lk 22:53). With this, it is significant that Jesus' petition on the cross assumes his executioners' guilt before God: "Father, forgive them, for they know not what they do" (Lk 23:34).[44]

Jesus' saying also presupposes some lack of understanding on the part of those who crucify him. Ernst Käsemann was very aware of this when he wrote that "the Cross is a misunderstanding on the part of the Jews, who have not properly understood Old Testament prophecy, and the Resurrection is the necessary correction of this human error by the Great Disposer."[45] Behind this statement stood Hans Conzelmann's sep-

---

Jesus (Nashville: Abingdon Press, 1971) 107-108; Paul S. Minear, "Luke's Use of the Birth Stories," *Studies in Luke-Acts,* ed. L. Keck and J. L. Martyn (Nashville: Abingdon, 1966) 119-20; Nils Dahl, "The Story of Abraham in Luke-Acts," *Studies in Luke-Acts,* 150; Lloyd Gaston, "The Theology of the Temple. The New Testament Fulfillment of the Promise of Old Testament Heilsgeschichte," *Oikonomia* (1967): 39ff.

[42]Ernst Lohmeyer, *Lord of the Temple,* trans. S. Todd (Edinburgh: Oliver and Boyd, 1961) 88. I. H. Marshall, following L. Goppelt (*TDNT* 6:149-53) connected the suffering of Jesus with the ideas of fate and judgment (*The Gospel of Luke,* 831). Martin Dibelius (*From Tradition to Gospel,* trans. Bertram L. Woolf [New York: Charles Scribner's Sons, 1935] 201) was more helpful when he pointed out "that Jesus at His arrest does not speak of the hour which God has sent nor, as in Matthew xxvi, 18, of 'my time'; rather He says: 'this is *your* hour and the power of darkness' (Luke xxii, 53)."

[43]Ernest Fremont Tittle, *The Gospel According to Luke* (New York: Harper and Brothers, 1951) 247-48.

[44]E. E. Ellis has pointed out that "ignorance" in the verse does not refer to "a deficient mentality or a lack of information but a sinful moral state" that exists in unbelief (*The Gospel of Luke,* 268).

[45]Ernst Käsemann, "The Problem of the Historical Jesus," *Essays on New Testament Themes,* trans. W. J. Montague (Naperville IL: Alec R. Allenson, 1964) 29.

aration of the "Passion" from the period when Satan was inactive and salvation was being manifested. With Conzelmann the Passion became a time of transition into the third epoch of redemptive history, which begins with the ascension.[46] Thus, the Passion took on a purely historical character for Conzelmann—as a setback to the plan of salvation history, which God nevertheless straightens out with the resurrection.

But this view shows too much of the influence of the narrator. It is true that those who kill Jesus in Luke do not fully understand who he is—and this creates a tremendous amount of irony in the story. While Jesus does not claim to be the Son of God, the council nevertheless condemns him for being the Son of God, all along sure that he is not the Son of God, when actually Jesus is the Son of God. Or again, Pilate orders Jesus to be crucified for being the king of the Jews, while at the same time being convinced that he is not the king of the Jews, in part convinced because Jesus does not claim to be the king of the Jews—when all along Jesus really is the king of the Jews.

But, in Luke, Jesus' death does not simply result from a misunderstanding. There is real opposition to Jesus. This is evident in the intricate plot to kill Jesus. The gospel is organized around the theme of the temple. It begins in the temple and ends with the temple. In Luke Jesus comes to take back God's temple for God. It is immediately following Jesus' appearance in the temple that the chief priests, scribes, and principal men of the people seek to destroy him (Lk 19:47).[47] In Luke, the death of Jesus does not result from his disobedience to the Law.[48] The confrontation centers on the temple.[49] It is because the temple au-

---

[46]Conzelmann, *The Theology of St. Luke,* 16-17, 185-206.

[47]Conzelmann has correctly joined Jesus' act of taking possession of the temple with the temple authorities' plot to kill Jesus (ibid., 71). It is significant that all earlier statements in Mark's gospel concerning a plot to kill Jesus are muted in Luke; cf. Augustin George, "Israel dans l'oeuvre de Luc," 502.

[48]Ibid., 503. The clearest example of this is Luke's redaction of Mk 3:6 (cf. Lk 6:11 and F. W. Beare, *The Earliest Records of Jesus,* 93).

[49]Neill Q. Hamilton has argued on socioeconomic grounds that the death of Jesus was historically occasioned by the cleansing of the Temple ("Temple Cleansing and Temple Bank," *Journal of Biblical Literature* 83 [1964]: 365-72). C. Van der Waal was more helpful, however, when he showed that the

thorities recognize what Jesus is about and feel themselves and their religious ideal of the temple threatened that they seek his death. This is perhaps clearest in Jesus' parable of the vineyard (Lk 20:9-18).[50] It is because the scribes and chief priests understand the parable that they want to kill Jesus (Lk 20:19).

Jesus' innocence and the duplicity of his accusers indicate the same thing. It really is because Jesus is teaching daily in the temple and all the people are coming to hear him that the chief priests and the scribes want to kill him (Lk 21:37-22:2). I have mentioned that there is no attempt to keep Jesus' identity a secret in Luke except in the mind of the narrator. Jesus' enemies fail to perceive him for who he is, not because his identity is hidden, but because they are stubborn men who refuse to accept God's call to the kingdom. Thus Jesus calls his generation an evil generation, and the opposition to Jesus is true opposition. The temple authorities plot to kill a man whom they know to be innocent of wrongdoing. It is interesting that in the trial they do not accuse Jesus of blasphemy—as is the case in Mark and Matthew, where there is a clear lack of understanding of Jesus' mission.[51] It is the opposition to Jesus that Luke wishes to emphasize. That is why, as Con-

---

cleansing of the temple fits within a broader scheme in Luke in which Jesus fights a final eschatological battle for the temple ("The Temple in the Gospel According to Luke," *Neotestamentica* 7 [1973]: 53ff.). Cf. my articles, "Confrontation in the Temple: Luke 19:45 20:47," *Perspectives in Religious Studies* 11,2 (1984): 153 65, and "Entre Cesar e Deus (Lc 20, 20-26)," *Revista Eclesiastica Brasileira* 44 (1984): 391-93.

[50]To Lohmeyer, the vineyard was a symbol of the Temple (*Lord of the Temple*, 44ff.).

[51]Luke has often been understood as attempting to correct an impossible historical treatment by Mark; cf. Marshall, *The Gospel of Luke*, 847; R. W. Husband, *The Prosecution of Jesus: Date, History, and Legality* (Princeton: University Press, 1916); H. Danby, "The Bearing of the Rabbinical Criminal Code on the Jewish Trial Narratives in the Gospels," *Journal of Theological Studies* 21 (1920): 51-52. This probably is the case, but one must not minimize the different views of Luke and Mark concerning the rejection of Jesus. In Mark, the rejection is very much tied to a lack of understanding. In Luke the rejection takes on much more of the character of willful opposition from the temple authorities.

zelmann pointed out, there are no witnesses at Luke's trial, and why the accusation that the Council takes to Pilate is deliberately false (Lk 23:2).[52] The rejection of Jesus in Luke is full rejection. That is, it is a full denial of what he is about and not simply a misunderstanding of his identity.

The narrative structure of Luke supports Jesus' view of rejection in other ways also. Noticeably, the crowd turns against Jesus and joins the chief priests and the rulers in demanding Jesus' crucifixion and the release of Barabbas (cf. Lk 23:13, 18, 21, 23). The disciples also abandon him. Judas betrays Jesus (Lk 22:47) and is held responsible by him for his actions (Lk 22:22).[53] Peter, who says that he is ready to go with Jesus to prison and to death (Lk 22:33), denies him (Lk 22:54-62). Jesus dies alone, abandoned, his acquaintances and the women who had followed him from Galilee standing at a distance, watching (Lk 23:49).

And again, with the disciples, the denial of Jesus cannot be assigned to a lack of understanding. From the first they are part of the believing community. To this effect it is significant that when compared with Mark the disciples' speech is toned down and made deferential in Luke. Whereas Mark's disciples accuse Jesus, "Teacher, do you not care if we perish?" (Mk 4:38), in Luke they plea for help, "Master, Master, we are perishing!" (Lk 8:24); and whereas Mark's Peter is sarcastic, "You see the crowd pressing around you, and yet you say, 'who touched me?' " (Mk 5:31), Luke's Peter gently reminds Jesus, "Master, the multitudes surround you and press upon you!" (Lk 8:45). It is also significant that the disciples half expect Jesus' resurrection.

---

[52]Conzelmann, *The Theology of St. Luke,* 84.

[53]I. H. Marshall, while holding that the second part of Lk 22:22 indicated the responsibility of Judas, saw the first part as an explanation that Jesus' destiny was appointed by God (*The Gospel of Luke,* 809). But the divine plan for Jesus' death belongs to the view of the narrator and not to Jesus. In the context of the passage and of the character Jesus, the phrase κατὰ τὸ ὡρισμένον pertains not to God's predetermined fate for Jesus, but to what Judas and the temple authorities plotted. The close association of Lk 22:22a with Lk 22:21 and 22b makes this very clear, especially as Mark has been edited in such a way as to remove any idea of a scriptural prescription for the betrayal (Mk 14:21: "For the Son of man goes as it is written of him . . . "; Lk 22:22: "For the Son of man goes as it has been determined . . . ").

Cleopas and his companion emphasize that "it is now the third day," that is, the expected day of Jesus' reappearance,[54] that the empty tomb had been found, and that angels had appeared in a vision saying that Jesus was alive. They admit to having been amazed (ἐξέστησαν, aorist) at the women's report of the empty tomb, but end their own summary of events on a wistful, rather than disclaiming note: "but Jesus they did not see" (Lk 24:24).[55] In a stronger way, the inclusion of ὄντως in the speech of the disciples in Jerusalem indicates the completion of a half-expected event, rather than complete surprise: "The Lord has risen indeed, and has appeared to Simon!" (Lk 24:34).[56]

The attitude of the disciples is much the same at the end of the narrative as it is at the beginning. The tone is set by Simon's opening words in the story. Humbly, almost reverently, he complies with Jesus' request: "Master, we toiled all night and took nothing! But at your request I will let down the nets" (Lk 5:5). They know throughout who Jesus is. They are fully aware before the resurrection that he is the Lord. Peter speaks for the group: "(You are) the Christ of God" (Lk 9:20). And once more one sees that with Peter's definition of Jesus the Markan source has been so edited as to remove from Luke any indication of a possible misunderstanding on the part of the disciples of the intended nature of the messiah. Luke's Peter qualifies his concept of the messiah by adding "of God" to the answer of his Markan counterpart, thereby minimizing the political connotations of the claims. Likewise, Peter does not rebuke Jesus for speaking of the Son of man's suffering, rejection, death, and resurrection in Luke as he does in Mark (cf. Mk 8:32). Neither does Jesus, in Luke, call Peter "Satan" (cf. Mk 8:33).[57]

---

[54]Alfred Loisy saw the difficulty that Lk 24:21 presents to the narrator's position that the disciples did not expect the resurrection. What else could the phrase refer to? (L'évangile selon Luc, 577).

[55]This verse holds an important place in the Emmaus account. A central motif in the account is the hiddenness of Jesus. Cleopas and his companion long to see Jesus—and yet, even though they look straight at him, they do not see him.

[56]Cf. the use of ὄντως in Lk 23:47.

[57]Hans Conzelmann, "History and Theology in the Passion Narratives of the Synoptic Gospels," Interpretation 24,2 (1970): 195; Helmut Flender, St. Luke: Theologian of Redemptive History, trans. Reginald and Ilse Fuller (London: SPCK, 1967) 66.

The point in Luke is that Jesus is abandoned even by his closest followers—those who believe in him and perceive him for who he really is. It is the deferential attitude of the disciples throughout the narrative and their full realization that Jesus is the Lord that makes their denial so heinous. That is why the narrative emphasizes that Peter wept bitterly after denying Jesus.[58] In Mark, Jesus is abandoned at the crucifixion by disciples who followed him but never really understood him. In Luke, Jesus is abandoned by the believing community itself. The rejection, just as Jesus himself sees it, is a real rejection. Jesus dies, not primarily in accordance with a divine plan or because there is a lack of understanding of his true identity, but because an evil generation opposes the will of God and rejects his son. And even the believing community becomes part of the rejection.

Conclusion

Thus the structure of Luke supports Jesus' view of events instead of the narrator's view. As Jesus would have it, he really is the rejected one, abandoned by all. Likewise, John the Baptist is more than the forerunner figure proposed by the narrator. In keeping with Jesus' view, he is the messenger entrusted with calling Israel to the kingdom. It is unlikely, then, that the author so carefully distinguished between the language and views of Jesus and his narrator solely because he was a historian interested in doing justice to the Jesus tradition. He seems to have had something else in mind.

---

[58]Lk 22:62 presents a well-known textual difficulty as it agrees with Mt 26:75 against Mk 14:72, and as it is omitted in some manuscripts, including (apparently) one Greek manuscript; cf. B. M. Metzger, *A Textual Commentary on the Greek New Testament* (London: Oxford University Press, 1971) 178.

Confusion in Luke

Chapter 7

Jesus' view, then, to a great extent mediates the gospel. The narrator is a believer, and the view different from that of Jesus that he holds is relative to his position as a participant in the cult. Broadly speaking, he has his eyes fixed on the image of the exalted Jesus and filters the gospel story through his confession that Jesus is Lord. Thus the narrator tones down Jesus' view of complete rejection by associating the crucifixion primarily with the temple authorities and Satan and by introducing a divine plan of secrecy that keeps "all the people" from fully perceiving who Jesus is and the disciples from completely understanding why he has to suffer. Likewise, the narrator changes Jesus' emphasis on the presence of the kingdom and tends to push the kingdom into the future. He is mainly interested in the good news that will accompany the day of judgment, when Jesus will reappear.

Again, the narrator's interpretation of Jesus fits easily with what one might expect from a second-generation Christian. Accompanying the narrator's emphasis on a future kingdom is a diminished concern for the periodization of salvation history that is so much a part of Jesus' view. Jesus is no longer primarily the prophetic messenger of God who has come to announce the rejection of Israel and call its outcasts into the kingdom. Jesus is the exalted Lord of "all the people." He has become manifest in a specific historical time, and has promised to return on the day of judgment. It is not surprising, therefore, that the narrator has deemphasized the role of John the Baptist in salvation history, or has extended the Christ title to cover the entirety of the ministry of Jesus. It is quite natural that he should see the meaning of Jesus in terms of his own generation, and not only of Jesus' generation. One could hypothesize that the delay of the parousia and the lack of clear evidence of a present kingdom outside of the realm of faith would have lent themselves to the narrator's interpretation.[1] It is also not surprising that a believer would experience some difficulty with the concept of a rejected Lord and attempt to make of the rejection something less than it really was.[2]

Thus it is possible, without too great an effort, to place the characterization of the narrator within the context of the developing thought of the early Church. Were it not for a curious aspect of the gospel's redaction, I should without hesitation attribute it to some such tendency on the part of the author himself. Both form criticism and redaction criticism have had great success in this enterprise of distinguishing and analyzing the layers of the Jesus tradition.

But the attempt to identify the author of the gospel too closely with its narrator falls short in Luke, for the author's hand can be seen with equal force in the characterization of Jesus. Moreover, he constructed his story around Jesus' view. The author purposefully distinguished Jesus' point of view from that of the narrator. The confusion in the narrative does not so much stem from the natural accretion of a growing tradition as from the different views purposefully held in tension in the story.

The Story's Framework of Confusion

The Gospel of Luke concerns the manifestation of the Lord Jesus. Hans Frei was not off target when he focused on the identity of Jesus

---

[1]So Hans Conzelmann, *The Theology of St. Luke,* trans. Geoffrey Buswell (New York: Harper and Row, 1961) 95-106.

[2]Martin Dibelius, *From Tradition to Gospel,* trans. Bertram L. Woolf (New York: Charles Scribner's Sons, 1935) 178-217; David Tiede, *Prophecy and History in Luke-Acts* (Philadelphia: Fortress Press, 1980) 108-25; William Wrede, *The Messianic Secret,* trans. J. C. G. Greig (Cambridge: James Clarke, 1971) 164-80.

as a central concern in the gospel story.[3] One of the main purposes in presenting the gospel, then as now, was to allow the community of believers to be confronted again with the Lord who appeared in history, and quite naturally a governing question of the narrator is "who is Jesus?" This is well illustrated by Luke's redactional treatment of the Pharisees. Frank Beare has pointed out that they are noticeably different from their counterparts in Mark—and we have already noted the narrator's tendency to soften their posture toward Jesus.[4] Thus Mark's statement, early in Jesus' ministry, that "the Pharisees went out, and immediately held counsel with the Herodians against him, how to destroy him" (Mk 3:6), is toned down in the mouth of the Lukan narrator: "But they were filled with fury and discussed with one another what they might do to Jesus" (Lk 6:11). Likewise Mark's statement that the chief priests and the scribes and the elders "sent to him *some of the Pharisees* and some of the Herodians to entrap him in his talk" (Mk 12:13) is changed in the speech of Luke's narrator, who writes that the scribes and chief priests "sent spies, who pretended to be sincere, that they might take hold of what he said" (Lk 20:20). According to the narrator, the Pharisees do not oppose Jesus to the point of seeking his death.

Nonetheless, it is also clear that the narrator places the Pharisees among those who reject Jesus. The Pharisees murmur against Jesus' disciples (Lk 5:30); they watch Jesus in order to find an accusation against him (Lk 6:7); they reject the purpose of God for themselves (Lk 7:30); they question in their minds whether Jesus is a prophet (Lk 7:39); and they provoke Jesus, trying to catch him through something he might say (Lk 11:53-54). Although they are not responsible for Jesus' death, the Pharisees are clearly his opponents.[5]

Yet this view of the Pharisees held by the narrator is not quite the view of the Pharisees themselves. What is interpreted by the narrator

---

[3]Hans W. Frei, *The Identity of Jesus Christ* (Philadelphia: Fortress Press, 1975) 85-152.

[4]F. W. Beare, *The Earliest Records of Jesus* (Nashville: Abingdon Press, 1962) 94, 212.

[5]Richard J. Cassidy, *Jesus, Politics, and Society* (Maryknoll NY: Orbis Books, 1978) 52, 156 n8.

as opposition to Jesus, through the direct speech of the Pharisees, takes on more the tone of complaining. "Why do you eat and drink with tax collectors and sinners?" (Lk 5:30). "The disciples of John fast often and offer prayers and so do the disciples of the Pharisees, but yours eat and drink" (Lk 5:33). "Why are you doing what is not lawful to do on the sabbath?" (Lk 6:2). "This man receives sinners and eats with them" (Lk 15:2). "Teacher, rebuke your disciples" (Lk 19:39). The Pharisees, through their own speech, appear as not fully understanding who Jesus is and what he is about. They complain. Nevertheless, they accompany Jesus from Galilee (cf. Lk 5:17; 6:2) to Jerusalem (cf. Lk 19:39); they invite him into their houses (cf. Lk 7:36; 14:1); they eat with him (cf. Lk 7:36; 11:37; 14:1); and they warn him of danger: "Get away from here, for Herod wants to kill you" (Lk 13:31).

The interesting question concerns the motive for the Pharisees' close association with Jesus. According to their own speech, and the run of the story, their purpose is not to oppose him. They question Jesus' actions (cf. Lk 5:30, 33), and they assume that he is breaking the law (Lk 6:2) and is even blaspheming (Lk 5:21). But they do not condemn Jesus. Even their assumption of blasphemy does not lead to condemnation, but rather to awe: "We have seen strange things today" (Lk 5:26).[6]

Significantly the Lukan source has been edited at this point. Whereas the speech in Mark emphasizes the accusation of blasphemy, the speech of the Pharisees in Luke emphasizes their desire to discover Jesus' identity.

Mk 2:7	Lk 5:21
Why does this man speak thus? It is blasphemy! Who can forgive sins but God (εἷς) alone?	Who is this that speaks blasphemies? Who can forgive sins but God only (μόνος)?

And that really is the attitude of the Pharisees in Luke. They complain and certainly never believe but nevertheless follow Jesus and seem genuinely concerned to discover who he is and what he is about.

The question of the Pharisees' opposition to Jesus is important. I will return to it in the next chapter. Now I can say that their opposition to Jesus seems to fit within a larger pattern in the gospel in which char-

---

[6]Heinz Schürmann, *Das Lukasevangelium* (Freiburg: Herder, 1969) 1:285.

acters reject Jesus without really being aware of what they are doing. This pattern also includes the rejection of Jesus by the disciples.

But there are more forthright opponents to Jesus in Luke, people who in the end are directly responsible for his death, and these also show a keen interest in finding out who Jesus is. Thus, Herod's speech in Mark is so altered in Luke as to change the assumption that Jesus is John-redivivus into a question concerning Jesus' true identity: "But, who is this man?" (Lk 9:9, cf. Mk 6:16). The speech of the chief priests and the rulers of the people is also more insistent in Luke than in Mark.[7]

| Mk 14:61 | Lk 22:67 |
| Are you the Christ, The Son of the Blessed? | If you are the Christ, tell us. |

Likewise the introduction of a followup question in Lk 22:70 ("Are you the son of God, then?") accentuates the attempt to find out who Jesus is.

Ironically, however, the view of "those who kill Jesus" is governed by the assumption that they already know who he is not. Certainly, the mocking tone of those who hold Jesus ("Prophesy! Who is it that struck you?" Lk 22:64), the rulers ("He saved others; let him save himself, if he is the Christ of God, his Chosen One!" Lk 23:35), and the soldiers ("If you are the king of the Jews, save yourself," Lk 23:37) indicates that they did not consider him to be a prophet, God's chosen one, or the king of the Jews.[8] It is their certainty that Jesus is not the Son of God, in fact, that seals his guilt in the eyes of the council.[9] Pilate's inquiry into the identity of Jesus is governed from the outset by the as-

---

[7]The use of the imperative εἰπὸν ἡμῖν makes unlikely Helmut Flender's position that the question is insincere (*St. Luke: Theologian of Redemptive History*, trans. Reginald and Ilse Fuller [London: SPCK, 1967] 45).

[8]The use of σῴζω by the mockers in Lk 23:35, 37 shows their complete lack of understanding of what salvation means to Jesus. To the mockers, "salvation" refers to salvation from death. To Jesus, "salvation" refers to incorporation into a kingdom where society is turned upside down and where the suffering Jesus is exalted.

[9]Flender's insight into the confessional nature of Lk 22:71 is helpful. The Sanhedrin denies that which it involuntarily confesses: "what further testimony do we need? We have heard it ourselves from his own lips" (*St. Luke: Theologian of Redemptive History*, 45-46).

sumption that Jesus cannot possibly be the king of the Jews. Even though Jesus does not deny the accusation, Pilate quickly dismisses any possibility that it is true (cf. Lk 23:4). While the taunts of those who hold Jesus—the rulers and the soldiers—imply some possibility of conviction, Pilate's speech is condescending. His repeated offer to chastise Jesus (παιδεύω, Lk 23:16, 22) carries with it connotations of giving guidance or instruction—of a superior to an inferior.[10] Not for one second does he allow that Jesus might be the one who it is claimed he is. Jesus is innocent, but he is put to death anyway. In Pilate's view, Jesus is of little consequence. In this sense, Pilate's repeated statements that Jesus is not guilty ("I find no crime in this man," Lk 23:4; "I did not find this man guilty of any of your charges against him," Lk 23:14; "I have found in him no crime deserving death," Lk 23:22) are doubly purposeful, for while they show that he thought Jesus blameless, they also are a constant and ironic reminder of Pilate's ultimate responsibility.[11]

Thus the view of those who kill Jesus is cross-focal. On the one hand, these characters openly inquire more than any other narrative group about the true identity of Jesus. But, on the other hand, they falsely assume that Jesus cannot be who he is claimed to be. It is fair to say that these characters are not so much interested in knowing Jesus as in placing him in an already established category. This is very true of Pilate, who declares Jesus innocent of charges without hearing evidence—and even though, in actuality, Jesus is "the King of the Jews." But it is also true of such a character as Simon the Pharisee,

---

[10]Walter Bauer, F. W. Gingrich and F. Danker, *A Greek-English Lexicon of the New Testament and Other Early Christian Literature* (Chicago: University of Chicago Press, 1979) 603-604.

[11]Hans Conzelmann popularized the notion of a political apologetic at work in the trial scene (*The Theology of St. Luke,* 85ff.); so also Henry J. Cadbury, *The Making of Luke-Acts,* (New York: Macmillan, 1927) 308-16; Augustin George, "Israel dans l'oeuvre de Luc," *Revue Biblique* 75 (1968): 503. But the contrast that is set between Pilate, who declares Jesus innocent, and the Jews who call for Jesus' death (cf. Cassidy, *Jesus, Politics, and Society,* 68ff.) is a false contrast, since the gospel of Luke emphasizes the chain by which authority is handed down (cf. Paul Minear, *To Heal and Reveal* [New York: Seabury Press, 1976] 16-18).

who decides that Jesus is not a prophet because Jesus allows the sinful woman to anoint his head and kiss his feet.

Jesus and Elijah. In fact, much of Luke is concerned with the attempt of its characters to mold Jesus in some way to fit a preconceived idea of what he should be like. One cannot help thinking that this is behind the use of the different titles for Jesus in Luke. It is evident in John the Baptist's attempt to categorize Jesus as the expected Elijah. John the Baptist does not see himself as the prophet of the end-time predicted by Malachi (cf. Mal 3-4). He sends his disciples to ask if Jesus might not be the prophet who is to come (Lk 7:19-20). That John does not consider himself to be the expected Elijah is clear from his self-identification as the one who baptizes with water. The "coming one" is the one who will baptize with fire, according to John—and in Malachi, it is the messenger who is "like refiner's fire" (Mal 3:2) and who "will sit as a refiner" (Mal 3:3) immediately preceding the day of judgment that "comes, burning like an oven, when all the arrogant and all evildoers will be stubble" (Mal 4:1).

Conzelmann correctly perceived that through his own speech John appears in the narrative as one (a) proclaiming God's demand for social justice (Lk 3:11, 13, 14), and (b) using the expected time of judgment as a lever with which to add urgency to the appeal for repentance.[12] His message, in effect, is that there is still time to "bear fruits that befit repentance" (Lk 3:8). The sequence of expected events with Luke's John is strictly conditional. The phrase "after me" of Mk 1:7 has been omitted from Lk 3:16, so making indefinite the expected time of arrival of the "mightier one";[13] and the verbs, which in Mt 3:12 are found in the future indicative—"he will clear," "he will gather," (διακαθαριεῖ, συνάξει)—are in Lk 3:17 infinitives (διακαθᾶραι, συναγαγεῖν) so emphasizing the possibility rather than the inevitability of action.

It is the report that "a great prophet has arisen among us" (Lk 7:16) that reaches John and urges that the question be put to Jesus (Lk 7:19):

---

[12]Conzelmann, *The Theology of St. Luke*, 102.

[13]Ibid., 24-25; Erick R. Egerston, "John the Baptist in Lucan Theology" (Th.D. dissertation, Graduate Theological Union and the Pacific Lutheran Theological Seminary, Berkeley, 1968) 76.

"Are you he who is coming?" But Jesus does not answer John's messengers directly. Instead, he points to his activity of bringing the outcasts of society into the kingdom.

> In that hour he cured many of diseases and plagues and evil spirits, and on many that were blind he bestowed sight. And he answered them, "Go and tell John what you have seen and heard: The blind receive their sight, the lame walk, lepers are cleansed, and the deaf hear, the dead are raised up, the poor have good news preached to them. And blessed is he who takes no offense at me." (Lk 7:21-23)

One of the interesting aspects of this scene is Jesus' obdurate refusal to accept the Elijah typology. J. A. T. Robinson was quite right in calling attention to Jesus' concluding remark to the messengers: "And blessed is he who takes no offense at me" (Lk 7:23).[14] Jesus distinguishes his mission to the outcasts of society from the expected role of Elijah, and, in effect, does not allow himself to be categorized in any way other than through his own saving activity.

But there is a second curious aspect to this incident. John's question is not imposed on Jesus, but rather grows naturally out of the similarity of Jesus to Elijah. It is because Jesus' resuscitation of the widow's son at Nain (Lk 7:11-17) reminds the people of Elijah's encounter with the widow at Zarephath (1 Kings 17:8-24) that John sends messengers to ask if Jesus might be the "one who is to come" (Lk 7:17-20).

The gospel is constructed on the paradox of Jesus—and this is, in part, the play of confusion in Luke. Jesus is like Elijah, but he is not like Elijah. John Drury has ably pointed out how Lk 9:52-62 was composed with this paradox in mind.[15] While Elijah called down fire from heaven to consume the messengers of the king of Samaria (2 Kings 1:10), Jesus refuses James's and John's suggestion that he call down fire from heaven to consume Samaritans (Lk 9:52-56). And although Elijah, when he met Elisha plowing in the field, gave him leave to say good-bye to his household before following him, Jesus refuses to let a would-be disciple say good-bye to his household with a proverb about

---

[14]J. A. T. Robinson, "Elijah, John and Jesus," *New Testament Studies* 4 (July 1958): 271.

[15]John Drury, *Tradition and Design in Luke's Gospel* (Atlanta: John Knox Press, 1977) 66ff.

plowing: "No man, having put his hand to the plow, and looking back, is fit for the kingdom of God" (Lk 9:59-62). Jesus is like Elijah—but he is different.

Jesus and Moses. Besides Elijah, two other prominent figures from Israel's history are used as both types and antitypes for Jesus. One is Moses—and we have already seen something of the Moses typology in the third chapter. Like Moses, Jesus teaches the crowds after coming down from the mountain, sends out twelve, and chooses seventy.[16] More important, he announces release to the captives and good news to the oppressed. But, unlike Moses, Jesus is not primarily a lawgiver or a national figure.[17]

It is the devil who most attempts to join Jesus to the type, Moses. The setting of the testing episode (Lk 4:1-13), with Jesus spending forty days in the wilderness (Lk 4:2), is obviously reminiscent of the Moses event. The devil's saying in Lk 4:3 especially recalls the miracle performed by Moses when he brought forth water from the rock (Ex 17:1-7; Num 20:2-13)—soon after God "had rained bread (ἄρτος) from heaven" (cf. Ex 16:4).[18] Likewise, his saying in Lk 4:6-7 recalls Moses atop Pisgah, where "the Lord showed him all the land" (Deut 34:1-4). I cannot agree with J. A. T. Robinson, who thought that the showing of the world's kingdoms is almost incidental to the meaning of the temptation.[19] A comparison of Lk 4:6-7 with Mt 4:9 makes clear the emphasis that Luke places on the kingdoms.[20]

---

[16]Although Jesus is not a lawgiver in Luke, there is no polemic against the law (cf. George, "Israel dans l'oeuvre de Luc," 490).

[17]G. W. H. Lampe, "The Lucan Portrait of Christ," *New Testament Studies* 2 (1955-1956): 168ff.; J. Manek, "The New Exodus of the Books of Luke," *Novum Testamentum* 2 (1957): 20-21.

[18]T. W. Manson, *The Sayings of Jesus* (London: SCM Press, 1949): 43-44; Petr Pokorny, "The Temptation Stories and Their Intention," *New Testament Studies* 20 (1974): 124.

[19]J. A. T. Robinson, "The Temptations," in *Twelve New Testament Studies* (Naperville IL: Alec R. Allenson, 1962) 57.

[20]H. Schürmann argued that Matthew abbreviated the originally longer saying found in Luke (*Das Lukasevangelium* 1:211). This is not clear, however; cf. J. Dupont, *Die Versuchungen Jesu in der Wüste* (Stuttgart: Katholisches Bibelwerk, 1969) 53-56.

Lk 4:6-7	Mt 4:9
To you I will give *all this authority and their glory: for it has been delivered to me, and I give it to whom I will.*	All these I will give you
If you, then, will worship me, *it shall all be yours.*	if you will fall down and worship me.

Jesus, like Moses, is shown the promised land. Although Matthew's parallel account of the saying might also be appropriate to the type, Abraham, the claim that "all authority (and their glory) has been delivered to me" which is peculiar to Luke, seems to indicate Moses to be the intended model.[21] In this case, the devil appears as Moses and typecasts Jesus as the new Joshua. The conditional form of Lk 4:7 is a vivid reminder that Moses was not allowed to enter the promised land, because he was held responsible for the people of Israel not worshiping the Lord (Num 20:12-13).

Although it is not as obvious, the third temptation also stresses the Moses typecast. Robinson has helpfully shown how there is a thematic connection between the attempt to compel God to prove the election of Jesus with the threat of "casting yourself against the stone," and the attempt to compel God to prove the election of Israel by threatening to stone Moses at Massah (Ex 17:1-7).[22] But typecasting of Jesus is also more direct at this point. The devil's saying in Lk 4:9-11 is a quotation taken from Ps 91, which in the Septuagint as we now know it (Ps 90) is attributed to David but which is traditionally of uncertain superscription, as the second psalm of a fourth division of the Psalter, which division is headed by Ps 90 (89) "A Prayer of Moses, the man of God."[23]

---

[21]"And he [that is, the Lord] said, 'Hear my words.' If there is a prophet among you, I the Lord make myself known to him in vision, I speak with him in a dream. Not so with my servant Moses; he is entrusted (πιστός) with all my house. With him I speak mouth to mouth, clearly, and not in dark speech; and he beholds the form (τὴν δόξαν) of the Lord" (Num 12:6ff.).

[22]J. A. T. Robinson, "The Temptations," 56.

[23]On the division of the Psalter, see Sigmund Mowinckel, *The Psalms in Israel's Worship,* trans. D. R. Ap-Thomas (Nashville: Abingdon Press, 1967) 1:197-206; Artur Weiser, *The Psalms,* trans. H. Hartwell (Philadelphia: Westminster Press, 1962) 21.

Even with the ascription of Ps 91 (90) to David, however, the content of the psalm recalls Moses. For example, it would be hard for one versed in Israel's tradition to read Ps 91:1, "He that dwells (κατοικῶν) in the help of the Highest, shall sojourn under the shelter (σκέπη) of the God of heaven" without remembering that "the Lord used to speak to Moses face to face," offering him help in the tent of the meeting, and that Joshua did not depart from the tent (cf. Ex 33:11), or remembering that "throughout all (Israel's) journeys (in the wilderness) the cloud of the Lord was upon the Tabernacle by day" (cf. Ex 40:38).[24] Thus, midrashim on Ps 91 often indicate that Moses was the true author of the

---

[24]Some other instances of Moses imagery brought to mind by the psalm follow. In Ps 91:2: (a) after Moses was asked by God to write for a memorial in a book and speak in the ears of Joshua that he would utterly blot out the memorial of Amalek, Moses built an altar to the Lord and called it κύριος καταφυγή μου (Ex 17:15), and (b) Ps 22 (21):4-5 also phrases the attitude of the "fathers who were delivered" in terms of ἐπὶ σοὶ ἤλπισαν. In Ps 91:3: (a) God delivered Moses and the people of Israel from the Egyptians (cf. Ex 14:30) and (b) Joshua promised the people of Israel that if they did not turn back, God would deliver them from the snares of the nations (Jos 23:13). In Ps 91:4: (a) God led ἐκύκλωσεν) Israel in the wilderness, and as an eagle, spread his wings and took the people up onto his back (Deut 32:10-11) and (b) Moses and Joshua perceived this as God's true works (ἀληθινὰ τὰ ἔργα αὐτοῦ, Deut 32:4). In Ps 91:5: (a) during the night the cloud God stood between the people of Israel and the terrifying army of Egypt (Ex 14:10, 20) and (b) Joshua credited the victories of Israel to God and not to the bow (Jos 24:12). In Ps 91:6: (a) God killed the firstborn of Egypt at midnight (Ex 12:29) and (b) Moses and Joshua prophesied that it was sacrifice to demons and turning from God that would bring calamity. In Ps 91:7: (a) the same numbers are used by Moses and Joshua in Deut 32:30 and (b) Moses and Joshua were kept safe by God. In Ps 91:8: (a) because Moses sinned, he was not allowed to enter the promised land, but only allowed to see it (Deut 32:48ff.) and (b) Joshua witnessed the payment of Moses' sin, and entered the promised land (Deut 34:9). In Ps 91:14: (a) Moses and Israel hoped in God, and so were delivered from Egypt and (b) Moses knew God's name (Ex 6:2-3). In Ps 91:15: (a) God listened to Israel's cry and delivered the people through Moses and Joshua (Ex 3:8) and (b) when Moses came down from Sinai, his appearance was glorified (Ex 34:29ff.). In Ps 91:16: (a) Moses and Joshua lived long lives (Deut 34:7; Jos 24:29) and (b) through a variety of ways Moses and Joshua saw the salvation of God.

psalm. The midrash Tehillim on Ps 91 locates the psalm with Moses seven different times.[25] The midrash Tehillim on Ps 90 claims that Moses composed "eleven psalms appropriate to eleven tribes"; Ps 91 is the one appropriate to the tribe of Levi.[26]

Given the natural identification of Joshua and Jesus—both names are the same in Hebrew and in Greek—and the strong identification of Moses and the three temptations by the devil, it is immediately noticeable that Jesus is tempted by the devil to do what Moses did (first temptation), what Moses should have done and Joshua did (second temptation), and what Moses was prophetically claimed to have been able to do (third temptation),[27] and the Jesus refuses the devil by quoting the Torah (Lk 4:4∥Deut 8:3; Lk 4:8∥Deut 6:13; Lk 4:12∥Deut 6:16). Clearly, the one temptation that binds all three is the subtle attempt on the part of the devil to get Jesus to see himself as the Son of God who comes in the spirit and tradition of Moses. And again, it is significant that this attempt to categorize Jesus as the successor to Moses, the new Joshua, is refuted through an appeal to Moses. Jesus is like Moses, but he is not like Moses.[28] He is the new Joshua, but also the antitype of Joshua.

Jesus and David. The other prominent figure from Israel's past who is used as both type and antitype for Jesus is David. Jesus, although not a military and political sovereign, is the awaited king of Israel, a descendant of David, born in the town of Bethlehem. Jesus is called "Son of David" by the blind beggar near Jericho, but the David typology is strongest with the speech of the angel—for example, in his statement that Jesus

---

[25]*The Midrash on Psalms,* trans. William G. Braude (New Haven CT: Yale University Press, 1959) 2:100-107.

[26]Ibid., 87.

[27]Perhaps an even closer alliance between the third temptation and Moses could be reconstructed, had we a greater knowledge of that portion of *The Assumption of Moses* dealing with the angels' lifting up Moses' spirit to heaven; cf. Joachim Jeremias in *Theological Dictionary of the New Testament,* 10 vols. (Grand Rapids MI: William B. Eerdmans, 1964-1976) 4:853ff.

[28]J. Manek, "The New Exodus of the Books of the Luke," 21-22; Petr Pokorny, "The Temptation Stories and their Intention," 123-25.

will be great, and will be called the Son of the Most High; and the Lord God will give to him the throne of his father David, and he will reign over the house of Jacob for ever; and of this kingdom there will be no end. (Lk 1:32-33)

I have pointed out some of the formal parallels between the announcements of the births of John and Jesus. Raymond Brown has especially noted how closely these announcements parallel one another and fit with Old Testament stories of this genre.[29] But it is interesting that the formal parallels do not completely agree when the angel's proclamation to Zechariah and to Mary are placed by side.

Lk 1:13-17	Lk 1:30-33
Do not be afraid,	Do not be afraid,
Zechariah,	Mary,
for your prayer is heard	for you have found favor with God.
and your wife Elizabeth	And behold, you will conceive in your womb
will bear you a son,	and bear a son,
and you shall call his name John	and you shall call his name Jesus
And you will have joy and gladness, and many will rejoice at his birth;	
for he will be great before the Lord,	He will be great, and will be called the Son of the Most High;
and he shall drink no wine nor strong drink,	
and he will be filled	and the Lord God will give
with the Holy Spirit,	to him the throne
even from his mother's womb.	of his father David,
And he will turn many	and he will reign over
of the sons of Israel to the Lord their God,	the house of Jacob for ever;
and he will go before him in the spirit and power of Elijah,	

---

[29]Raymond E. Brown, *The Birth of the Messiah* (Garden City NY: Doubleday, 1977) 292ff. See also C. T. Ruddick, Jr., "Birth Narratives in Genesis and Luke," *Novum Testamentum* 12 (1970): 343-48.

to turn the hearts of the fathers to the children, and the disobedient to the wisdom of the just, to make ready for the Lord a people prepared.	and of his kingdom there will be no end.

Three dissimilarities in the form of the announcements become evident (see the italicized passages). Only one, however, is neither the result of the different functions of the future Jesus and John, nor the result of the different scriptural verses applied to them. The Angel announces that Zechariah "will have joy and gladness," and that "many will rejoice" at John's birth (Lk 1:14). This is not paralleled in his speech to Mary, and only partly paralleled later in his announcement to the shepherds.

But why does the Angel make his announcement of joy to the shepherds and not to Mary?[30] Clearly Mary is excluded. Nevertheless the contrary claim that the Angel thinks that Mary will not experience joy and gladness is unwarranted—especially in light of Mary's own perception of events (cf. Lk 1:47).[31]

Certainly helpful at this point is the angel's enjoyment of typologies. He links Elizabeth with Sara (Lk 1:37‖Gen 18:14), John with Elijah (Lk 1:16-17‖Mal 4:5), and Jesus with David (Lk 1:32-33‖2 Sam 7:13).[32]

---

[30]H. Gressmann (*Das Weinachts-Evangelium auf Ursprung und Geschichte untersucht* [Göttingen: Vandenhoeck und Ruprecht, 1914]) argued that the Lukan birth story of the manger and the shepherds was a reworking of a legend of the birth of Osiris that passed over into Judaism. Thus the announcement of joy to the angels finds its place in Luke because of an earlier form of the story in which the shepherds discover the child in their manger and are told by an angelic voice that he is the promised messiah. But see Rudolf Bultmann, *The History of the Synoptic Tradition,* trans. John Marsh (New York: Harper and Row, 1963) 297-99; J. Gresham Machen, *The Virgin Birth of Christ* (London: Macmillan, 1949) 348-58.

[31]P. L. Bernadicou has pointed out that the Magnificat is a statement of joy occasioned by the presence of salvation ("Programmatic Texts of Joy in Luke's Gospel," *The Bible Today* 44 [December 1969]: 3101-3102).

[32]I. H. Marshall, *The Gospel of Luke* (Grand Rapids MI: William B. Eerdmans, 1978) 71-72, 56, 67-68. According to M. D. Goulder and M. L. Sanderson, Mary appears in the narrative as the new Hannah of 1 Sam 1:11; cf. "St. Luke's Genesis," *Journal of Theological Studies* n.s. 8 (1957): 20.

Therefore the announcement to the shepherds places the birth of Jesus within the messianic tradition of 1 Sam 16.[33] As David's anointing by Samuel was a hidden event that took place among shepherds, so Jesus' birth is a hidden event, first announced to shepherds. Governing this identification is a strong sense of historical propriety. The message of joy is announced to the shepherds because they are its proper recipients.[34] Emphasis is shifted away from the individual, Mary, to a social group, the shepherds, who symbolize not only the Davidic kingdom (cf. Ez 37:24ff.) but also Israel's genetic and therefore essential nature (cf. Deut 26:5) and Israel's understanding of God's true and desired relation with his people (cf. Ps 23:1; Ez 34; Jer 23:3-4; Is 40:11).[35] Actually, it is the two latter connotations that are emphasized by the heavenly host; they contextually connect the ἀνθρώποις εὐδοκίας, "people with whom God is pleased" (Lk 2:14) with the shepherds of Lk 2:8.[36]

But again, as with the Elijah and Moses typologies, the curious point about all of this is that Jesus refuses to be encompassed by the Davidic type. In Lk 20:41-44 it almost seems that he wishes to repudiate completely the conception that the Christ is David's son and heir.[37]

> But he [that is, Jesus] said to them, "How can they say that the Christ is David's son? For David himself says in the Book of Psalms,
> *The Lord said to my Lord,*
> *Sit at my right hand,*
> *till I make thy enemies a stool for thy feet.*
> David thus calls him Lord; so how is he his son?"

---

[33]J. M. Creed, *The Gospel According to St. Luke* (London: Macmillan, 1957) 31-32; Drury, *Tradition and Design,* 54ff.

[34]The shepherds receive the joyous message in name of the people; see Bernadicou, "Programmatic Texts of Joy in Luke's Gospel," 3202ff.

[35]B. D. Napier, "Sheep; Shepherd," *Interpreter's Dictionary of the Bible,* 5 vols. (Nashville: Abingdon Press, 1962, 1976) 4:314-15.

[36]Ernest Vogt, " 'Peace among Men of God's Good Pleasure,' Lk. 2:14," *The Scrolls and the New Testament,* ed. Krister Stendahl (New York: Harper and Brothers, 1957) 114-17.

[37]Creed, *The Gospel According to St. Luke,* 250.

Really, however, Jesus only wishes to repudiate the view of the Davidic Christ held by the Sadducees. Jesus' saying fits in the context of the discussion concerning the resurrection. Lk 20:41 intends to say, "How can *the Sadducees* say that the Christ is David's son?" The issue concerns the nature of the kingdom.[38] Since the Sadducees do not believe in resurrection, they think of the Christ entirely in terms of this world. It is this view of the Davidic Christ held by the Sadducees that Jesus refutes.

He is like . . . but he is not like. . . . This is the paradox of Jesus. And the plot of the gospel revolves around the confusion that results, as the characters in Luke attempt to typecast Jesus into predetermined roles, and Jesus refuses to play his part.

Many of the gospel's confrontation scenes fit this pattern. The question of the scribes and Pharisees about fasting and Jesus' answer with the parables of unshrunken cloth and the old wineskins illustrate the point (Lk 5:30-39). New wine needs to be put in new wineskins. Jesus' biting humor comes out in Lk 5:39, which is peculiar to Luke. "The problem with you Pharisees," Jesus says, "is that you are so satisfied with the old way of thinking that you are unable to understand something new."[39] What Jesus is getting at is the attempt to force him into a mold that does not fit. The old conceptual framework will not encompass the new event of Jesus.

Jesus' silence before his accusers seems to make the same point. Jesus is not simply being obstinate or secretive.[40] This is made clear by his statement in Lk 22:67-68, which has been edited into the text.[41] Rather, Jesus refuses to let his accusers fit him neatly into their prearranged categories. Thus while Jesus is the king of the Jews, he refuses to answer Pilate because he is not the kind of king that Pilate has in

---

[38]Cf. James M. Dawsey, "Confrontation in the Temple: Luke 19:45–20:47," *Perspectives in Religious Studies* 11 (1984): 153-65.

[39]Elton Trueblood, *The Humor of Christ* (San Francisco: Harper and Row, 1964) 94-98.

[40]So W. Grundmann, *TDNT* 9:532-33 n274.

[41]Oscar Cullmann, *The Christology of the New Testament,* trans. Shirley Guthrie and Charles A. M. Hall (Philadelphia: Westminster Press, 1957) 120ff.; E. E. Ellis, *The Gospel of Luke* (London: Nelson, 1966) 262.

mind. Jesus is also a miracle worker, but he refuses to answer Herod, because he is not the kind of miracle worker that Herod has in mind. Likewise, Jesus is a prophet, but he refuses to answer his mockers because he is not the kind of prophet that they have in mind. The motif plays itself out most fully in the exchange between the assembly of the elders and Jesus at his trial (Lk 22:67-70).

> The assembly: "If you are the Christ, tell us."
>
> Jesus: "If I tell you, you will not believe; and if I ask you, you will not answer. But from now on the Son of man shall be seated at the right hand of the power of God."
>
> The assembly: "Are you the Son of God, then?"
>
> Jesus: "You say that I am."

Jesus battles to keep himself from being typecast into a ready-made role. The whole gospel revolves around this point. Many see but do not see; they hear but do not hear. The drama of the Jesus story is centered on the purposeful confusion surrounding Jesus' identity. This is why the titles of Jesus play such a prominent role in the gospel's redaction. Different groups of characters refer to Jesus by different names. Jesus recognizes them all, and none at the same time. Jesus is a teacher and a prophet and a king and the messiah and the Son of God and the new Elijah, Moses and David—but he is also different. None of the titles fully define him or explain who he is.

Jesus is who he is. He resists all attempts at categorization, and defines himself through his story. He is the awaited one, but wholly other, who appears in the cult, confronting the community with the mystery of his person, meeting humanity always as the unexpected Lord.

Recognizing Jesus

That the paradox of Jesus, his hiddenness and mysterious presence, is at the heart of the gospel is evident through the account of the resurrection appearance at Emmaus (Lk 24:13-32). This is the denouement scene of the gospel, and for it the author selected and shaped his materials to unravel certain important strands in the plot.[42]

---

[42]George Rowland Brunk III, "The Concept of the Resurrection According to the Emmaus Account in Luke's Gospel" (Th.D. dissertation, Union Theological Seminary in Virginia, 1975).

Since the most curious aspect of the Emmaus account is the hiddenness of Jesus, C. H. Dodd identified its dramatic center in the disciples' moment of recognition.[43] Jesus walks beside the two, talking to them, and interpreting "in all the Scriptures the things concerning himself," and yet he is not recognized until he takes the bread, blesses, breaks, and gives it to them. Bultmann and others have suggested that the presence of the Lord at the Lord's Supper was at this point projected back into the account.[44] And this is really the play of the gospel: Jesus is the Lord who appears unexpectedly confronting the community with his mysterious presence, recognized only in the cultic memory of his deeds. As Nigel Turner pointed out, the emphatic use of αὐτῶν at the beginning of Lk 24:31 is best explained by its connection with the αὐτοῖς at the end of 24:30.[45] Enlightenment is directly related to receiving the broken bread. This is also the sense of 24:35: "and how he was known to them in the breaking of the bread."[46]

But the important question concerns the exact meaning of the incident of the bread. What were the two disciples made conscious of when Jesus broke the bread and gave it to them? Eric Franklin has argued that the bread was "a sign of fellowship with the risen, exalted Lord . . . empowering them with the life of the kingdom and with the promise of its fullness in the future."[47] His main evidence is found in

---

[43]C. H. Dodd, "The Appearances of the Risen Christ: An Essay in Form Criticism of the Gospels," *More New Testament Studies* (Grand Rapids MI: William B. Eerdmans, 1968) 103-33; first published in 1955 in *Studies in the Gospels*, ed. D. E. Nineham.

[44]Bultmann, *The History of the Synoptic Tradition*, 291; H. D. Betz, "The Origin and Nature of Christian Faith according to the Emmaus Legend," *Interpretation* 23 (January 1969): 37-38; but see Oscar Cullmann, "The Meaning of the Lord's Supper in Primitive Christianity," in *Essays on the Lord's Supper*, trans. and ed. J. G. Davies (Richmond VA: John Knox Press, 1958) 8-16.

[45]Nigel Turner, *Grammatical Insights into the New Testament* (Edinburgh: T and T Clark, 1965) 79.

[46]So Brunk, "The Concept of the Resurrection," 296 n 371; Robert Tannehill, A Study in the Theology of Luke-Acts," *Anglican Theological Review* 43 (1961): 200.

[47]Eric Franklin, *Christ the Lord* (Philadelphia: Westminster Press, 1975) 149.

Luke's treatment of the Last Supper (Lk 22:14-23). He followed A. R. C. Leaney in accepting the shorter reading of 24:19 and the omission of 24:20, which associates the cup with the death of Christ and concluded that Luke understood the Lord's Supper not as looking back to incorporate people into the death of Christ but as looking forward in anticipation of full incorporation into the kingdom.[48]

But perhaps Franklin need not have separated these two concepts. As Robert Tannehill pointed out, the fellowship of the church in Luke is formed on the basis of suffering.[49] The shorter reading of the eucharistic words removes not the idea of death but the idea of a *sacrificial* death from the event of Jesus.[50] As I have pointed out several times, for Luke's Jesus the exaltation depends on the Passion. Thus, in Luke, the necessity of suffering is edited into, and not out of, Jesus' words at the Last Supper (cf. Lk 22:15). Jesus' path to glory leads through suffering.

That is the path that is also demanded of the disciples in Luke. To this effect, the author has relocated to this same setting the sayings about the greatest being like the youngest, and the leader like one who serves (Lk 22:24ff.‖Mk 10:42ff.). The disciple, following his master, is the one who takes up his cross (Lk 9:23; 14:27) and loses his life in order to save it (Lk 9:24; 17:33). The one who humbles himself is exalted (Lk 14:11; 18:14).

It is exactly this pattern reversal of the humble being exalted that is emphasized by the Emmaus account. After hearing from the two disciples that before Jesus' death they had hoped that he was the one who was to redeem Israel, Jesus answers, "O foolish men. . . . Was it not necessary that the Christ should suffer these things and enter into his glory?" (Lk 24:25-26). This is the mystery that is disclosed at Emmaus. The glorious Christ is the one who suffered. The risen Jesus is not recognized until Cleopas and his companion shift their gaze from the

---

[48]Ibid., 214 n 8.

[49]Tannehill, "A Study in the Theology of Luke-Acts," 198-201.

[50]Hans Conzelmann, "History and Theology in the Passion Narrative of the Synoptic Gospels," *Interpretation* 24 (1970): 196. See the discussion by Walter E. Pilgrim, "The Death of Christ in Lukan Soteriology" (Th.D. dissertation, Princeton Theological Seminary, 1971) 213ff.

"prophet mighty in deed" to the memory of Jesus' suffering death. Then they finally see him for who he is. Thus attention focuses on the one who before his death took bread, and when he had given thanks, broke it and gave it to the disciples saying, "This is my body" (Lk 22:19). In the unexplained mystery of his appearance in the breaking of the bread, Jesus is Christ, the redeemer, the Lord who confronts his community as other than expected, not in his glory, but in his humiliation.

Irony and the Purpose of Luke

Chapter 8

The suffering of Jesus, his rejection, and his death show Jesus for who he really is—and it is at this point that one begins to understand the strain with which the narrator relates the story of Jesus. He speaks the language of the worshiping community, calling Jesus "Lord," but as I have pointed out in detail, he does not really understand the humiliation of Jesus. In one sense his perspective is the very opposite of Jesus'. Instead of seeing the exalted Christ through the focus of Jesus' suffering death, the narrator sees the story of Jesus through the focus of the exalted Lord.

In part, of course, this is a natural consequence of the believer's adoration of Jesus. The narrator's comment concerning the Samaritan leper (Lk 17:15-16) nicely illustrates the innocence with which he concentrates on the Lord of worship: "Then one of them, when he saw that he was healed, turned back, praising God with a loud voice; and he fell on his face at his feet (παρὰ τοὺς πόδας αὐτοῦ) giving him thanks (εὐχαριστῶν αὐτῷ)." The comment has a built-in ambiguity that obfuscates the lines separating Jesus from God. The use of pronouns instead of nouns in the last phrase leaves the grammatical antecedent, God, to temper the audience's commonsense inference that the leper knelt at Jesus' feet. In the eyes of the narrator, Jesus and God are almost indistinguishable, and both are worshiped.[1]

But also, in part, the tendency to focus on the exalted Jesus is a denial of the very essence of the gospel pattern. For instance, in the same account of the Samaritan leper Jesus attempts to direct attention away from himself and toward God—"Was no one found to return and give praise to God except this foreigner?" (Lk 17:18). And, actually, this is a general concern of the Lukan Jesus. He plays down attempts of the community to worship him and emphasizes the message that he is delivering from God.

> Why do you call me "Lord, Lord," and not do what I tell you? Every one who comes to me and hears my words and does them, I will tell you what he is like: he is like a man building a house, who dug deep and laid the foundation. . . . But he who hears and does not do them is like a man who built a house on the ground without a foundation.(Lk 6:46ff.)
> As he said this, a woman in the crowd raised her voice and said to him, "Blessed is the womb that bore you, and the breasts that you sucked!" But he said, "Blessed rather are those who hear the word of God and keep it!" (Lk 11:27-28)

In line with the prophetic tradition of the Old Testament, Jesus focuses attention on what God is doing. In this respect, the main purpose of the story of the Samaritan leper is not to show that the proper relationship of the believer to Jesus should be governed by an attitude of adoring gratitude. The story's final statement—"Rise and go your way; your faith has made you well" (Lk 17:19)—fits within a larger context that includes the apostles' request, "Increase our faith!" (Lk 17:5), and Jesus' question, "Nevertheless, when the Son of man comes, will he find faith on earth?" (Lk 18:8).[2]

Most recent commentators, following Bultmann, have regarded Jesus' response to the leper to be a schematic addition by the redactor.[3] This indicates its significance for his thought—but what exactly could

---

[1]Alfred Loisy, *L'évangile selon Luc* (Paris: Nourry, 1924) 427.

[2]Eric Franklin, *Christ the Lord* (Philadelphia: Westminister Press, 1975) 16.

[3]Rudolf Bultmann, *The History of the Synoptic Tradition,* trans. John Marsh (New York: Harper and Row, 1963) 33; I. H. Marshall, *The Gospel of Luke* (Grand Rapids MI: William B. Eerdmans, 1978) 652.

he have intended? J. Reiling and J. L. Swellengrebel suggested that faith in the passage refers to "faith in Jesus' implied promise of healing (v. 14) and its fulfillment."[4] But this view is hardly tenable in light of the deferential petition and trusting obedience of all the lepers. As E. E. Ellis pointed out, the concept must be in some way related to the thankful attitude of the Samaritan.[5] All ten lepers trusted that Jesus would heal them.

In chapter 4 I indicated that Jesus' phrase ἡ πίστις σου σέσωκέν σε, "your faith has made you well" (Lk 17:19), connotes not only healing but also incorporation into the divine kingdom.[6] I had already indicated in chapter 3 that Jesus understood himself to be commissioned to bring the outcasts of society into the kingdom. Specifically he mentions his ministry of cleansing lepers (Lk 7:22). While the narrator focuses on the worshiped Lord, Jesus draws attention to the reversal being wrought by God— the humble are being exalted. In this sense, the story of the Samaritan leper is appropriate to its context between the story of the rich man and Lazarus (Lk 16:19-31) and the story of the Pharisee and the Publican (Lk 18:9-14).[7] God is turning society upside down.

This reversal of society is also consonant with the main theme of Jesus' message as seen, for example, in the Sermon on the Plain (Lk 6:20-49). In Matthew's Sermon on the Mount, Jesus radicalizes the law. He pushes it further and makes it more difficult, so that it encompasses attitudes and not just actions. But in the final analysis, Jesus' new law is only an extension of Moses' law, and Jesus' sermon is a com-

---

[4]J. Reiling and J. L. Swellengrebel, *A Translator's Handbook on the Gospel of Luke* (Leiden: E. J. Brill, 1971) 585.

[5]E. E. Ellis, *The Gospel of Luke* (London: Nelson, 1966) 208-209; J. M. Creed, *The Gospel According to St. Luke* (London: Macmillan, 1957) 216-17.

[6]Similarly, Hans Dieter Betz, "The Cleansing of the Ten Lepers (Luke 17:11-19)," *Journal of Biblical Literature* 90 (1971): 315, 318, 325.

[7]Source theories run aground in this section of Luke. See the great difficulties encountered by John Drury, *Tradition and Design in Luke's Gospel* (Atlanta: John Knox Press, 1977) 162-63.

pendium of ethical guidelines.[8] Luke's introduction of "woes" and his use of the second person directed to the disciples in the presence of the multitude (Lk 6:17, 19-20) give to Jesus' sermon much more of the flavor of a statement about how God is reversing the order of society.[9] The rich have their consolation, but now is time for the poor.

Moreover, in chapter 3 I indicated in detail how Jesus relates incorporation into the kingdom to receiving or perceiving the kingdom. The kingdom is present but hidden and will not be fully visible until its consummation at the judgment. Until then, a few see what God is doing, but many do not.

Against this background, it seems clear that when Jesus speaks of the leper's faith, he is not referring to a belief in Jesus' power to perform miracles, but to the leper's realization that in the healing miracle God was acting to incorporate the outcasts of society into the kingdom. As Minear pointed out, the leper's understanding is contrasted in the next pericope to the blindness of the Pharisees who do not perceive what is before their eyes (Lk 17:20).[10] The Samaritan leper realized the true implication of the miracle and returned praising God.

There is also a second important element in the reversal in Luke's story. Jesus calls attention to the fact that the leper who perceived was ἀλλογενὴς οὗτος, "this foreigner" (Lk 17:18), that is, part of the group

---

[8]Joachim Jeremias attempted to read "the law" out of the Sermon on the Mount, but he only succeeded by drawing heavily on the Lukan account (*The Sermon on the Mount*, trans. Norman Perrin [Philadelphia: Fortress Press, 1963]). In Matthew, the law becomes gospel only at the time of Jesus' resurrection appearance in Galilee, when he closes his ministry with the words "Go therefore and make disciples . . . teaching them to observe all that I have commanded you; and lo, I am with you always to the close of the age."

[9]So P. L. Bernadicou, "Programmatic Texts of Joy in Luke's Gospel," *The Bible Today* 44 (December 1969): 3102ff. This, of course, is also very evident in the Matthean sermon; cf. F. W. Beare, *The Earliest Records of Jesus* (Nashville: Abingdon Press, 1962) 52ff.

[10]Paul Minear, "Jesus' Audience According to Luke," *Novum Testamentum* 16 (1974): 101. Awareness leads to salvation; see Betz, "The Cleansing of the Ten Lepers (Lk 17:11-19)," 315, 325.

excluded from the inner barrier of the temple.[11] It is the rejected ἀλ-λογενής who has perceived and become the chosen guest.

This also is characteristic of Jesus' thought. It is the one who has no hope or resources of his own who paradoxically sees the in-breaking kingdom. Faith, therefore, is also a recognition of one's unworthiness before the God who acts (Lk 17:5-10)—of being completely dependent on him (Lk 18:10-30). Only the one who is truly humble sees the kingdom. Thus, for example, after the joyous references concerning the defeat of the powers of evil in Lk 10:17-20, Jesus says, "I thank thee, Father, Lord of heaven and earth, that thou hast hidden these things from the wise and understanding and revealed them to babes; yea Father, for such was thy gracious will" (Lk 10:21). Unlike the parallel in Matthew where the "hidden things" refer to the coming judgment, in Luke they refer to the presence of the kingdom. Babes see what God is doing, while the wise and understanding do not.[12]

At this point one may begin to perceive the irony at play in Luke. There is tremendous incongruity between Jesus' words that God has hidden the kingdom from the wise and understanding and revealed it to babes, and the words of the prologue written in high Attic style to a "most excellent Theophilus," so that he might "know the truth concerning the things of which [he] has been informed" (σοι γράψαι, κράτιστε Θεόφιλε, ἵνα ἐπιγνῷς περὶ ὧν καταχήθης λόγων τὴν ἀσφάλειαν, Lk 1:3-4). On the one hand, the pattern of reversal stands at the center of Jesus' view. Society is being turned downside up, and only the very simple recognize that the awaited time of salvation has come. But on the other hand stands the dedication of the gospel, perhaps to a rich patron or even a provincial governor, κράτιστε Θεόφιλε, written in a highly cultured style appropriate for an educated audience.[13]

---

[11]Walter Bauer, F. W. Gingrich and F. Danker, *A Greek-English Lexicon of the New Testament and Other Early Christian Literature* (Chicago: University of Chicago Press, 1979) 39.

[12]Cf. a similar attitude in Sir 3:19; Wis 10:21; Bar 3:9ff.; 1 QS 11:6-7; 1Qp Hab 12:4; 1QH 2:8-10. See the list in Marshall, *The Gospel of Luke*, 434.

[13]Henry J. Cadbury, "The Purpose Expressed in Luke's Preface," *The Expositor* 21 (1921): 431-41. E. D. Burton's position that Theophilus was a real

Of course, the different voices in the gospel are the most telling indicators of the irony. In chapter 2 and Appendix C I have discussed at length the popular style of Jesus' speech. I pointed out that he uses a number of words that are included on Phrynichus's list of condemned vulgarisms; that he prefers the more common ὡς in questions to the more classical πῶς used by the narrator; that he uses ἄλλος and ἕτερος incorrectly; that he prefers μετά with genitive to the more proper σύν ; that the phrase with the missing copula in Lk 22:20 is part of his speech; that he uses a variety of foreign words; that his speech includes many Semitic elements; and so on. I also pointed out that many of these elements cannot be credited to a source. The author purposefully characterized Jesus through his voice. Jesus does not speak the language of worship or of the cultured, but he speaks the language of the common people. This is an important aspect of the gospel, for Jesus' language matches his message of deliverance to the oppressed. Jesus speaks to the outcasts in their own language, revealing the secrets of the kingdom, which babes see but the wise and understanding do not.

It would be hard to exaggerate the contrast that exists between Jesus' language and the narrator's prologue. The latter, as I pointed out in chapter 1, fits with the best tradition of classical Greek. It displays proper balance and symmetry and an Attic vocabulary. In a glorious language, the narrator promises to pass on to Theophilus a knowledge of the truth.

But, in fairness to the narrator, he abandons his elaborate style almost immediately and shifts into a specialized language reminiscent of the Septuagint. In the first chapter I discussed this change of voice extensively, pointing out that it was accomplished principally through the use of parataxis and the appropriation of certain formulas. I also pointed out that, excluding those elements, the narrator's speech is generally of a proper Hellenistic style.[14] Thus, the narrator uses a pro-

---

person representative of the social class for whom the book was written has been a common one ("The Purpose and Plan of the Gospel of Luke," *Biblical World* 16 [1900]: 257); cf. Helmut Flender, *St Luke: Theologian of Redemptive History,* trans. Reginald and Ilse Fuller (London: SPCK, 1967) 66.

[14]Henry J. Cadbury, *The Style and Literary Method of Luke* (Cambridge MA: Harvard University Press, 1920); *The Making of Luke-Acts* (New York: Macmillan, 1927) 213-38.

portionate number of significant Attic words comparable to Lucian, Aelian, and Philostratus; he uses the optative; he uses τοῦ with infinitive to express purpose; he uses the more classical ὡς and never the later πῶς in indirect questions; he prefers σύν to the more popular μετά with genitive; he tends to avoid barbarisms; and so on.

Again, the language of the narrator is appropriate to his view of Jesus. He speaks an exalted language rooted in Christian worship, and focuses on the glorious Lord, who performs miracles, is recognized by the masses, and will return on the day of judgment to destroy the evil and save the just. But it is the very thoroughness of this characterization that most emphasizes the different views of Jesus and the narrator. There is immense irony at play in this portrait of a narrator who has little understanding for the humiliation of Jesus, but who nevertheless sets out to pass on to the most excellent Theophilus, in his educated, cultic language, a knowledge of things that the wise and understanding cannot see.

The irony is increased when we recall that the narrator is not the only one in the story who speaks a language commensurate with a high position in society. In chapter 4 I pointed to Pilate's cultured speech: his Attic vocabulary; his use of the dative agent αὐτῷ in the classical construction with πεπραγμένον; and so on. And like Pilate, other characters directly involved in killing Jesus use a socially correct speech. For instance, the spies in Lk 20:21-22 do not use Mark's difficult καὶ οὐ μέλει σοι περὶ οὐδενός (Mk 12:14)[15] and substitute φόρος for Mark's Latin loanword κῆνσος ;[16] Luke's chief priests, scribes, and elders use the nicely phrased πεπεισμένος γὰρ . . . εἶναι (Lk 20:6) instead of Mark's ἅπαντες γὰρ εἶχον τὸν Ἰωάννην ὄντως ὅτι προφήτης ἦν (Mk 11:32); and Luke's "whole company" speaks a nicely balanced sentence in which the infinitives διδόναι and εἶναι are used at the end of clauses, headed by paralleling participles κωλύοντα, λέγοντα (Lk 23:2).[17]

---

[15]Cf. Marshall, *The Gospel of Luke*, 734.

[16]F. Blass and A. Debrunner, *A Greek Grammar of the New Testament and Other Early Christian Literature*, trans. Robert W. Funk (Chicago: University of Chicago Press, 1961) 4-5.

[17]Τοῦτον εὕραμεν διαστρέφοντα τὸ ἔθνος ἡμῶν καὶ κωλύοντα φόρους καίσαρι διδόναι καὶ λέγοντα ἑαυτὸν Χριστὸν βασιλέα εἶναι.

The Purpose of Luke's Irony

The incongruity in the gospel story is perhaps sharpest when we compare the narrator's optimism concerning the number of people who followed Jesus with Jesus' pessimism about the number who will be saved. As I pointed out in chapters 4 and 5, the narrator sees a Jesus surrounded by "all of the people," that is, by the believing community, who "glorify God," and offer Jesus such support that his few opponents are afraid and send spies to try to entrap him. It is this same large group of followers that with justification, according to the narrator, looks forward to the day of judgment (compare Lk 3:18; 7:19).

Yet over against this view stands Jesus' indictment of the believing community in Lk 13:23-30. Someone asks, "Lord, will those who are saved be few?" And Jesus replies:

> Strive to enter by the narrow door; for many, I tell you will seek to enter and will not be able. When once the householder has risen up and shut the door, you will begin to stand outside and to knock at the door, saying, "Lord, open to us." He will answer you, "I do not know where you come from." Then you will begin to say, "We ate and drank in your presence, and you taught in our streets." But he will say, "I tell you, I do not know where you come from; depart from me, all you workers of iniquity!" There you will weep and gnash your teeth, when you see Abraham, and Isaac, and Jacob and all the prophets in the kingdom of God and you yourselves thrust out. And men will come from east and west, and from north and south, and sit at tables in the kingdom of God. And behold, some are last who will be first, and some are first who will be last.

I. H. Marshall's position concerning this passage—that Jesus does not have the believing community in mind, but rather the Jews of his time who did not respond to his teachings[18]—is extremely difficult. I pointed out in the Introduction that the titles used for Jesus form a pattern in the gospel. "Lord" is used only by the believing community. Therefore, contra Marshall, the question in Lk 13:23, "Lord, will those who are saved be few?" originates with a believer; and, contra Marshall, Jesus' answer disavowing those who will call him Lord and will

---

[18]Marshall, *The Gospel of Luke*, 565-66; cf. Bultmann, *The History of the Synoptic Tradition*, 117.

say "We ate and drank in your presence, and you taught in our streets" (Lk 13:25ff.) is directed to the believing community.

Earl Ellis was right in that this passage has in mind later Christians.[19] It refers to those who perhaps are exalted in the church, who knew Jesus personally and, like the narrator, call him Lord. The sense of the passage is, "In the church, too, some of the first will be last." This also fits with other sayings that, as we have seen, distinguish between those who worship Jesus, calling him "Lord, Lord," and those who do the will of God (compare Lk 6:46ff.; 11:27-28). Jesus in Lk 13:23-30 is disavowing that part of the worshiping community that exalts him but does not respond to the will of God.[20] It is to his own followers that Jesus says, "Strive to enter by the narrow door; for many, I tell you, will seek to enter and will not be able" (Lk 13:24).

Another of Jesus' sayings is of this same type. Jesus concludes his promise to the disciples that God is not going to delay before vindicating his elect by asking, "Nevertheless, when the Son of man comes, will he find faith on earth?" (Lk 18:8). The use of the interrogative particle ἆρα suggests that Jesus expects a negative answer:[21] "No, the Son of man will not find faith on earth." And again, to Jesus, faith is perceiving and participating in the reversal that is taking place in the kingdom. Although many will call Jesus "Lord," few will understand what it really means to be completely dependent on the God who acts.[22]

---

[19]Ellis correctly pointed to the broadening influence of Lk 13:30 on the pericope. "Originally Jesus' prophecies referred both to his opponents and to the Jewish masses who made no ultimate commitment to him. By his conclusion (30) Luke appears to broaden the application to all followers of Jesus who do not strive to enter 'the narrow door' (cf. 2 C. 13:5; 2 Pet. 1:10)" (*The Gospel of Luke*, 188). Paul Hoffmann ("παντες ἐργαται ἀδικιας. Redaktion und Tradition in Lc. 13:22-30," *Zeitschrift für die Neutestamentliche Wissenschaft* 53 [1967]: 188-214) saw a double meaning in Lk 13:22-30. The passage refers to the time of Jesus and to the time of the church.

[20]Flender, *St. Luke*, 110-11.

[21]The force of the ἆρα really indicates anxiety or impatience, and of course is not to be confused with μη(τι), which demands a negative answer; cf. Bauer, Gingrich, and Danker *A Greek-English Lexicon*, 104.

[22]It is not at all obvious, as Flender thought, that πίστις "means man's

The rejection that Jesus experienced in his own lifetime is extended into the future. In the same way that, before his crucifixion, Jesus finds himself surrounded by many who do not really understand that his way is the way to the cross, after the resurrection many will surround the "Lord" who will not understand that the humble will be exalted.

This emphasis is not one that can easily be traced to a source. All of the sayings to which I have drawn attention are either peculiar to Luke or show only distant connections with some Q sayings in Matthew. It was the author's purpose to distinguish between the cultic adoration of Jesus and following his path of humiliation.

We have come full circle. On the one side stands the narrator, who is part and in some sense leader of the worshiping community, who calls Jesus Lord, remembers his miraculous power, speaks a special language, and looks forward to the day of judgment when the exalted Jesus will return, doing away with evil and saving the believers—but who does not understand the humiliation of Jesus. On the other side stands the Lord himself, who deemphasizes cultic adoration in favor of obedience to God's word, and asks his community, "When the Son of man comes, will he find faith on earth?" On the one side, the focus is firmly fixed on the exalted Christ; on the other, on the call to renunciation, to taking up the cross (compare Lk 9:23; 14:27; 16:13; 18:14), with the promise that the humble will be exalted.

Who is Jesus? In the end, the gospel is claiming that Jesus cannot be found in preestablished categories, or by pointing to his titles. Jesus meets the believer always as a paradox. He is the Son of David, but he is not the exalted king of Israel. He is the new Joshua, but he is not the victor who conquers a promised land. In many ways he is like Elijah, but so different that he warns "blessed is he who takes no offense at me" (Lk 7:23).

---

receptivity for the coming Lord" (*St. Luke,* 79). Rather, faith in Luke is a perception of the new order that Jesus announces. Thus the promise in Lk 18:1-8 is that God will vindicate his elect speedily (ὅτι ποιήσει τὴν ἐκδίκησεν αὐτῶν ἐν τάχει). The construction with ποιέω emphasizes the idea of justice (cf. Bauer, Gingrich, and Danker, *A Greek-English Lexicon,* 238). Happy are the poor! Woe to the rich!

Jesus is the unexpected Christ. He meets the believer also in paradox. He is the Lord, but not the Lord who is known in glory. Rather, Jesus is the one who calls his disciples into a kingdom where society and all of its values are turned upside down. He is recognized when he is seen as the suffering Lord who dies on the cross—the outcast dying for the outcasts.

But what is the purpose of the irony in Luke? Why did the author build into the story such sharp incongruity between the call of the suffering Jesus on the one hand and the belief in the glorious Lord on the other? Was he setting up his own narrator as an absurd character who sees but does not see?

In his book *The Humor of Christ* Elton Trueblood pointed out how Jesus often made deliberately preposterous statements in order to get the opposite point across. In this regard, Jesus' statement in Lk 16:9, "And I tell you, make friends for yourselves by means of unrighteous mammon, so that when it fails they may receive you into eternal habitations," is so obviously absurd, according to Trueblood, "that the sensitive hearer is supposed to be able to see that the clear intent is the exact opposite of the literal statement." Trueblood holds that the same is true of Jesus' saying in Lk 8:10 (compare Mk 4:11-12||Mt 13:11-13), "To you it has been given to know the secrets of the kingdom of God; but for others they are in parables, so that seeing they may not see, and hearing they may not understand," and his saying in Lk 22:36, "And let him who has no sword sell his mantle and buy one."[23]

This general insight, that Jesus' words in the gospels are sometimes ironic, is very helpful—especially with the parable of the Unjust Steward (Lk 16:1-13).[24] Nevertheless, two points need to be brought forward about Trueblood's study. The first is this: although the author intended to recapture the humor of the historical Jesus, most of his best examples come from Luke and show no parallels in the other gospels. Some striking examples are the ironic addition to the end of the parable of the new wineskins (compare Lk 5:39); the Lukan version of the parable of the talents (Lk 19:12-27); and the idea of rulers who have

---

[23]Elton Trueblood, *The Humor of Christ* (San Francisco: Harper and Row, 1964) 102, 91, 93.

[24]Ibid., 98-110.

authority being called benefactors (Lk 22:25). Matthew's Jesus, in particular, seems to use little wit.

The second point about this use of the "absurd" by the Lukan Jesus is that it fits well with the gospel's pattern of reversal. In Luke, Jesus appears as other than expected. As Trueblood pointed out, this is the real meaning of Jesus' chiding remark concerning the men of his generation in Lk 7:32ff.[25]

> They are like children sitting in the market place and calling to one another, "We piped to you, and you did not dance; we wailed, and you did not weep." For John the Baptist has come eating no bread and drinking no wine; and you say, "He has a demon." But the Son of man has come eating and drinking; and you say, "Behold, a glutton and a drunkard, a friend of tax collectors and sinners!" Yet wisdom is justified by all her children.

Here again is an attempt by characters in the gospel to categorize Jesus, and Jesus refuses to play the appointed role. But as Trueblood observed, Jesus' humor was not sarcastic or vindictive at this point but was of a teasing kind, the purpose of which was to make his hearers examine their own presuppositions.[26] This is characteristic of the Lukan Jesus. He confronts his audience with ironic statements in order to elicit a change in perspective.

One can imagine that the purpose of the irony at play in the views of the narrator and of Jesus would likewise be to chafe the audience into a change in perspective. And this makes sense, for the ironic stance of the narrator is instrumental to the gospel's function of making the event of salvation alive to the community of believers. To encounter the Lord means to meet the suffering Jesus, and it is in this confrontation of the community with the Jesus of the cross that the narrator plays his role.

As already mentioned, one of the significant motifs in the gospel is that its characters reject Jesus without being fully aware of what they are doing. Pilate, of course, is the most obvious example: he claims the innocence of Jesus, but at the same time hands him over to his death. This pattern, to some degree, is repeated by all of the story's

---

[25]Ibid., 21, 58.

[26]Ibid., 56-59.

characters. Thus the Pharisees do not see themselves as Jesus' enemies; neither does Herod, nor "all the people." Even the chief priests
do not realize that they are rejecting the Son of God. Only Peter, after
his denial, recognizes his culpability.

And that is the pattern that repeated itself in Luke's church. It, like
the church of every generation, categorized Jesus as Lord and was un-
aware of any complicity in his death. As the narrator speaks for his
generation, Jesus died at the hands of a few evil men and Satan. But
in the Church, each new generation must come face to face with the
suffering Jesus. The Lord who manifests himself is not the one the
community exalts, but the one whom it has rejected. Again, this is the
paradox of Jesus.

Without too much effort, one can imagine a variety of settings and
ways in which the Third Gospel could have been read or presented in
the early Church so that the ironic stance of the narrator would have
allowed the community to be confronted again with the saving humiliation of Jesus. For example, through the narrator, a proud church
might have relived its own tendency to exalt Jesus, and therefore its
denial of the suffering Son of God. Through the narrator, a socially in-
sensitive community might have experienced its own blindness in perceiving the present kingdom. Through him, believers might have
confessed that Jesus was Lord, and played the part of "all the people,"
until finally they joined in shouting "Crucify crucify him!" (Lk 23:21).
Through him, they might have relived the lack of understanding of the
first disciples, who also knelt at Jesus' feet, but nevertheless did not
see his path of suffering. And at every point, Jesus would have confronted the community, saying, "If any one would come after me, let
him deny himself and take up his cross daily and follow me" (Lk 9:23).

It might be, then, that the narrator's misunderstanding of Jesus was
the bridge that allowed for full participation in the story and led to decision. The meeting of Jesus and his community would have become
possible when the community became so immersed in the character
of the narrator that it could be confronted by the incongruity between
its words and Jesus' words. When Christians so lived the story that Jesus' use of the second person became direct address to them, then they
encountered Jesus. The irony in Luke would have made the transition
into faith possible. As the distance between the hearers' view and Jesus' view was laid bare through the narrator, Jesus appeared.

Thus almost two thousand years ago Jesus might well have confronted his community—in the hearing of the gospel as he had in the flesh—as other than expected, and his followers would have seen what only babes can see. The Christ of the oppressed, the one who suffered, came forward and called his Church to participate in the mystery of God's reversal. God's Son appeared not in glory but in humility.

And as the community relived its own founding story it was confronted then, as it is in every age, with the paradox of Jesus' identity. Jesus is the Christ—but not the expected Christ. He is the Son of David, born in Bethlehem, the king of Israel; he is the new Joshua, a prophet like Moses; and he is like Elijah. But Jesus is also the one who refuses to be a new David, Moses, and Elijah. He is the herald of a new age in which the structures of society are turned downside up. He is the fulfillment of the Scriptures, but also the new insight into what had been promised of old. He not only announces the advent of the kingdom, but himself appears as a manifestation of the paradox of the new order. At once, Jesus is the rejected man, hung on the cross, and the Son of God; simultaneously humiliated and exalted.

"Function Words" in Luke

Appendix A

The best indicators of speech patterns are what Robert Funk calls "function words," that is, words that are nearly empty lexically, but which are grammatically significant in indicating the structure of language.[1] The individual's preferences in regard to these so-called "particles" give to his or her speech a distinctive imprint. Included in this appendix is a complete statistical analysis of the use of particles in the Gospel of Luke, the statistical results of which are highly significant.[2]

Jesus and the third-person narrator prefer different function words in the formation of their sentences.[3] Some of their preferences can be

---

[1]Robert W. Funk, *A Beginning-Intermediate Grammar of Hellenistic Greek*, 2 vols. (Missoula MT: Scholars Press, 1973) 2:475-526.

[2]As this appendix shows, the statistical evidence indicates a very strong probability of design for the observed distribution of the group of function words in narration in Luke. Individual particles that show very strong indications of design are ἀλλά, ἄν, γάρ, δέ, ἐάν, ἤ, καί, μή, ὅταν, οὐ, and οὖν.

[3]Jesus prefers ἀλλά, ἄν, γάρ, γέ, ἐάν, ἕως (as a conjunction), ἤ, μή,

traced to Luke's sources (for example, Jesus' bountiful use of negatives), but others are clearly imposed by the author. Thus, for example, the occurrence of γάϱ (a conjunction used to express cause, inferences, continuation, or to explain—most often translated "for") in the speech of the characters accords easily with an expected random distribution in Mark, while not at all in Luke. As best I can ascertain, the particle appears sixty-seven times in Mark (out of 11,022 words), thirty-four times in the speech of the narrator (out of 5,826 words, with an expected random occurrence of thirty-five), twenty-eight times in the speech of Jesus (out of 3,944 words, with an expected random occurrence of twenty-four), and five times in the speech of the other characters (out of 1,252 words, with an expected random occurrence of eight). But in ninety-five instances in Luke (out of 19,165 words),[4] γάϱ appears only twelve times in the speech of the narrator (out of 7,690 words, with an expected random occurrence of thirty-eight), sixty-six times in the speech of Jesus (out of 9,038 words, with an expected random occurrence of forty-five), and seventeen times in the speech of the other charaacters (out of 2,437 words, with an expected random occurrence of twelve).[5] While the pattern in Mark eas-

---

ὅταν, ὅτι, οὐ, οὐδέ, οὖν, πλήν, and ὡς (as a conjunction denoting comparison). The narrator prefers δέ, καί, ὡς (as a temporal conjunction), and ὡσεί.

[4]The word counts are all approximate with some small variation granted by textual uncertainty. The approximate nature of the counts is not enough, however, to detract from the statistical significance of the distribution. My count of γάϱ is based on the *Concordance to the Greek Testament,* 5th ed., ed. W. F. Moulton, A. S. Geden, and H. K. Moulton (Edinburgh: T. and T. Clark, 1978). My count of total words was made in *The Greek New Testament,* ed. K. Aland, et al. (Stuttgart: Deutsche Bibelstiftung, 1981). In *Statistik des neutestamentlichen Wortschatzes* (Zürich: Gotthelf-Verlag, 1958), Robert Morgenthaler indicated that Mark used γάϱ sixty-four times (167) out of 11,229 words (166) and that Luke used γάϱ ninety-seven times (167) out of 19,404 words (166).

[5]F. C. Grant counted 101 instances of γάϱ in Luke ("Editorial Style in the Synoptic Gospels: II. St. Luke," *Anglican Theological Review* 3 (1920-1921): 57).

ily fits within the statistical boundaries of a chance distribution, the pattern in Luke strongly indicates design.[6]

The scarcity of γάϱ in the speech of Luke's narrator and its abundance in the speech of Jesus and the other characters results from the extensive redaction of Mark. Twenty-eight times γάϱ was removed from the speech of the narrator,[7] while clearly it was added to Jesus' speech at Lk 5:39; 8:46, 52; 9:44; 18:25, 32; 19:21; 20:38, 42; 21:26; and 22:18, and perhaps added in numerous other places.[8] In general, the author of the gospel removed explanatory clauses formed with γάϱ from the speech of the narrator while allowing and often inserting the construction in Jesus' speech.[9] It is interesting that the author of Luke completely omitted the construction "for they/he said," ἔλεγον γάϱ, ἔλεγεν γάϱ, from the speech of the narrator (cf. Mk 3:21; Mk 5:8‖Lk 8:29; Mk 5:28‖Lk 8:44; Mk 6:18, Mk 14:2‖Lk 22:2), while often inserting the construction "for I say," "for he says," λέγω γάϱ, λέγει γάϱ, into the speech of Jesus (cf. Lk 5:39; 10:24; 14:24; 20:42; 22:16, 18, 37).[10]

But one must be cautious when handling statistical evidence, especially when trying to hypothesize the hidden motives behind even significant variations. For example, Luke's omission of γάϱ from the speech of the narrator actually involves three distinct types of redaction: (1) Luke rewrote a clause and omitted the γάϱ (cf. Mk 1:16, 22; 2:15; 3:10; 5:42; 6:17, 31; 9:6 [one occurrence]); (2) Luke omitted a clause that in Mark contains γάϱ (cf. Mk 6:14, 18, 20; 9:6 [one occurrence] 16:4, 8, 8); and (3) Luke omitted a whole passage that in Mark contains γάϱ (cf. Mk 3:21; 5:28; 7:3; 11:13; 14:40, 56). While it seems

---

[6]According to the Chi-square test, there is a 99.5 percent chance that the distribution of γάϱ per character in Luke is not random.

[7]Mk 1:16, 22; 2:15; 3:10, 21; 5:28, 42; 6:14, 17, 18, 20, 31, 48, 50, 52; 7:3; 9:6 (twice), 31; 34; 11:13, 32; 14:40, 56; 15:10; 16:4, 8 (twice).

[8]Γάϱ is found 66 times in the speech of Luke's Jesus and only 28 times in the speech of Mark's Jesus.

[9]For the removal of explanatory clauses with γάϱ from the speech of the narrator see Mk 2:15‖ Lk 5:29; Mk 3:10‖Lk 6:18; Mk 5:28‖Lk 8:44; Mk 6:14‖Lk 9:7; Mk 9:6‖Lk 9:33; Mk 9:31‖Lk 9:43-44; Mk 9:34‖Lk 9:46; Mk 16:4‖Lk 24:2; Mk 16:8‖Lk 24:8-9.

[10]Λέγω γάϱ was also inserted into the speech of the Baptist at Lk 3:8.

likely that omissions of the first two types might often have hinged on the conjunction itself, this would not have been the case with omissions of the third type. We can scarcely conceive of Luke having omitted an entire section of Mark because it had a γάρ in it.

Luke's patterned use of particles does not necessarily imply, therefore, that the author in all cases consciously chose to characterize his speakers by imprinting each voice with a peculiar language. Perhaps such a conscious effort best explains the insertion of πλήν ("but," "nevertheless") and γέ ("indeed") into the speech of Jesus since these are emphatic particles associated with prophecy, but it hardly explains the nonrandom distribution of γάρ or the also nonrandom distributions of ἀλλά, "but"; ἄν, a particle that usually adds indefiniteness to a sentence; ἤ, "or," "than"; ὅταν, "whenever"; and οὖν, "then."[11] It seems to me that these nonrandom distributions are especially important in establishing a contrasting pattern with the καί and δέ, "and," "but," overwhelmingly preferred by the narrator. The overall pattern of the particles in Luke is more significant, in this case, than the idiosyncratic values of the individual particles.

With these general cautions about statistical analysis in mind, and with great hesitancy about any attempt to quantify literary studies, let us look at the data. I will employ three narrational groups in order to display statistically the use of particles in the Gospel of Luke: (1) the narrator, (2) Jesus, and (3) a composite group of the remaining characters in the gospel. The Chi-square test that will be used is a standard statistical tool for determining if a distribution is significantly different

---

[11]The patterns for ἀλλά, ἄν, ἤ and ὅταν were already present in Mark. The patterns for ἀλλά and ὅταν were emphasized in Luke, as was also the pattern for οὐ. Generally these particles were omitted from the speech of the narrator. The pattern for οὖν was not established in Mark and received its emphasis in Luke through frequent insertion of the particle into the speech of the characters. Of course, it is difficult to explain why the author might have thought γάρ to be appropriate to Jesus' speech and not to the narrator's speech. Walter Bauer, F. W. Gingrich, and F. Danker (*A Greek-English Lexicon of the New Testament and Other Early Christian Literature* [Chicago: University of Chicago Press, 1979] 152) have suggested that there was a movement by later Greek writers to substitute δέ for γάρ, and this matches the tendency of the narrator.

than an ∞ -0 association model.[12]   That is, it will tell us if the narrator, Jesus, and the composite group of the remaining characters in the gospel have significantly different distributions in the use of particles.

Test 1

A preliminary test will show us if there is a significant difference in "function word" and "nonfunction word" frequencies of the narrational groups. As best I can determine, there are fifty-one particles in Luke.[13] They are listed with the number of narrational occurrences in Table 1.

TABLE 1

THE NARRATIONAL USE OF FUNCTION WORDS IN LUKE				
PARTICLES	NARRATOR	JESUS	OTHERS	TOTAL
1. ἀλλά	1	29	4	34
2. ἄν	5	28	4	37
3. ἄρα	1	3	2	6
4. ἆρα	0	1	0	1
5. ἄχρι	1	2	1	4
6. γάρ	12	66	17	95
7. γέ	0	8	1	9
8. δέ	366	157	15	538
9. δή	0	0	1	1

---

[12]Cf. H. J. Loether and D. G. McTavish, *Descriptive and Inferential Statistics: An Introduction*, 2nd ed. (Boston: Allyn and Bacon, 1980) 198, 461-62.

[13]The list of particles, with two exceptions, is gleaned from Friedrich Blass's listing for the entire New Testament (see F. Blass, *A Grammar of New Testament Greek*, trans. Henry St. John Thackery, 2nd ed. [London: Macmillan, 1905] 60). The exceptions are the division of ὡς—which accords with W. Moulton, A. Geden, and H. Moulton's division (*Concordance to the Greek New Testament*, 1026-1031)—and the inclusion of a separate category for ἕως when used as an improper preposition. The number of occurrences of the particles with the exceptions of καί and δέ accords with Moulton, Geden, and Moulton's edition of the *Concordance to the Greek Testament* (1978); καί and δέ occurrences were counted in the K. Aland, M. Black, B. Metzger, and A. Wikgren edition of *The Greek New Testament* (New York: American Bible Society, 1975).

PARTICLES	NARRATOR	JESUS	OTHERS	TOTAL
10. διό	0	0	2	2
11. διότι	1	1	1	3
12. ἐάν	0	19	7	26
13. ἐὰν μή	0	3	0	3
14. εἶτα	0	1	0	1
15. ἐπάν	0	2	0	2
16. ἐπεί	1	0	1	2
17. ἐπειδή	1	1	0	2
18. ἐπειδήπερ	1	0	0	1
19. ἔπειτα	0	1	0	1
20. ἕως, conjunction	0	15	0	15
21. ἕως, improper preposition	6	4	2	12
22. ἤ	1	35	4	40
23. ἤδη	3	5	2	10
24. ἵνα	10	20	8	38
25. καθότι	1	1	0	2
26. καθώς	6	7	4	17
27. καί	698	587	150	1,435
28. μέν	3	5	2	10
29. μή	12	68	11	91
30. μηδέ	0	5	1	6
31. μήτε	0	6	0	6
32. μήτι	0	1	1	2
33. ναί	0	4	0	4
34. ὁπότε	0	1	0	1
35. ὅπως	2	3	2	7
36. ὅταν	0	26	2	28
37. ὅτε	7	5	0	12
38. ὅτι	53	98	27	178
39. οὐ	24	116	19	159
40. οὐδέ	0	17	3	20
41. οὖν	3	19	9	31
42. οὔτε	0	5	0	5
43. πλήν	0	15	0	15
44. πρίν	2	0	0	2
45. τέ	4	4	1	9
46. τοίνυν	0	1	0	1

PARTICLES	NARRATOR	JESUS	OTHERS	TOTAL
47. ὡς, denoting comparison	5	21	2	28
48. ὡς, temporal conjunction	17	5	3	25
49. ὡσει	8	1	0	9
50. ὡσπερ	0	2	0	2
51. ὡστε	5	0	0	5
TOTALS	1,260	1,424	319	3,003

The total number of spoken words in each narrational group is shown in Table 2.[14]

Thus the narrator employs 1,260 function words and 6,430 nonfunction words; Jesus employs 1,424 function words and 7,614 nonfunction words; and the composite group employs 319 function words and 2,118 nonfunction words. This is displayed in Table 3.

H_0: There is no difference in word use frequencies (among the three groups).

H_A: There is a difference.

H_0: $P_{1,1} = p_{1,1}$ (observed); $P_{i,j} = p_{i,j}$ (observed); $P_{k,e} = p_{k,e}$ (observed); where: $P_{k,e}$ is the expected probability of occurrence for the total number of rows and columns.

TABLE 2

USE OF WORDS BY THE GOSPEL'S SPEAKERS	
The Narrator	7,690
Jesus	9,038
Others	2,437
TOTAL	19,165

TABLE 3

THE NARRATIONAL USE OF FUNCTION AND NONFUNCTION WORDS IN LUKE				
	NARRATOR	JESUS	OTHERS	TOTAL
Function Words	1,260	1,424	319	3,003
Nonfunction Words	6,430	7,614	2,118	16,162
TOTALS	7,690	9,038	2,437	19,165

---

[14]The word count was made in *The Greek New Testament,* ed. Aland, et al.

$p_{k,e}$ is the observed occurrence for the total number of rows and columns.

If an α of .01 is selected for a table with two rows and three columns, df $= (2-1) \times (3-1) = 2$, where "α" is the level of significance selected by the experimenter (in this case $= 0.01$, which corresponds to a ninety-nine percent confidence that a Type 1 error has not been committed), then x^2 needs to be 9.21 or larger before we will conclude that there is a difference in the frequency that the narrational groups use the function and nonfunction words.

In fact,
$$x^2 = \frac{\Sigma (f_i - F_i)^2}{F_i} = 15.4$$

$$x^2 = 15.4 > (0.01) = 9.21$$

$\therefore$ The Chi-square test shows a significant difference in function word and nonfunction word frequencies at the 0.01 level.

Test 2

My primary purpose is to test for evidences of characterization in the choice of particles of the three narrational groups. Because it is generally agreed that the inclusion of cells on which the expected frequency is less than about five tends to distort the analysis, this part of our study will be limited to the function words numbered 1, 2, 6, 8, 12, 22, 24, 27, 29, 36, 38, 39, 41, and 47 in Table 1. The distribution of these particles is displayed in Table 4 on page 165.

H_0: There is no difference in word use frequencies (by the three narrational groups).

H_A; There is a difference.

If an α of .01 is selected for a table with fourteen rows and three columns, df. $= (14-1) \times (3-1) = 26$, then X^2 needs to be 45.64 or larger before we will conclude that there is a difference in the frequency that the narrational groups use function words in Luke.

In fact,
$$x^2 = \frac{\Sigma (f_i - F_i)^2}{F_i} = 452.618$$

$$x^2 = 452.618 > \alpha \, (p < .01) = 45.64$$

$\therefore$ The Chi-square test indicates at the 0.01 level that the distribution of the population of particles in narration in Luke is purposeful.

Test 3

It is possible to carry the statistical analysis a little further by testing the individual word frequencies for particles number 1, 2, 6, 8, 12, 22,

24, 27, 29, 36, 38, 39, 41 and 47 against the already determined total "function word" frequencies. This is actually a "goodness of fit" application, df. $= (c-1) = 2$ for each particle: α (.01) $= 9.21$. Thus, X^2 for each word needs to be 9.21 or larger before we will conclude that that particular function word is used in a nonrandom way in Luke.

$$x^2 \ (\dot{\alpha}\lambda\lambda\dot{\alpha}) \qquad = \quad 23.6 \ > \quad \alpha \ (p < 0.01)$$
$$x^2 \ (\ddot{\alpha}v) \qquad = \quad 14.2 \ > \quad \alpha \ (p < 0.01)$$
$$x^2 \ (\gamma\dot{\alpha}\varrho) \qquad = \quad 36.7 \ > \quad \alpha \ (p < 0.01)$$
$$x^2 \ (\delta\dot{\epsilon}) \qquad = \quad 141.1 \ > \quad \alpha \ (p < 0.01)$$
$$x^2 \ (\dot{\epsilon}\dot{\alpha}v) \qquad = \quad 22.4 \ > \quad \alpha \ (p < 0.01)$$
$$x^2 \ (\ddot{\eta}) \qquad = \quad 29.6 \ > \quad \alpha \ (p < 0.01)$$
$$x^2 \ (\ddot{\iota}v\alpha) \qquad = \quad 7.4 \ < \quad \alpha \ (p < 0.01)$$
$$x^2 \ (\varkappa\alpha\dot{\iota}) \qquad = \quad 20.6 \ > \quad \alpha \ (p < 0.01)$$
$$x^2 \ (\mu\dot{\eta}) \qquad = \quad 34.7 \ > \quad \alpha \ (p < 0.01)$$
$$x^2 \ (\ddot{o}\tau\alpha v) \qquad = \quad 25.0 \ > \quad \alpha \ (p < 0.01)$$
$$x^2 \ (\ddot{o}\tau\iota) \qquad = \quad 14.5 \ > \quad \alpha \ (p < 0.01)$$
$$x^2 \ (o\dot{\upsilon}) \qquad = \quad 52.9 \ > \quad \alpha \ (p < 0.01)$$
$$x^2 \ (o\ddot{\upsilon}v) \qquad = \quad 20.7 \ > \quad \alpha \ (p < 0.01)$$
$$x^2 \ (\dot{\omega}\varsigma \text{ as conjunction} \qquad = \quad 9.2 \ < \quad \alpha \ (p < 0.01)$$
$$\text{denoting comparison})$$

TABLE 4

THE NARRATIONAL USE OF FUNCTION WORDS IN LUKE				
PARTICLES	NARRATOR	JESUS	OTHERS	TOTAL
1. ἀλλά	1	29	4	34
2. ἄν	5	28	4	37
6. γάρ	12	66	17	95
8. δέ	366	157	15	538
12. ἐάν	0	19	7	26
22. ἤ	1	35	4	40
24. ἵνα	10	20	8	38
27. καί	698	587	150	1,435
29. μή	12	68	11	91
36. ὅταν	0	26	2	28
38. ὅτι	53	98	27	178
39. οὐ	24	116	19	159
41. οὖν	3	19	9	31
47. ὡς, denoting comparison	5	21	2	28
TOTALS	1,190	1,289	279	2,758

∴ The "goodness of fit" application of the Chi-square test indicates at the 0.01 level that the distributions ἀλλά, ἄν, γάρ, δέ, ἐάν, ἤ, καί, μή, ὅταν, ὅτι, οὐ and οὖν in narration in Luke are purposeful.

Conclusions

1. The Chi-square test shows a significant difference in "function word" and "nonfunction word" frequencies at the 0.01 level for three narrational groups: the narrator, Jesus, and a composite group made up of the remaining characters in the gospel.

2. The distribution of function words in narration in Luke, as a group, gives very strong indications of design.

3. Individual particles that show very strong indications of design are ἀλλά, ἄν, γάρ, δέ, ἐάν, ἤ, καί, μή, ὅταν, ὅτι, οὐ and οὖν.

Other Elements of the Narrator's Language

Excluding those elements mentioned in chapter 1 the narrator's voice is generally of a proper Hellenistic style. By appropriating Cadbury's study of the "Literary Standard of Luke's Vocabulary" to the narrator only, one notes that it is comparable in proportion of significant Attic words to the standard of Lucian, Aelian, and Philostratus. (See Tables 1 and 2.)

Also indicating a relatively high standard of speech, the narrator uses the optative, with ἄν in Lk 1:62; 6:11; 9:46; 18:36, and without ἄν at Lk 1:29; 3:15, 8:9; 22:23.[1] He uses the τοῦ with infinitive to express

---

[1]The optative is not common in the New Testament, as it was generally obsolescent in the first century. While its use in Luke gives some indication of a "literary" style, it should be noted that the gospel's author never uses the optative in a final clause—so breaking with proper Attic practice; F. Blass and A. Debrunner, *A Greek Grammar of the New Testament of the New Testament and Other Early Christian Literature,* trans. Robert W. Funk (Chicago: University of Chicago Press, 1961) 36; John M. Creed, *The Gospel According to St. Luke* (London: Macmillan, 1957) lxxxi-lxxxii.

purpose at Lk 2:24, 27; 24:45.[2] He uses the more classical ὡς (compare Lk 8:47; 23:55; 24:35) and never the later πῶς in indirect questions.[3] He uses πρίν with the subjunctive correctly following a negative at Lk

TABLE 1

SIGNIFICANT VOCABULARY IN LUKE-ACTS			
CLASS OF WORDS	LUKE & ACTS	LUKE ONLY	NARRATOR
A. Common Attic words or words affected by the Atticists	137	81	43
B. Words used chiefly by one of the ancient writers	27	17	6
C. Words first or chiefly in poetry	87	58	34
D. Words belonging to the postclassical prose, including Aristotle	202	118	55
E. Words first used by Luke	22	7	4
TOTALS	475	281	142

TABLE 2

CLASS	A COMPARISON OF THE STANDARD OF THE VOCABULARY (α-ε) OF THE "NARRATOR TO THEOPHILUS" WITH SOME HELLENISTIC AUTHORS							
	DIO CHRYSOSTOM	LUCIAN	ARISTIDES	AELIAN	PHILOSTRATUS	LUKE AND ACTS	LUKE ONLY	NARRATOR TO THEOPHILUS
A	47%	29%	52%	25%	33%	29%	29%	30%
B	13%	10%	10%	9%	7%	6%	6%	4%
C	16%	27%	23%	32%	27%	18%	21%	24%
D	21%	20%	9%	23%	16%	42%	42%	39%
E	3%	14%	6%	11%	17%	5%	2%	3%
TOTALS	100%	100%	100%	100%	100%	100%	100%	100%

---

[2]While τοῦ with infinitive to express purpose was classical Greek, it was also used occasionally in the papyri; cf. Creed, *The Gospel According to St. Luke,* lxxxi. Nigel Turner has argued that the use in Luke is only "a pretense to style." The author was really more interested in imitating the Septuagint's

2:26.[4] He uses the article before an indirect question, transforming the clause into a quasi substantive at Lk 1:62; 9:46; 19:48; 22:2, 4, 23, 24.

Out of twenty-three times that σύν appears in the gospel, eighteen times it is spoken by the narrator.[5] On the other hand, μετά with genitive, which was more frequent in later Greek and perhaps indicates a more popular style, appears fifty times in the gospel, but only fourteen times in the voice of the narrator.[6] The missing copula (Lk 22:20) is not part of his speech; of ten instances of ellipsis in the gospel (Lk 1:30, 3:5; 5:19, 7:45; 12:47; 13:32, 33; 14:28; 17:24; 19:4), only three are in the speech of the narrator (Lk 3:5; 5:19; 19:4);[7] and of eleven times that εἰς is confused with ἐν in the gospel (Lk 4:23, 44; 6:8; 7:50; 8:48; 9:61; 11:7; 13:9, 21; 14:8, 10), only once does it appear in the speech of the narrator (Lk 4:44).[8]

---

very common use of τοῦ with infinitive; cf. J. H. Moulton, R. Howard, and N. Turner, *A Grammar of New Testament Greek,* 4 vols. (Edinburgh: T. and T. Clark, 1908-) 3:8,142.

[3]In late Greek, ὡς became more or less interchangeable with πῶς, which in turn assumed the meaning of ὅτι ; cf. Blass and Debrunner, *Grammar,* 230-31.

[4]The papyrus writers did not always use πρίν properly, cf. Moulton, *A Grammar of New Testament Greek,* 1:169 n1.

[5]Σύν appears in the narrator's speech at Lk 1:56; 2:5, 13; 5:9, 19; 7:6, 12; 8:1, 38, [45]; 9:32; 20:1; 22:14; 23:11, 32; 24:10, 29, 33. Otherwise σύν appears in the speech of Jesus at Lk 19:23; 24:44; the speech of the maid who identifies Peter at Lk 22:56; and the speech of the two men on the Road to Emmaus (Lk 24:21, 24).

[6]Μετά with genitive appears in the speech of the narrator at Lk 1:39, 58, 66; 2:36, 51; 5:29; 6:17; 7:36; 10:17; 13:1; 17:15; 23:12; 24:30, 52. Otherwise it appears twenty-seven times in the speech of Jesus, and nine times in the speech of the other characters.

[7]Ellipsis is sometimes a helpful indication of the formality or informality of speech, cf. Blass and Debrunner, *Grammar,* 291-95.

[8]The narrator also uses εἰς for ἐν at Lk 21:37—but in this case he seems to do so because of the "double pregnant force" of εἰς; cf. James H. Moulton and George Milligan, *The Vocabulary of the Greek Testament Illustrated from the Papyrus and Other Non-Literary Sources* (London: Hodder and Stoughton, 1914-1929) 1042, 1047. The narrator confuses ἐν with εἰς at Lk 23:19.

The narrator tends to avoid barbarisms. While Latinisms appear in the gospel,[9] they never appear in the voice of the narrator. Other foreign words are also not common to his language. He does use the Egyptian or Semitic-rooted σινδών, "linen cloth" (Lk 23:53), the Hebrew Ἰουδαῖος, "Jew" (Lk 7:3; 23:51), the Aramaic names Βαρθολομαῖος, "Bartholomew" (Lk 6:14), and Βηθσαϊδά, "Bethsaida" (Lk 9:10), and the Hebrew or Aramaic πάσχα, "Passover" (Lk 2:41; 22:1, 7, 13), Σάββατον, "Sabbath" (Lk 4:16, 31; 6:1, 6, 7; 13:10, 14; 14:1, 23:54, 56; 24:1), and Σατανᾶς, "Satan" (Lk 22:3). But of these, only the use of σινδών and Σατανᾶς is not necessitated by the subject of his narrative.[10] The first is appropriated from Mk 15:46 as the technical term for the wrapping placed around Jesus' body. It portrays a close connection with the memory of the worshiping community, and one notes that the term's noncultic appearances in Mk 14:51, 52 are omitted from Luke. Σατανᾶς, which is introduced by the narrator as part of his explanation of Judas' betrayal, is also related to the cultus. Likewise, while necessitated by the subject matter of his story, Βαρθολομαῖος, πάσχα, and σάββατον are words tied to the cultic experience of the early Church,[11] and are not attempts to give local color to the narrative as perhaps is the case with Matthew's Ἐμμανουήλ (Mt 1:23).

The true extent of this characterization can be quickly illustrated. Cadbury rightly pointed out that Luke's use of Bethsaida (Lk 9:10) is softened by the use of the participle καλουμένην, "called."[12] To Cadbury this indicated that the author, in good Hellenistic style, tended to apologize for his use of foreign words. As Cadbury analyzed the usage of foreign words,

> 1) Sometimes, while retaining the foreign word [of Mark or Q], he [that is, the author of Luke] apologizes for it by the use of a participle mean-

---

[9]For a list see C. F. D. Moule, *Idiom Book of New Testament Greek* (Cambridge: Cambridge University Press, 1959) 192.

[10]The author could have used χιτῶν and διάβολος, for example.

[11]Βαρθολομαῖος was one of the twelve apostles; πάσχα was the religious festival at which Jesus was killed, and σάββατον was the day for worship of the Jewish synagogue.

[12]Henry J. Cadbury, *The Style and Literary Method of Luke* (Cambridge MA: Harvard University Press, 1920) 154.

ing "named" or "called," or by ὀνόματι or by some similar expression (Lk 9:10; 22:1, 3).

2) So also in passages not from Mark, the participle and other forms of the verb are used with foreign names, and particularly with foreign surnames (Lk 2:4; 7:11; 8:3; 10:39; 19:2).

3) Even if the foreign word is omitted or translated by Luke the apologetic participle is still retained (Lk 6:15; 19:29; 22:47; 23:33).

4) The use of ὀνόματι or ᾧ (ᾗ) ὄνομα makes the introduction of names less abrupt (Lk 5:27; 23:50).

5) In this connection should be compared the verbless clause ᾧ (ᾗ) ὄνομα used by Luke with foreign names in a similar way (Lk 1:26, 27; 2:25; 8:41; 24:13).

6) In addition to the apologetic expressions mentioned, many of the examples already cited still further soften the use of foreign words by adding the common or class noun, like city, feast, man, woman (Lk 4:31; 23:51; 9:30, 54).[13]

What is striking about Cadbury's discovery is that it represents a tendency of the narrator's voice only, and not a tendency of the gospel as a whole. Although Cadbury did not draw attention to this point, all of the cases that he enumerated come from the narrator's speech. The other characters in Luke do not so carefully avoid barbarous language.[14] When they do, however, one notices a very different method used by the author.[15] The other narrative characters do not explain or apologize for their vocabulary.

Of course, this is exactly what one would expect. The characters speak "in character." While it is fitting that Jesus or John the Baptist do not apologize for their Semitic vocabulary, it is also fitting that the author, when speaking through his Hellenistic narrator, softens his use of barbarous language.

---

[13]Ibid., 154-56.

[14]Cadbury (ibid., 154) gives five instances in which the author of Luke took over, without apology, a foreign word from Mark or Q: Mk 5:9‖Lk 8:30; Mk 4:21‖Mt 5:15‖Lk 11:33; Mt 10:28‖Lk 12:5; Mt 10:29‖Lk 12:6; Mk 12:14-17‖Lk 20:22-25. In every case, the word was part of the speech of one of the dramatic characters in the story: the demoniac, Lk 8:30; Jesus, Lk 11:33; 12:5, 6; and Jesus and his accusers, Lk 20:22-25.

[15]Cf. the omission of ὡσαννά in Lk 19:38‖Mk 11:9-10.

The Narrator's Place in the Christian Community

As Cadbury seemed to indicate, the qualifying of foreign words is probably a stylistic trait on the narrator's part, and is not an attempt to explain something that was unfamiliar to his hearers. True attempts to explain unfamiliar elements in the story seem to be very rare in the narration of Luke. As best I can ascertain, only the following might fit that category. Regarding Palestinian geography, the narrator perhaps makes an effort to explain that Nazareth is in Galilee (Lk 1:26), that Bethlehem is in Judea (Lk 2:4), that Capernaum is in Galilee (Lk 4:31), that the country of the Gerasenes is opposite Galilee (Lk 8:26), and that Arimathea is a Jewish town (Lk 23:51). He further indicates that Judah is hill country (Lk 1:39), and that the way to Jerusalem leads through towns and villages (Lk 13:22) and between Samaria and Galilee (Lk 17:11).[16]

The narrator also might want to clarify certain aspects of Jewish history when he indicates that Bethlehem is the city of David (Lk 2:4), that Herodias was Herod the tetrarch's brother's wife (Lk 3:19), that Pilate had "mingled the blood" of some Galileans with their sacrifices (Lk 13:1), that the temple was adorned with noble stones and offerings (Lk 21:5), and that Barabbas was imprisoned "for an insurrection started in the city, and for murder" (Lk 23:19). Also the narrator might be interested in explaining Jewish practices and customs when he indicates that Zechariah was on duty in the temple according to the custom of the priesthood (Lk 1:9), that Jesus' circumcision took place after eight days (Lk 2:21), that the time of purification is established by the law of Moses (Lk 2:22), that Jerusalem was the place to present the boy to the Lord (Lk 2:22-23), that a sacrifice was demanded by the law of the Lord (Lk 2:24), that Jesus was brought into the temple according to the custom of the law (Lk 2:27), that Jesus' family went to Jerusalem every year at the feast of Passover, according to custom (Lk 2:42), that the Scribes and the Pharisees considered it unlawful to heal on the

---

[16]This passage was one of the cornerstones of Hans Conzelmann's view that the redactor of the Third Gospel had an incorrect conception of the geographical relationship of Galilee, Samaria, and Judea; cf. Conzelmann, *The Theology of St. Luke,* trans. Geoffrey Buswell (New York: Harper and Row, 1961) 68-73.

sabbath (Lk 6:7), that teaching in the synagogue occurred on the sabbath (Lk 13:10),[17] that it was because Jesus healed on the sabbath that the ruler of the synagogue was indignant (Lk 13:14), that the Sadducees said that there is no resurrection (Lk 20:27), that the feast of Unleavened Bread is called the Passover (Lk 22:1), that the Passover lamb had to be sacrificed on the day of the Unleavened Bread (Lk 22:7), and that the assembly of the elders of the people was composed of both chief priests and scribes (Lk 22:66).

But again, many of those elements listed above might only be examples of church language, or stylistic traits, or formulations whose purpose was a particular rhythmic effect. On the whole there are very few, if any, indications in Luke that the narrator was interested in explaining unfamiliar aspects of the geography, history, tradition and customs of Israel. On the contrary, the narrator seems to assume that his audience is very well informed about such matters.[18] This is clear already in the first paragraph of his story as the narrator assumes some understanding of (1) the historical referent Herod, King of Judea, (2) the Jewish priesthood, (3) the division of Abijah, (4) Aaron, (5) the commandments and ordinances of the Lord. What this shows is that the Gospel of Luke was not an evangelical tract. According to the prologue (Lk 1:1-4), Theophilus was already informed about the story of Jesus. The narrator, in fact, assumes more than a passing familiarity with it. The narrator assumes that his audience knows the context and the texture of the story. All of this makes good sense, given the characterization of the narrator as one speaking to the Christian community (70-90 C.E.).

Thus it is not surprising that the narrator does not clarify aspects of his narrative that have implications for Christian worship. Of course, he consciously passes on great quantities of information concerning

---

[17]The use of the plural ἐν τοῖς σάββασιν is confusing. Possibly it is intended literally; cf. H. Schürmann, *Das Lukasevangelium* (Freiburg: Herder, 1969) 1:227 n45. Generally, however, it is regarded as indicating a particular sabbath; cf. A. Plummer, *St. Luke,* International Critical Commentary (Edinburgh: T. and T. Clark, 1922) 31.

[18]So also E. D. Burton ("The Purpose and Plan of the Gospel of Luke," *Biblical World* 16 [1900]: 258), who remarks on "the familiarity with Jewish affairs which [Luke] assumes on the part of his readers."

the birth, life, death, resurrection, ascension, and meaning of Jesus. Part of this information concerns the Christian rituals of baptism and communion, and the Christian concept of the Holy Spirit. But the information is given as if to insiders who are familiar with it. For example, the narrator assumes that his audience understands what "a baptism of repentance for forgiveness of sins" (Lk 3:3) means; that all agree that the promise of one who will baptize with the Holy Spirit and with fire is "good news to the people" (Lk 3:18); that Jesus' command concerning the Last Supper, "do this in remembrance of me" (Lk 22:19), and Jesus' reference to "the new covenant in my blood" do not need further explanation;[19] and that all understand the final command of Jesus, "stay in the city until you are clothed with power from on high," and so the great joy of the eleven and those with them as they returned to Jerusalem.

The narrator's perception of his audience as part of the Christian community is buttressed also by the way he introduces Simon Peter into the narrative. Generally, when the narrator first introduces a character by name into the narrative, he also in some other way characterizes him or her, thereby helping the hearers better locate the characters in the story. So Zechariah was a priest, of the division of Abijah, and so on (Lk 1:5); Elizabeth was Zechariah's wife, a daughter of Aaron, and so on (Lk 1:5); Gabriel was the angel of the Lord, sent by God (Lk 1:26, 11); Mary was of Nazareth, a virgin betrothed to Joseph, and so on (Lk 1:26-27); Joseph was of the house of David, betrothed to Mary (Lk 1:27); John was the son of Zechariah and Elizabeth, and so on (Lk 1:58-59); Jesus was the Son of Mary and Joseph, and so on (Lk 2:21); Simeon was righteous and devout, and so on (Lk 2:25); Anna was a prophetess, daughter of Phamuel, and so on (Lk 2:36); James was a partner of Peter, son of Zebedee, and so on (Lk 5:10); John was a partner of Peter, son of Zebedee, and so on (Lk 5:10); Levi was a tax collector (Lk 5:27); Andrew was Simon's brother, one of the twelve (Lk 6:14); Philip was one of the twelve (Lk 6:14); Bartholomew was one of the twelve (Lk 6:14); James was the Son of Alphaeus, one of the twelve (Lk 6:15); Simon was called the Zealot, one of the twelve (Lk 6:15);

---

[19]The text is confused at this point and E. Nestle (*Novum Testamentum Graece* [London: United Bible Society, 1971] 217) considered both phrases to be later additions to the original.

Matthew was one of the twelve (Lk 6:15); Thomas was one of the twelve (Lk 6:15); Judas was the Son of James, one of the twelve (Lk 6:16); Judas Iscariot became a traitor, and was one of the twelve (Lk 6:16); Mary was called Magdalene, seven demons had gone out from her, and so on (Lk 8:2); Joanna was the wife of Chuza, and so on (Lk 8:2-3); Suzanna accompanied Jesus, had been healed, and so on (Lk 8:2-3); Jairus was the ruler of the synagogue (Lk 8:41); Mary and Martha were sisters (Lk 10:38-39); Zacchaeus was chief tax collector, rich, and so on (Lk 19:2); Simon was of Cyrene and came in from the country (Lk 23:26); Joseph was from Arimathea, a member of the council, and so on (Lk 23:51); Cleopas was one of the eleven and those with them, and so on (Lk 24:18, 9ff.).

Only a few characters in the narrative are first introduced by the narrator without some accompanying description. They are Simon (Lk 4:38), Moses (Lk 9:30), Pilate (Lk 23:1), and maybe Herod the tetrarch (Lk 9:7). The assumption on the part of the narrator seems to be that his hearers already possess some working definition of these characters.[20] And again, a general knowledge of the "Christian story" gives familiarity with Simon Peter.

---

[20]So also J. Delorme, "Luc v. 1-2: Analyse structurale et histoire de la redaction," *New Testament Studies* 18 (1971-1972): 333.

The Language
and Style of Jesus

Appendix C

In Luke, Jesus speaks the language of the people. By appropriating
Henry J. Cadbury's study of the standard of language of Luke-Acts to
Jesus and the narrator, one may compare significant words in Luke.

TABLE 1

CLASSIFICATION OF SIGNIFICANT WORDS IN LUKE			
CLASS OF WORDS	LUKE	NARRATOR	JESUS
A. Common Attic words or words affected by the Atticists	81	43	36
B. Words used chiefly by one of the ancient writers	17	6	13
C. Words first or chiefly in poetry	58	34	32
D. Words belonging to the postclassical prose, including Aristotle	118	55	71
E. Words first used by Luke	7	4	3
TOTALS	281	142	155

The percentage of significant vocabulary of Jesus and the narrator is compared in Table 2.

This point is perhaps illustrated by Jesus' use of words and phrases included in Phrynichus's list of condemned vulgarisms.[1] There are twenty-six words on Phrynichus's list found in the gospel. Nineteen of these are used by Jesus.

αἰχμαλωτισθήσονται	(Lk 21:24)
ἀλέκτωρ	(Lk 22:34, 61)
ἀπεκρίθεις	(Lk 10:28; 11:7; 13:25; 22:68)
βασίλισσα	(Lk 11:31)
γρηγοροῦντας	(Lk 12:37)

TABLE 2

COMPARISON OF SIGNIFICANT VOCABULARY: JESUS AND THE NARRATOR		
CLASS OF WORDS	NARRATOR	JESUS
A. Common Attic words or words affected by the Atticists	30%	23%
B. Words used chiefly by one of the ancient writers	4%	8%
C. Words first or chiefly in poetry	24%	21%
D. Words belonging to the postclassical prose, including Aristotle	39%	47%
E. Words first used by Luke	3%	2%
TOTAL	100%	100%

[1]On Phrynichus and his work, see John Edwin Sandys, *A History of Classical Scholarship* (New York: Hafner, 1958) 1:323-25. The narrator uses the following words from Phrynichus's list of condemned vulgarisms (see *Phrinichi Eclogae Nominum et Atticorum,* ed. Chr. August Lobeck [Lipsiae; Weidmannia, 1820]): ἀλέκτωρ (Lk 22:60); γογγύζειν (Lk 5:30); ἐγκάθετος (Lk 20:20); εὐχαρίστειν (Lk 17:16); νοσσός (quoting Scripture, Lk 5:24); ὄρθρος of the dawn (Lk 24:1); παιδίσκη of a maidservant (Lk 22:56); and ποταπός for ποῖος (Lk 1:29). The twelve use οὐθείς (Lk 22:35); Pilate uses οὐθείς (Lk 23:14); and the Pharisees use ποταπός for ποῖος (Lk 7:39). J. M. Creed listed the Lukan uses of condemned vulgarisms in *The Gospel According to St. Luke* (London: Macmillan, 1957) lxxxiv. Those words on Phrynichus's list that appear in Luke but are not used by Jesus, are γογγύζειν, ἐγκάθετος, εὐχαρίστειν, νοσσός, ὄρθρος, and ποταπός for ποῖος.

δύνῃ in a principal sentence	(Lk 16:2)
ἐμπτυσθήσεται	(Lk 18:32)
καθώς	(Lk 5:14; 6:31, 36; 11:1, 30; 17:26, 28; 22:29; 24:39)
κρούειν τὴν θύραν	(Lk 13:25)
λυχνίας	(Lk 8:16; 11:33)
μενοῦν at the beginning of a sentence	(Lk 11:28)
μεσονυκτίου	(Lk 11:5)
νοσσίαν	(Lk 13:34)
οἰκοδεσπότης	(Lk 12:39)
παιδίσκας of maidservants	(Lk 12:45)
πανδοχεῖον spelled with χ	(Lk 10:34)
πανδοχεῖ spelled with χ	(Lk 10:35)
σινάπεως	(Lk 13:19; 17:6)
σκορπίζει	(Lk 11:23)

Jesus, in Luke, prefers the more common πῶς (Lk 6:42; 10:26; 11:18; 12:56; 20:41, 44) in questions to the more classical ὡς used by the narrator; he uses ἄλλος and ἕτερος incorrectly (compare Lk 4:43; 6:29); and out of twelve times that εἰς is used incorrectly for ἐν in Luke, nine appear in the speech of Jesus (Lk 4:23; 6:8; 7:50; 8:48; 11:7; 13:9, 21; 14:8, 10). In contradistinction to the narrator, Jesus prefers μετά with genitive to the more proper σύν. The first appears twenty-seven times in the mouth of Jesus out of fifty times in the gospel (Lk 5:34; 6:3, 4; 8:13; 10:37; 11:7, 23, 31, 32; 12:46, 58; 14:9, 31; 15:29, 30, 31; 17:20; 21:27; 22:11, 15, 21, 28, 33, 37, 52, 53; 23:43); the second appears only twice in the speech of Jesus out of twenty-three times in the gospel (Lk 19:23; 24:44). Also υἱοί with genitive to indicate "People worthy of or associated with" appears five times in the gospel, all in the speech of Jesus (Lk 5:34; 6:35; 16:8; 20:34, 36);[2] ἄρχομαι with infinitive to represent the future appears four times in the speech of Jesus (Lk 13:25, 26; 14:9; 23:30) out of five times in the gospel;[3] anacoluthon appears in Jesus' speech at Lk 9:3; out of ten ellipses in the gospel, six are in

---

[2]C. F. D. Moule, *An Idiom Book of New Testament Greek* (Cambridge: Cambridge University Press, 1959) 175.

[3]Henry J. Cadbury, *The Style and Literary Method of Luke* (Cambridge MA: Harvard University Press, 1920) 162-63.

the speech of Jesus (Lk 7:45; 12:47; 13:32, 33; 14:28; 17:24); the phrase with the missing copula in Lk 22:20 is part of the speech of Jesus.[4]

The determination of non-Greek influence on the Greek language is difficult. But according to the studies of Robertson and Moule, several non-Greek influences appear in the speech of Jesus. Latinisms include ἀσσάριον (Lk 12:6), δηνάριον (Lk 7:41; 10:35; 20:24), ἔχω (Lk 14:18), μόδιος (Lk 11:33), σουδάριον (Lk 19:20), and δὸς ἐργασίαν (Lk 12:58). Cyrenaic and Sicilian influence are in βουνός (Lk 23:30), and παράδεισος (Lk 23:43); oriental influence is in χιτών (Lk 6:29; 9:3); Macedonian influence is in ῥύμη (Lk 14:21); and Phoenician influence is in μνᾶ (Lk 19:13, 16, 18, 20, 24), βίβλος (Lk 20:42), βύσσος (Lk 16:19), and σίναπι (Lk 13:19; 17:6).[5] And as expected, there are a number of Hebrew and Aramaic words in Jesus' speech. So ἀμήν (Lk 4:24; 12:37; 18:17, 29; 21:32; 23:43), βάτος (Lk 16:6), βεελζεβούλ (Lk 11:15, 18, 19), βηθσαϊδά (Lk 10:13), βύσσος (Lk 16:19), γέεννα (Lk 12:5), κάμηλος (Lk 18:25), κόρος (Lk 16:7), μαμωνᾶς (Lk 16:9, 11, 13), πάσχα (Lk 22:8, 11, 15), σάββατον (Lk 6:5, 9; 13:14, 15, 16; 14:3, 5; 18:12), Σατανᾶς (Lk 10:18; 11:18; 13:16; 22:31), σάτον (Lk 13:21), Σιλωάμ (Lk 13:4), and συκάμινος (Lk 17:6).[6]

Other likely Semitic elements in Jesus' speech include the superfluous ἀφείς (Lk 10:30), ἐλθών (Lk 14:9; compare 10:32; 19:23), καθίσας (Lk 16:6, compare 14:28, 31), ἀναστάς (Lk 15:18, 20, compare 6:8), and ἐγερθείς (Lk 11:8); the phrase θέτε οὖν ἐν ταῖς καρδίαις ὑμῶν (Lk 21:14);[7] εἰρήνη as a salutation (Lk 10:5, 6); ὁμολογήσῃ ἐν with dative (Lk 12:8); and ἰδού used almost with the meaning of "since" (Lk 13:7, 16).[8] Also υἱοί with genitive is probably Semitic, as are the adversative use of καί in the phrases καὶ ἐδικαιώθη ἡ σοφία (Lk 7:35) and καὶ μακροθυμεῖ ἐπ' αὐτοῖς (Lk 18:7);[9] the periphrasis for the direct mention of God (Lk 6:38; 12:20; 16:9; com-

---

[4]Ibid., 148-49.

[5]Moule, *An Idiom Book*, 192.

[6]Creed, *The Gospel According to St. Luke*, lxxix.

[7]Ibid.

[8]Ibid. lxxxi.

[9]Moule, *An Idiom Book*, 178.

pare 12:48);[10] the use of a substantive following the construct case as the equivalent of a qualifying adjective in the phrases τὸν οἰκονόμον τῆς ἀδικίας (Lk 16:8) and ὁ κριτὴς τῆς ἀδικίας (Lk 18:6);[11] the use of προσέθετο in place of an adverb (Lk 20:11, 12);[12] a command expressed by the future indicative (Lk 4:8);[13] the use of ἐνώπιον as an improper preposition with genitive (Lk 12:6, 9; 13:26; 14:10; 15:10, 18, 21; 16:15 [twice]);[14] and the constructions καὶ ἰδού (Lk 13:30; 24:49; compare 11:31, 32, 41);[15] καὶ ἐγένετο ἐν τῷ with infinitive (Lk 19:15); ἀποκριθεὶς εἴπη (Lk 11:7); ἀστραπὴ ἀστράπτουσα (Lk 17:24) and ἐπιθυμίᾳ ἐπεθύμησα (Lk 22:15);[16] ἐπὶ πρόσωπον (Lk 21:35);[17] and ἐρχόμενος ἤγγισεν (Lk 15:25).[18] Even if some of these constructions simply represent popular koine style rather than actual Semitisms, the overall presence of Semitic influence in the diction and style of Luke's Jesus is clear.

It is surprising to learn how much of the material indicative of the popular standard of Jesus' speech, when compared with the gospel as a whole, cannot be accounted for by appealing to Luke's accepted sources, Mark and Q. For example, Jesus' πῶς at Lk 10:26 has been edited into Mk 12:28-31; πῶς at Lk 11:18 has been added to Mk 3:26-28 (but compare Mt 12:26); and πῶς at Lk 12:56 is not part of the parallel material in Mt 16:3. The incorrect ἕτερος (Lk 4:43) has been added to Mk 1:38. The incorrect εἰς (Lk 4:23) has been added to Mk 6:1-6. Lk 6:4 changes Mark's more proper σύν (Mk 2:26) to μετά with genitive (but compare Mt 12:4), and the μετά with genitive is perhaps

---

[10]W. L. Knox, *Some Hellenistic Elements in Primitive Christianity* (London: Oxford University Press, 1944) 9 n1.

[11]Creed, *The Gospel According to St. Luke*, lxxxi.

[12]Ibid.

[13]Moule, *An Idiom Book*, 178-79.

[14]Creed, *The Gospel According to St. Luke*, lxxix.

[15]Ibid.

[16]Moule, *An Idiom Book*, 178.

[17]Creed, *The Gospel According to St. Luke*, lxxix. One could also add the idiom πρὸ προσώπου σου (Lk 7:27, Jesus quoting Scripture).

[18]Ibid., lxxx.

added at Lk 22:28 to Mk 10:45-46 and clearly added at Lk 22:53 to Mk 14:49. Words on Phrynichus's list of vulgarisms not explained by recourse to source theories include αἰχμαλωτισθήσονται (Lk 21:24), which is added to Mk 13:19-20; ἀποκρίθηναι (Lk 22:68; 10:28), which is added to Mk 14:61-62 and Mk 12:31-32; καθώς (Lk 5:14), which is added to Mk 1:44 and does not appear in the parallel material in Matthew at Lk 6:31‖Mt 7:12; Lk 6:36‖Mt 5:48; Lk 11:1‖Mt 6:9; Lk 11:30‖Mt 12:40; Lk 17:26‖Mt 24:37; Lk 17:28‖Mt 24:38-39; Lk 22:29‖Mt 19:28; κρούειν τὴν θύραν (Lk 13:25), which is not in the parallel material at Mt 25:10-11; and παιδίσκας (Lk 12:45), which is not in the parallel material at Mt 24:48-49. Also υἱοί with genitive to indicate "people worthy of or associated with" at Lk 20:34, 36 is added to Mk 12:24-25; ἄρχομαι with infinitive to represent the future at Lk 13:25, 26 is not in the parallel material at Mt 25:10-11 and Mt 7:22; the ellipsis at Lk 17:24 is not present in the parallel Mt 24:27; the anacoluthon at Lk 9:3 is not present in Mk 6:8-9; and the missing copula (Lk 22:20) is not by reason of Mk 14:22. The Latinisms ἔχω (Lk 14:18), σουδάριον (Lk 19:20), and δὸς ἐργασίαν (Lk 12:58) are not in the parallel material at Mt 22:4; 25:24; 5:25. Other foreign words, ῥύμη (Lk 14:21), μνᾶ (Lk 19:13, 16, 18, 20, 24), and βίβλος (Lk 20:42) are not found in the parallel material of Mt 22:8-9, Mt 25:16ff., and Mk 12:36. The Semitic ἀμήν (Lk 4:24) is added to Mk 1:4 and συκάμινος (Lk 17:6) is not in the parallel material at Mt 17:20. θέτε ἐν ταῖς καρδίαις (Lk 21:14) is inserted into Mk 13:11; εἰρήνη as a salutation (Lk 10:5) is not in the parallel material at Mt 9:11; the periphrasis for the direct mention of God (Lk 6:38) is not in the parallel material at Mt 7:2; προσέθετο in place of an adverb (Lk 20:11, 12) is inserted into Mk 12:4, 5; ἐνώπιον as an improper preposition with genitive (Lk 12:6, 9; 13:26) is not in the parallel material at Mt 18:29, 33; 7:22; καὶ ἰδού (Lk 13:30, compare 11:41) is not found in the parallel material at Mk 10:31 (and Mt 23:23-24); καὶ ἐγένετο ἐν τῷ with infinitive (Lk 19:15) is not found in the parallel material at Mt 25:19; and ἀστραπὴ, ἀστράπτουσα (Lk 17:24) is not found in the parallel material at Mt 24:27.

To this evidence can be added those possibly Semitic elements listed above which are in that part of Jesus' speech that is in material peculiar to Luke and might or might not be the result of sources. Luke's special material includes εἰς used incorrectly for ἐν (Lk 7:50; 11:7; 13:9; 14:8, 10); μετά with genitive (Lk 10:37; 11:7; 14:9, 31; 15:29, 30,

31; 17:20; 22:15, 21, 33, 37); ἀλέκτωρ (Lk 22:34); ἀποκρίθηναι (Lk 11:7; 12:37, but compare Mt 25:13); δύνῃ in a principal sentence (Lk 16:2); καθώς (Lk 24:39); μενοῦν at the beginning of a sentence (Lk 11:28); μεσονυκτίου (Lk 11:15); πανδοχεῖον (Lk 10:34); πανδοχεῖ (Lk 10:35); υἱοί with genitive to indicate "people worthy of or associated with" (Lk 16:8); ἄρχομαι with infinitive to represent the future (Lk 14:9; 22:30); ellipses (Lk 7:45; 12:47; 13:32, 33); δηνάριον (Lk 7:41; 10:35); βουνός (Lk 23:30); παράδεισος (Lk 23:43); ἀμήν (Lk 12:37; 23:43); βάτος (Lk 16:6); βύσσος (Lk 16:19); κόρος (Lk 16:7); μαμωνᾶς (Lk 16:9, 11, 13); πάσχα (Lk 22:15); σάββατον (Lk 13:14, 15, 16; 14:3, 5; 18:12); Σατανᾶς (Lk 10:18; 13:16; 22:31); Σιλωάμ (Lk 13:4); the superfluous ἀφείς (Lk 10:30); the superfluous ἐλθών (Lk 14:9, compare Lk 10:32); the superfluous καθίσας (Lk 16:6, compare 14:28, 31); the superfluous ἀναστάς (Lk 15:18, 20); the superfluous ἐγερθείς (Lk 11:8); ἰδού used almost with the meaning of "since" (Lk 13:7, 16); the adversative use of καί (Lk 7:35; 18:7); the periphrasis for the direct mention of God (Lk 12:20; 16:9; compare 12:48); the substantive following the construct case as the equivalent of a qualifying adjective (Lk 16:8; 18:6); ἐνώπιον as an improper preposition with genitive (Lk 14:10; 15:10, 18, 21; 16:15 [twice]); καὶ ἰδού (Lk 24:49); ἀποκριθεὶς εἴπῃ (Lk 11:7); ἐπιθυμίᾳ ἐπεθύμησα (Lk 22:15); ἐπὶ πρόσωπον (Lk 21:35); and ἐρχόμενος ἤγγισεν (Lk 15:25).

It is certainly significant that approximately two-thirds of these instances indicating the popular standard of Jesus' speech cannot be attributed to any known sources. As tabulated from the listings in this appendix, out of 212 instances of the popular standard of Jesus' speech in the gospel, forty-seven come from material that parallels either Mark or Matthew but are not in Mark or Matthew, and eighty-seven are in material peculiar to Luke. Certainly it is not demonstrable that the popular style of Jesus' speech in Luke is the result of slovenly editorial work on Mark and Q. Rather, Jesus' speech characterizes him in the narrative. He does not speak as the narrator speaks. His language is the common language of the people.

Name Index

Scripture Index